Identity Complex

Identity Complex

Making the Case for Multiplicity

Michael Hames-García

University of Minnesota Press
Minneapolis
London

The University of Minnesota Press gratefully acknowledges financial support provided for the publication of this book from the Oregon Humanities Center and the College of Arts and Sciences at the University of Oregon.

Portions of an early version of chapter 1 were published as "Who Are Our Own People? Challenges for a Theory of Social Identity," in *Reclaiming Identity: Realist Theory and the Predicament of Postmodernism*, ed. Paula M. L. Moya and Michael Hames-García, 102–29 (Berkeley: University of California Press, 2000). Portions of an early version of chapter 2 were published as "How Real Is Race?" in *Material Feminisms*, ed. Stacy Alaimo and Susan Hekman, 308–39 (Bloomington: Indiana University Press, 2008). Portions of an early version of chapter 3 were published as "What's at Stake in 'Gay' Identities," in *Identity Politics Reconsidered*, ed. Linda Martín Alcoff, Michael Hames-García, Satya Mohanty, and Paula M. L. Moya, 78–96 (New York: Palgrave MacMillan, 2006).

Published by the University of Minnesota Press
111 Third Avenue South, Suite 290
Minneapolis, MN 55401-2520
http://www.upress.umn.edu

Library of Congress Cataloging-in-Publication Data

Hames-García, Michael Roy.
    Identity complex : making the case for multiplicity / Michael Hames-García.
        p. cm.
    Includes bibliographical references and index.
    ISBN 978-0-8166-4985-3 (hc : alk. paper)—ISBN 978-0-8166-4986-0 (pb : alk. paper)
    1. Group identity. 2. Identity (Philosophical concept). 3. Race awareness. 4. Gender identity. 5. Prisons—United States. I. Title.
    HM753.H36 2011
    305—dc22   2010049335

Printed in the United States of America on acid-free paper

The University of Minnesota is an equal-opportunity educator and employer.

18 17 16 15 14 13 12   10 9 8 7 6 5 4 3 2

For Ernesto Martínez

Contents

Preface

*Since subject position is everything in my analysis of the law, you deserve
to know that it's a bad morning.*

—Patricia J. Williams, *The Alchemy of Race and Rights*

The Book

Taking a cue from legal scholar Patricia Williams, I should probably introduce this book by introducing myself, its author. The questions the book
considers, after all, matter to me for many personal reasons, although I
believe them to have a broader significance than merely their importance for
me. Let me begin, however, by introducing the subject of the book itself. In
essence, *Identity Complex: Making the Case for Multiplicity* examines, from
a humanistic theoretical perspective, the interrelatedness of different forms
of *social identity* (understood as a concept distinct from both, on the one
hand, *personal identity*, or *the self*, and, on the other hand, the more social
scientific category of *social groups*). Whereas personal identities and selves
contain infinite complexity and variety, social groups—either as political
actors or as demographic categories—tend toward a reductive homogeny.

This book proposes a theory of *multiplicity* that can account for how
social identities take shape through processes of racial and gender formation, mutually constituting one another. That theory seeks to analyze
the necessary social interdependence of identities and, therefore, to enable
the creation of deep relations of solidarity across differences. I develop
the outlines of this theory in the first chapter. The second chapter considers the meaning of race as a social category and the significance of racial
identities, or "racial identity projects." In asking basic questions about the
reality of race, I seek to make sense of how race as a concept has come
to influence social structures and personal experiences over the past five
centuries and to understand the possibilities for its future development.
I argue, in part, that one can only adequately understand race in relation to other kinds of social identity rather than in isolation from them.

The third chapter asks how one might best understand the political substance of sexual identities. I consider, for example, recent debates about whether, particularly from an anticolonial perspective, sexual identities are politically desirable. In seeking answers, I consider the long, mutually constitutive history of race, gender, and sexuality within a world economic system. I propose that the desirability of liberatory sexual identities should be understood as a question that bears on histories of colonialism and racism as well as homophobia and sexism. The final chapter brings an analysis of multiplicity and social identities to bear on the contemporary U.S. prison crisis. The chapter turns to cultural representations of the prison to understand how their treatment of class, gender, race, ability, and sexuality relates to the larger histories explored in earlier chapters.

Identity Complex argues that social identities matter fundamentally to the operation of social processes of exploitation and oppression, and that one must understand precisely how identities operate in relation to these otherwise abstract and impersonal historical processes in order to undo their legacies. The importance of this project results from its simultaneous intervention in a number of debates in the humanities and social sciences. An established tradition now exists—in the wake of the flowering of academic women-of-color feminism in the 1980s and 1990s—of social theorists gesturing to the importance of "intersections" of oppression or of identities.[1] However, it remains rare for this gesture to influence core assumptions about identity, history, experience, or knowledge unless women of color constitute the immediate object of inquiry. This book contributes to a theory of history that seeks to account for the ways that race and class (for people of all races and genders) in the colonial/modern era (at least since the sixteenth century) have developed in a way that makes them inextricably bound up with gender and sexuality, and vice versa. The studies of sexual identities and of U.S. prisons in this book illustrate the profound impact of that inextricability for questions not traditionally conceived of as (only) "women-of-color issues." Understanding multiplicity and mutual constitution therefore remains absolutely essential to the eventual eradication of discrimination and social inequality.

Scholars often describe the collective wisdom of women of color and others who attend simultaneously to class, gender, race, and sexuality as elaborating a theory of "intersectionality."[2] However, I argue in the first chapter of this book that scholars should not try to extend the metaphor of "intersections" to cover everything, thereby losing sight of its specificity and original context. As people often invoke them, theories of *intersectionality* can imply that people exist, like myself, who have "intersectional" experiences, identities, or both, while other people have experiences and identities that are not "intersectional." While this claim is important, I find it useful to think of intersectionality, in this formulation, as a theory that describes the intersections of oppressions (such as racism and homophobia) and the experiences of those of us who identify (or those whom others identify) with multiple oppressed groups and whose experiences, consequently, exist at the intersections of multiple oppressions. This use, however, leaves some things unaccounted for, such as how to explain the experience of a "straight, white, middle-class man." He, too, has a class position, a gender, a race, and a sexual preference. In addition to *intersectionality*, understood as a theory of oppression, I therefore argue for a rich conception of *multiplicity*, understood as a theory of identity rather than a theory of oppression. A theory of multiplicity that understands social identities as *mutually constitutive* (rather than as discrete and separable) forms an organizing principle for this book. *Identity Complex* is therefore not a work of history, although I am concerned with history and with how people use history to shape contemporary identities. Nor is this book an ethnographic or empirical study, although I have tried to draw wherever appropriate from empirical research in making my claims. Unlike my earlier book, *Fugitive Thought: Prison Movements, Race, and the Meaning of Justice*, this book is not about the agency of the oppressed or about the importance of identities for generating knowledge. In other words, this book does not seek primarily to illustrate how gays and lesbians of color, for example, have articulated experiences of multiplicity or negotiated the limits of cultural representation. Excellent examples of such books already exist.[3] Nor is it an intellectual history, concerned with tracing the development of theories of race, gender, and sexuality.[4] *Identity Complex* is a theoretical project that draws from empirical studies and a range of intellectual sources—including women-of-color feminism, queer of color critique, queer theory, political economy, disability studies, world systems theory, critical race theory, ethnic studies, and theories of coloniality—in order to explore the mutual constitution of gender, race, sexuality, and, to a lesser extent, disability and class, and to argue for the importance of a conception of multiplicity for understanding identity and cultural politics.

I regret the secondary nature of my emphasis on class as an aspect of social identity in this book.[5] One explanation might lie in the fact that contemporary social identity movements have not often taken class as an abstract category (understood either as socioeconomic status or as one's location within a society-wide mode of production) to be their primary rubric for organization. Notable exceptions include peasant movements, but most labor organization tends to form around specific occupations (for example, farm workers, textile workers, or teamsters) rather than taking a class-wide shape. The most successful recent class-based movements, furthermore, typically overlap strongly with other identities based on nation, race, ethnicity, or citizenship status (for example, immigrant or guest worker). Even successful peasant mobilizations often correlate strongly with indigenous, tribal, linguistic, ethnic, or national identities rather than take shape solely around a conception of class. This phenomenon in itself would make an excellent subject for study, but remains outside the scope of my present project. I have, however, made an effort throughout this book to remain attentive to economic factors. Most notably, I try to attend to capitalism as both a historical process and a present-day mode of production that dominates nearly everything in society. Thus, while I do not emphasize class as an identity throughout the book, the book does not lack a class consciousness, for I understand a central part of the processes influencing social identities to be the development and functioning of a class-stratified capitalist world system, or a "colonial/modern world system."[6]

The Author

Since I have already stated that my reasons for taking up these questions stem partly from personal interest, let me introduce myself, beginning with some of the more obvious basics. My mother gave birth to me at the end of the U.S. civil rights movement and toward the end of the Vietnam War. To be precise, I entered the world on November 6, 1971, less than two months after the tragic end of the rebellion at the Attica Correctional Facility in upstate New York, the same day that the United States detonated a nuclear warhead on Amchitka Island in the middle of the Bering Strait, and one year and a day before Richard Nixon won reelection to his second term as president of the United States. My father is a white man whose ancestors immigrated to Canada from England in the nineteenth century and crossed the border into the United States near the turn of the twentieth. My mother is a Mexican American woman who was born in the city of Toppenish, Washington, on the lands of the Yakima Nation, also known as the Yakima Indian Reservation. Her ancestors lived in present-day Southern California since at least the late 1700s—before there was a United States of America or an Estados Unidos Mexicanos. Quite literally, the border crossed *them*. Although I have heard stories on both sides of my family of Native American ancestors (Gabrieleño/Tongva on my mother's side and Cherokee on my father's), these held no more cultural meaning for me growing up than did the rumored link, through my paternal grandmother, to Jefferson Davis, president of the Confederacy.

Wrestling to relate issues of class, gender, race, and sexuality has occupied much of my intellectual and political life, although rarely through direct consideration of my own personal history. Yet I can see a motivation for my scholarly and activist life in some of my earliest personal experiences. Those experiences did not really occur to me as having anything to do with intellectual questions, however, until one or two professors introduced me to writings by women of color in college.[7] I grew up as a monolingual English speaker with "olive skin" and dark hair and eyes in the years immediately after the introduction of an official legal classification for "Hispanics" in the United States, but until age twenty I lived in the states of Montana and Oregon, which were overwhelmingly white. This combination of factors had two main consequences for me. First, the most culturally salient aspect of my ethnic identity was my mother's Mexican heritage. Second, I had little sense of what that heritage meant. I knew I was different, and I understood racism and prejudice when I encountered them (as when a grade-school teacher once told me that I had "greasy" hair), but for the most part I found it difficult as a child to separate my ethnic or racial difference from something else: the awareness from around age eight that I was "queer." I remember at an even younger age feeling frustrated by the Mother Goose nursery rhyme describing boys as made of "snips and snails and puppy dog tails" and girls as made of "sugar and spice and everything nice." As I did not want anything to do with snails or dog tails, it seemed profoundly unjust that I should not be able to identify with "nice," pretty things like sugar and spice. In short, I was an effeminate, nerdy boy with a growing attraction to other boys and men, and to make matters worse, I looked visibly (if ambiguously) different from most of my peers. In addition, I also often felt ashamed of my parents' working-class status. In reality, according to how most people in the United States think about class, my family would probably have been described as *lower-middle class*. We were not *poor*, in other words, but I saw the difference between my home and those of many of my classmates—a difference that became much more pronounced when I left home for a private regional college on a full scholarship, and still more pronounced when I left that college for an Ivy League graduate school on another full scholarship. I remember one Christmas—possibly the year that International Paper Company had laid off my mother from her secretarial job—when I unwrapped a gift under the tree only to discover a package of white underwear briefs. Although I understood that *really* poor kids did not get any presents at all, the idea of underwear as a Christmas present seemed unfair to me. Around the same time, or perhaps a few years later, I adopted a practice of stealing from department stores. What I stole was, ironically, underwear, but not like the white briefs I had received for Christmas. No, these were the new designer men's underwear that became popular in the early 1980s, and the apparel itself did not hold so much attraction for me (I don't know that I actually wore any of it) as did the pictures of handsome, scantily clad (white) male models on the packages that I kept hidden in my room.

Writing about the politics of identity and my own life reminds me of a popular education workshop I once attended in which participants were asked to introduce ourselves by telling about when we first discovered Latina feminism. Without hesitation, I thought of my mother and the time, while I was in grade school, that she went on strike. She was not a union worker, and this was not that kind of strike. Rather, she announced one day to my father, my two brothers, and me that she would not be cooking, cleaning, or doing laundry anymore. That act transformed our household, and although the strike formally lasted only a few weeks, my mother never returned to doing anyone's laundry but her own. I remember thinking how strange it was that other boys in junior high (and in college, for that matter) did not know how to do laundry. Her action was based on an understanding of her own experiences and her own identity. And yet it helped me to realize something about my own experiences and identity and about how I as a boy had taken my mother's labor for granted. Although neither of us would have identified as feminists at that time, I did gain a glimpse at the gendering of oppression. I discovered something not just about women, however, but also about boys and men. Her act resulted from her experiences as a woman, specifically as a mother and wife, but its significance was not limited to women's experiences. My mother's strike and my ability to learn from it represent the possibilities of identity politics rather than its limits. In the same way, I hope that my experiences in this introduction, as well as the other issues and questions that I examine throughout this book, will demonstrate the significance of identity and multiplicity while proving useful to those with different identities and experiences from mine and from those I explore in the pages that follow.

The Argument

I have lived with and written about the ideas in this book for years. Some of that writing is in print elsewhere, and some of what is in this book has been previously published in different forms. However, I have thoroughly revised every part of this book that has an origin elsewhere. There is continuity and consistency, but there is also much transformation, growth, and discontinuity. In many cases, the rewriting has sought to provide greater clarity and to simplify some of my language. I have eliminated many digressions, for example, that I thought too narrowly focused on esoteric academic debates. In other cases, I have substantively rethought my ideas. This has sometimes come from personal encounters with people whose intellectual perspectives have shaken some of my most fundamental beliefs about identity, multiplicity, and oppression: Tobin Siebers and his work on disability, for example, or María Lugones and her thinking about gender and colonialism.[8] Questions like those from my colleague Irmary Reyes-Santos about my economic explanations in chapter 4 have pushed me to make my scholarship more rigorous and to deepen my grounding in fields outside of my formal training. In other cases, I have first encountered new ideas through an intellectual's written work. In some instances, these thinkers have given me new grounds on which to build my arguments; in others, they have forced me to question some of my own presuppositions. Discovering the work of Walter Mignolo and others in the Coloniality Working Group is an example of the first instance; the work of Joseph Massad and others on sexuality and neocolonialism is an example of the second.[9] In each case, I believe that my work in its current form constitutes an extended argument that I could not have made earlier, keyed as it is to new conversations and new debates.

Chapter 1 reprises a question I asked in one of my first published works, "Who are our own people?"[10] At its base, this question seeks to understand the possibilities for solidarity, for coalition, and for the sustainability of political struggle against oppression and domination in all forms. In answering that question, I hold that one's own people are those people with whom one has made common cause; however, one cannot do this in an abstract way—as when one declares solidarity with "the Cuban people" without really knowing much about the Cuban people. Instead, solidarity or common cause of the kind I have in mind must take into account deeply embodied connections and relations among people. I argue that expansive social identities can form one resource, among others of course, for discovering these connections and relations that enable a rich and robust solidarity across differences. These expansive social identities include some elaborations of feminist, queer, black, and women-of-color identities, as well as antiracist and ally identities. In this chapter, I thus seek to explore a theory of identity that understands social identities as internally heterogeneous and as connective, thereby rejecting derisive characterizations of "identity politics" either as the stifling of difference or as "Balkanizing." The primary theoretical tools that I develop for this purpose are *multiplicity* and *mutual constitution*.

Chapters 2 and 3 continue to respond to concerns that scholars and activists have raised about identity as a valuable political and intellectual resource, while seeking better and subtler understandings of what identities are and can be. Chapter 2 asks, "How real is race?"[11] In this chapter, I focus primarily on racial identity, considering both challenges to racial identity as a legitimate basis for social and political organization and a number of defenses of the importance of understanding race as a factor in social relations. I argue against critics of race and propose that racial identities are real, even if they are also socially constructed and historically variable. I go on to argue, however, that many of those who defend the reality of race and its salience for how people live have also failed to grasp the full scope of its relevance and complexity insofar as they tend to separate it from its mutual constitution with gender and sexuality. This chapter thus begins my engagement with the theoretical model that philosopher María Lugones has dubbed the "colonial/modern gender system."[12] Chapter 3 continues that engagement, focusing on the elaboration of sexual identities within that system. It asks, "Are sexual identities desirable?"[13] The critics of identity with whom I engage in this chapter have charged that sexual identities, particularly those identities (such as gay and lesbian) that refer to sexual minority groups, have evolved very recently and only in "the West" (that is, Western Europe and its former settler colonies, particularly those in North America, Australia, and New Zealand).

Can such identities have any legitimacy outside of the cultural contexts in which they developed? If so, how? These questions carry great weight, and I do not presume to offer answers with regard to any specific cultural or social context. Rather, my interest lies in understanding the stakes in both asking and answering these questions. What legitimate challenges do the history of the colonial/modern gender system and the mutual constitution of race, nation, ethnicity, religion, gender, and sexuality pose to the elaboration of sexual identities? What might sexual minorities need to take into account in responding to charges that the elaboration of sexual identities in formerly colonized contexts amounts to a form of cultural imperialism? How can anti-imperialist gays and lesbians in the United States, for example, best bring to light and challenge the connections among capitalism, homophobia, imperialism, patriarchy, and racism?

Chapter 4 reflects an application of the theoretical models explored in the previous chapters—*multiplicity, mutual constitution,* and the *colonial/ modern gender system.* This "case study" is two headed, addressing the chapter's overarching question, "Do prisons make better men?"[14] On the one hand, I discuss the social, economic, and political underpinnings of the contemporary U.S. prison crisis. On the other hand, I analyze one of the most complex cultural representations of that crisis, the cable television drama series *Oz* (1997–2003).[15] Many scholarly and activist studies of the prison exist that take race and class as important identity categories. Fewer exist that understand gender as important to the operation of prisons, and even fewer consider sexuality. My discussion adds one more voice to those calling for a more multifaceted consideration of the social functions of incarceration in the United States. *Oz* offers a special opportunity to deepen this theoretical intervention given its own attentiveness to masculinity, race, and sexuality, despite its highly melodramatic depiction of prison life. The program's shortcomings also afford me a chance to consider the central role of white masculinity in determining some of the limits of mass media cultural representations for effectively challenging the underpinnings of oppression and domination in U.S. society. The conclusion of this book reflects briefly on the possibilities at this historical moment for moving beyond legacies of inequality and despair.

Who Are Our Own People?

Why Ask the Question?

I have never assumed identity to be a simple matter, and, in my own life, I have always treaded haltingly through the tangled thicket of class, gender, race, and sexuality. For example, as an assistant professor, I had the good fortune to connect with a senior white male colleague who shared some of my interests in teaching in prisons and together we worked to offer classes at a nearby maximum-security prison for men. As an activist–scholar, I considered this an extraordinary opportunity to make progressive scholarship available to a community I considered my own, despite having never spent time in prison myself. However, at the prison I suddenly found myself working far outside my comfort zone. As a gay man, I have spent at least half of my life living in terror of straight men. Beginning at a young age, this terror consumed much of each day as I navigated the public spaces of bus stops, school buses, hallways, classrooms, track fields, locker rooms, dormitories, cafeterias, and even my own home. Entering the prison, even in a position of relative authority, brought to the surface every bit of the trauma that makes up part of the experience of growing up as a queer youth.

My only comfort lay in the assumed class position of "professor," which offered an explanation other than sexuality for my inability to correctly navigate the rituals of heterosexual male socialization. I could thus laugh off my inability to get right the complicated straight-male ritual verbal greetings, handshakes, and hugs. My masculine failures actually resulted from my having diligently avoided the rituals of male bonding as a youth, but in this context I could hope that the men would attribute everything to my being a teacher rather than a "faggot." That misattribution, in turn, could allow me to retain respect and authority in an exclusively male and ostensibly heterosexual classroom where all the students came voluntarily and did not receive credit for the course. I also wanted to avoid any possible conflicts over sexuality with the (probably homophobic) prison administrators. So there I found myself: teaching work on gender, race, and sexuality to a class of men in a maximum-security prison. Then, just as I thought I had everything in hand, the prison's director of educational programs chose to observe my class on the day dedicated to writings by black gay men and lesbians. I received a call from her the next day. She did not mention the fact that we had discussed gay and lesbian sexuality, which surprised me since I took that to be the most salient aspect of class discussion. Instead, she had concerns that the class focused too much on oppression. "We don't want them talking about being oppressed, because they are. We are oppressing them," she told me.

Class, gender, race, sexuality: I find it difficult to single out any one for separate discussion. During my work at the prison, for example, I actively concealed my sexual orientation, but my decision to do so in many ways came as a consequence of considerations of gender, race, and class. Working in homophobic spaces often requires gay and lesbian people to engage in one of two activities. The first involves passing as straight. Barring that possibility, people can engage in a silent "don't ask, don't tell" pact by letting others assume that they are simply effeminate men or masculine women. Unlike passing, this pact involves a silence about the otherwise obvious fact of one's gender nonconformity. Other people must actively guard their ignorance at the same time that they knowingly test me in frequent, but individually trivial ways, asking questions about marriage or commenting on the attractiveness of a member of the opposite sex. These occasions then solicit from me either an equivocation or an outright lie, thereby enlisting my active participation in my own erasure.

In this case, I felt my compliance necessary because the last thing I needed as a volunteer, offering the only available college-level classes at a maximum-security men's facility, was to have homophobic prison officials shut down the class—especially when I was already teaching topics that the administration found uncomfortable, like "oppression." Of course, I pushed the envelope of the pact, bringing in texts on homophobia, for example. I tried to work within a narrow space, challenging the homophobia of others, on the one hand, and maintaining a tense silence about my own sexuality, on the other. My political commitments around race and class thus brought me to make different decisions regarding my sexual identity than I would in another context.

Those decisions had their costs, of course. Only once did a flamboyantly "out" gay or transgender person show up in a class I taught in a men's prison. She only attended a couple of classes but asked that we address her by using a feminine name and she dressed in either bright pink shoes or a pink sweater, both against regulations. Within the context of the class, as near as I could tell, she had some respect from her fellow prisoners, who at least listened to her intelligent contributions to class discussion. Indeed, the most remarkable thing about her seemed to be her ardent Afrocentrism rather than her gender nonconformity.

During the very few classes she attended, the topic of sexuality never came up and she never explicitly identified herself as gay or as transgender. I intended to find a time to speak to her directly about her experiences in the prison and in the class, but did not get a chance before she stopped attending with no further explanation. Did she lose interest in the class or did she simply receive a transfer to another facility, as sometimes happened? Would it have made a difference if I had been "out" during one of those first days? What might have been the costs in relation to my ability to work with the other prisoners if I had come out? I cannot answer these questions. I only know that she made very different choices in the context of the class than I did. Of course, we had different objectives in the class. She was serving a prison sentence; the class formed an extension of her life in prison. I came there as a visitor, offering something I see myself having to contribute as an educator to communities of color.

Part of my continued effectiveness in that space, it seemed to me, depended on the students in the class not dismissing me, or more importantly, on the administration not kicking me out. Had I been in her place, would I have dared to be as bold as she was? I cannot say. The fact is, however, that our social locations differed significantly. Had I gone into that classroom as flamboyantly as she did, I seriously doubt that I could have retained in the long run a high degree of effectiveness for the vast majority of the prisoners who came through the classes I offered there. At the same time, I am not convinced that my choices enabled me to offer *her* all that I could during the time she came to class. Unfortunately, the price I paid for privileging effectiveness with the other prisoners prevented me from developing solidarity with her; on the other hand, the price of privileging my responsibility to her could very easily have reduced my ability later to engage with the other prisoners in discussions of male privilege and heterosexism.

I hope to illustrate through this example the importance of a concept of multiplicity for understanding the ways that this student–prisoner and I found ourselves differently located in relation to the prison and to our respective class positions, genders, sexual orientations, and races. However, while we might seem completely different at the level of these different kinds of identities (middle class and poor, gay male and transgender, Chicano and black), I consider her one of my people in a profound way if for no other reason than that I see her fate and my own to be connected in a world riddled with economic inequality, homophobia, racism, and sexism. The heart of this chapter lies in elaborating some theoretical underpinnings for this kind of claim.

Multiplicity

It verges on the commonplace to say that no two people are the same—or, what amounts to the same thing, that everyone is different. This remains true for people who share similar social identities around gender, race, and sexuality. Consider a photograph by way of comparison. Photographs can portray endless shapes and variations of hue and contrast. While one album might contain hundreds of photographs, no two even remotely alike, all the photographs contain combinations of three primary colors: red, yellow, and blue. Each of the photographs might contain yellow, yet the yellow might appear in different densities and shapes. Thus, no two photographs contain yellow in the same way. In some photographs, one might not see the yellow; there might only be some green or orange. What the yellow looks like depends not only on its own shape and density but also on the shape and density of the red and the blue and their position in relation both to the yellow and to each other. Thus, yellow next to red looks different than yellow next to blue.

Thinking of a person's identity in a similar way, but with more than three variables, one can begin to get a sense of the challenges of multiplicity for an account of identity. *Personal identity* involves so many complexities and so much variability from one individual to another that it might seem that any attempt to group people together under larger categories of *social identity* can only amount to a kind of deceit. No person, after all, is just a man, or just white, or just middle class. We all amount to so much more than any one thing. One might justly ask, therefore, if it is a falsehood to imply that all men are the same, that all whites are the same, that all middle-class people are the same. Do not categories of social identity (black, white, male, female, straight, gay, disabled, able-bodied) simply cover up individual differences and falsely imply sameness among all members of each group?

This amounts to a matter of more than just individual quirks (Bob is unlike José because Bob is from Connecticut and is a family man, while José is from New York City and does not want to settle down). Rather, the problem of multiplicity within contemporary social theory entails something more like the challenge of defining yellow in my example of the photograph. Memberships in various social groups (or categories of social identity) combine with and mutually constitute one another. Membership in one group (for example, "womanhood") thus means something different in the context of one simultaneously held group membership (for example, "blackness") than in the context of another (for example, "motherhood"). The combination of these relations and their mutual constitution goes into the making of a personal identity, combined further with the "individual quirks" shaped by a history of personal experiences, the values of one's parents, friends, and community, and so on.

Identities thus emerge from, on the one hand, the mutual constitution of various social group memberships and, on the other hand, the mutual constitution of individuals and their environment, including social structures. To distinguish individual personal identity from group social identity, I will refer to personal identity as "the self." Of course, the self is a *social* self. In other words, one can never fully separate the self from its historical relationships to categories of social identity. Despite that inextricability, however, I focus more on social identity than on the self in the later chapters of this book. In my focus on social identity throughout this book, however, my interest is in identity as it is experienced by real, concrete people—individual selves.

The multiplicity of the self in relation to social identities lies in the inadequacy of understanding the self as the sum of so many discrete parts: femaleness + blackness + motherhood, for example. The mutual interaction and the relation of its parts to one another constitute the self. Social identities—or aspects of the self that have political significance in a given society and that one shares with a significant number of others in that society so as to result in a sense of shared fate (for example, ability, citizenship, class, ethnicity, gender, race, religion, and sexuality)—overlap in fundamental ways. These social identities, therefore, do not constitute essentially separate categories that occasionally intersect. As legal and logical categories, abstracted from the fleshy world of everyday life, one might understand social identities as separable and therefore as sometimes intersecting as well. When they do seem to intersect, one can see the inadequacy of conceiving of them as separable to begin with, especially when attempting to understand the richness of the self and its personal history.[1]

At this point, rather than thinking of them abstractly as separable categories, I would like to consider social identities from the perspective of the day to day. From this perspective, social identities do not simply intersect now and then. They blend, constantly and differently, like the colors of a photograph. From within this multiplicity, over the course of a history of experiences colored by social interaction, emerge personal identities, or concrete, fleshy selves. No one in U.S. society (or anywhere in the modern world, for that matter) ever exists without class, ethnicity, gender, sexuality, and so forth, even if someone's class, ethnicity, gender, or sexuality might be ambiguous, confusing, blurry, and multiple, or might vary across different contexts and locations.

As a result, one's ethnicity or race is always shaped by class, by gender, by sexuality, and so on, and these other identities are shaped by one another as well. Social identities, within the context of the self, expand one another and mutually constitute each other's meanings. In other words, the subjective experience of any social identity *always* depends fundamentally on relations to other social identities. Which social identities have the most influence, in turn, also varies across time and space and can include ability, age, citizenship, educational level, ethnicity, immigration status, nationality, occupation, religion, and countless other identities.

This is the challenge of multiplicity, elaborated eloquently in writings by women of color and others over the past three decades, often in response to the limitations of social movements organized around single categories of social identity such as the U.S. women's movement or the Black Power movement. In the United States, some of the earliest of these women included Gloria Anzaldúa, Toni Cade Bambara, Grace Lee Boggs, Jo Carrillo, Chrystos, Cheryl Clarke, the women of the Combahee River Collective in Boston, Angela Davis, hattie gossett, Joy Harjo, bell hooks, June Jordan, Yuri Kochiyama, Jenny Lim, Audre Lorde, María Lugones, Chandra Talpade Mohanty, Cherríe Moraga, Aurora Levins Morales, Rosario Morales, Margo Okazawa-Rey, Pat Parker, Bernice Johnson Reagan, Barbara Smith, Michelle Wallace, Nellie Wong, Merle Woo, and Mitsuye Yamada.[2] Their published texts, while invaluable, should not stand in for the entirety of women-of-color feminism, much of which has flourished in streets, homes, organizational spaces, and workplaces— sometimes written out in brochures, pamphlets, and flyers, but more often simply discussed and lived. However, these women's published works have become important documents that record the experiences and theories of women of color in the wake of a nation's great social movements.

Given the power of these women's challenges to the limits of civil rights and liberation movements based around single agendas or monolithic conceptions of identity, one can easily imagine why someone might take the challenge of multiplicity to mean that any politics based on identity inevitably proves too problematic to endorse. One might go further and claim that multiplicity exposes all categories of social identity as mere fictions that stand in the way of progressive social change. Need the concept of social identity always imply sameness throughout a social group, erasing internal differences? Does the reality of multiplicity require the rejection of the concept of social identity as a useless, if not harmful, fiction?

The need to respond to these questions has motivated not only this book but also much of my work as an academic and activist over the past decade and a half. Before I return to them, however, I want to consider the importance of multiplicity for breaking down restrictive, oppressive constructions of identity. Those oppressive constructions have been erected by global social structures and long histories of domination, and later reanimated by purportedly progressive movements of identity politics that have arisen in response to those dominating structures and histories. The violence of this dynamic has taken shape, in part, through a process that I call restriction.

Restriction

The multiplicity of the self becomes obscured through ways of thinking that accompany domination and oppression. (Although the obscuring of multiplicity that accompanies oppression affects everyone to some degree—not only those who face direct oppression—the consequences of this obscuring take different forms for the oppressed than for those with relatively more privilege.) Modern society tends to conceive of a person's complexity in a way that fractures it. Thus, the multiplicity of the self becomes restricted in a way that reduces people's "identities" to those aspects of themselves with the most political significance at a given time in a given context. People understood exclusively in terms of their race, gender, or sexuality, furthermore, come to be understood only in terms of the most dominant construction of that identity—that identity understood in a way that ignores variation and multiplicity. Those whose interests conform largely to dominant constructions of a given social identity have what one might call relatively *transparent* interests from this perspective. By contrast, others, possibly by virtue of membership in multiple politically significant and oppressed groups, often find themselves and their interests distorted by restricted definitions and understandings. This distortion resembles what happens to the polar regions of the earth in most two-dimensional maps; they find themselves perversely reshaped to accommodate the perspective of the viewer. The interests of such people, rather than being transparent, are *opaque*—more difficult to see, to understand, and to explain given the fragmenting logic of social oppression and its restriction of multiplicity.

Restriction thus misrepresents and misunderstands multiply oppressed people to an even greater extent than it does other people. For example, one might call an able-bodied, heterosexual, middle-class, white woman's interests *as a woman* in the United States *transparent*, insofar as U.S. society typically takes such a woman's interests as a woman to represent those of women as a group. (This is not to say that such women are not complex persons, of course, with complex personal histories, who might have political commitments different from what one might otherwise expect.) Black women, gay Chicano men, Asian American lesbians, and poor people with disabilities, by contrast, have memberships in multiple politically significant and oppressed groups in the United States. Their political interests thus often appear *opaque*, insofar as they typically differ from those of the more privileged members of the multiple social groups to which they belong.[3] Several issues arise from this kind of opacity. These include abstract questions of knowledge and representation as well as material questions of access and resources. These two kinds of questions are not unrelated, but I want here to consider primarily the first, more abstract questions (of knowledge and representation) as a way to allow for more productive discussions later as to how to address some of the material issues that arise around social identity and oppression.

Allow me to consider two brief examples of how multiplicity and restriction work—one personal, the other literary. As a graduate student, I often went with friends on the weekend to our small town's one and only gay bar. One such night, I happened to be there with a good friend, a working-class, black, gay man. This night, a white, gay male friend of his, who did not know me, saw us together. When I was away, the white man told my friend that he "had better watch his wallet" because he was with me. (My friend reported this to me later in the evening.) While, as far as I know, the white man did not refer to my ethnicity as Mexican American or Latino, I have difficulty imagining what else might have occasioned this warning. I had come to the bar dressed in standard "Friday going out" attire, and my youth in this college town would have typically marked me as a student rather than a hustler. Somehow, at this moment and in this context, my ethnicity and this white man's assumptions about its significance outweighed all other aspects of my identity (as gay or as a graduate student at an Ivy League university, for example).

A thorough understanding of this example, however, requires us to go beyond simply thinking of this man as racist. Most obviously, my friend's blackness complicates matters beyond the standard rhetoric of race and racism in the United States. In addition, the fact that we were all gay men in a predominantly gay and lesbian environment colors all aspects of the incident. For example, Latinos in a largely white gay culture in the United States often find that other gay men consider our sexuality exotic, dangerous, and risky. The identification of me as a hustler, and possibly a thief, emerges in this light as a practice of sexual objectification according to the norms by which all Latino men are eroticized within white gay culture, as much as a warning to my friend. As an instance of sexualized racism, the incident poses complex questions about what it means for the three of us to share a gay identity, as well as to be black, white, and Chicano. At the very least, how each of us experiences going to a small town gay bar, receiving attention from other men, and feeling sexual attraction to other men might vary widely, at least in part, due to the mutual constitution of our sexual and ethnic and racial identities.

A different example comes from Michael Nava's 1992 mystery novel, *The Hidden Law*, the fourth in his Henry Rios detective series.[4] The main character of the book is Henry Rios, a gay Mexican American lawyer. In the novel, someone shoots and kills a prominent Mexican American state senator from California, and suspicion descends on a troubled Mexican American teenager. Convinced of the boy's innocence, Henry takes the case. A subplot in the book deals with the deteriorating relationship between Henry and his white, HIV-positive lover, Josh. Throughout the novel, Henry encounters prominent Mexican American academics and politicians. In all his interactions with these other Mexican Americans, he experiences hostility directed toward him due to his sexuality. Because the case receives a great deal of publicity, however, the others must veil their hostility (however thinly) in order to project an image of Mexican American unity in the public eye. Such experiences for the main character make him feel like an outsider in the Mexican American community, a community that simultaneously purports to include him. At the same time, Henry feels *solidarity* and *connection* with the homophobic Mexican American characters based on their shared position as members of an embattled U.S. minority group. Ultimately, Henry prevails in his quest for justice, proving the boy's innocence and uncovering the real murderer.

Following from these two examples, I want to pose the following question: How can one account for such complexities and contradictions and also explain (and facilitate) the *expansion* of solidarity and group interests in a way that can help to overcome restriction and separation? Furthermore, how can one do this while also acknowledging the distinct political significance of different social identities and the *lived experiences* that give substance to class, disability, gender, race, sexuality, and so on? Similar calls for the expansion of solidarity and understanding emerging from the experience of a particular nexus of social identities suffuse many artistic and literary works by women of color and gay men of color, from author Toni Morrison's novel *Beloved* to the late independent filmmaker Marlon Riggs's documentary *Tongues Untied.*[5] Such calls demand that individuals see their own interests, their own people, as extending beyond narrow conceptions of themselves, beyond their own experiences, and beyond their immediate group identifications. To do justice to these varied calls, one must have recourse to a theory that accounts for multiplicity and social identity.

Mutual Constitution

What does it mean for both Henry and the politicians who disdain him because of his sexuality to identify as "Mexican American" or as "Chicano"? Certainly, they are neither "Chicano" nor "Mexican American" in the same way, nor assume themselves to be. Similarly, in my first example, my friend, his friend, and I all share a gay identity, but to share an identity is not necessarily to be identical or to hold something in common. The linguistic similarity between *identity* and *identical* should not lead one away from sensing distinctions in how the terms are used. Sharing an identity can mean sharing a stake in something beyond oneself that includes those who also share that identity but who still experience it differently. In *The Hidden Law*, for example, Henry's identity as a Chicano includes his victimization by homophobia within a community that claims to hold him as a member and to represent his interests. One might object that I am here confusing the specific experiences of being gay and of being Chicano, that I should conceptually separate sexuality from race and ethnicity in order to understand Henry's situation. Once I understand that Henry is subjected to homophobia within his community, I can understand that it has to do with sexual identity rather than ethnic or racial identity.[6] This objection, however, presupposes a preracialized, preethnic (or nonracial and nonethnic), "pure" sexual identity that then intersects with a presexualized (or nonsexual), "pure" racial identity. If one assumes that sexual meanings come to bear on (what must then be nonsexual) ethnic and racial identities, one posits in advance a separation between them.

The crucial error here comes from asking how two *separate* identities come to "intersect" rather than starting from the presumption of mutual constitution.[7] This is like assuming that one can have pure essences of blue and yellow and that green is nothing more than the combination of both. While this might make initial sense, on closer consideration one could ask whether green might be something more than the sum of its component parts. One could also ask how to determine which yellow (or blue) represents the true yellow (or blue). Yellow (or blue) against a white background, or a black one? Brightly lit, or dimly?

I do not intend to dismiss the substantial and valuable work done by people using the terminology of *intersections* and *intersectionality*, most notably legal scholar Kimberlé Williams Crenshaw in her work on gender and race. Rather, I want to identify precisely what this terminology describes and to suggest additional terms that might further account for phenomena not fully captured by *intersectionality*. The metaphor of intersections has had currency among feminists since at least the 1980s, with literary critic and gay studies theorist Eve Kosofsky Sedgwick writing about "intersections" in 1990, Crenshaw coining the term *intersectionality* in a very different context in 1989, and Chicana feminist Gloria Anzaldúa writing expansively about "the crossroads" in 1987.[8]

No one would suggest that any one term should be extended to cover everything, and yet scholars sometimes now invoke *intersectionality* as an umbrella for any and every theoretical contribution by a woman of color. The 2009 meeting of the National Women's Studies Association illustrated the confusion wrought by overextending the term. Even while Crenshaw and sociologist Bonnie Thornton Dill argued in a special session for clarity and care in the use and application of *intersectionality*—paying particular attention to the disciplinary specificities of Crenshaw's original use of the term to describe a phenomenon in antidiscrimination law—the term appeared in nearly every session title, serving primarily as a shorthand way of signaling that a panel addressed not only gender but also other questions of identity and oppression, such as race. That use is, of course, understandable given the need in that context to signal one's concern with multiple issues, but the repetition of a single term to cover sometimes radically different projects and contexts also speaks to the need for more concepts and terms to address the complexity and specificity of identity, experience, and oppression.

Furthermore, the overextension of *intersectionality* tends to downplay differences of shade and emphasis, nuance and insight between, for example, what Hortense Spillers describes as the "interstices" in 1984 and what Audre Lorde tries to get at in choosing to talk about "difference" and "fragmentation" in the same year.[9] That which concerns Spillers and Lorde may have a connection to intersectionality, as Crenshaw later uses the term, but each of these three theorists surely does not describe an *identical* phenomenon. Indeed, Crenshaw herself uses the term *multidimensionality* at one point in her 1989 article to describe black women's experiences, while using *intersectionality* to describe a concern that arises for her with regard to the narrowness of how courts think of discrimination.[10]

Philosopher María Lugones offers a useful account of the effort to supplement the vocabulary of intersections. In a careful reading of Crenshaw's work, she observes that "[i]ntersectionality reveals what is not seen when categories such as gender and race are conceptualized as separate from each other. The move to intersect the categories has been motivated by the difficulties in making visible those who are dominated and victimized in terms of both categories."[11] Lugones points out that "Crenshaw and other women-of-color feminists have argued that the categories have been understood as homogenous and as picking out the dominant in the group as the norm," such that "the logic of categorial separation distorts what exists at the intersection, such as violence against women of color."[12] She therefore concludes that "intersection misconstrues women of color" so that "once intersectionality shows us what is missing, we have ahead of us the task of reconceptualizing the logic of the intersection so as to avoid separability. It is only when we perceive gender and race as intermeshed or fused that we actually see women of color."[13] In other words, intersectionality reveals the inadequacy of restricted categories of thought, but one needs other concepts to account for the reality of multiplicity.

Indeed, any adequate theory of social identity must be able to account for multiplicity, understood as the mutual constitution and overlapping of simultaneously experienced and politically significant categories such as ability, citizenship, class, ethnicity, gender, race, religion, and sexuality. Rather than existing as essentially separate axes that sometimes intersect, social identities blend, constantly and differently, expanding one another and mutually constituting one another's meanings. The white gay man in my first example, my African American gay friend, and I all find ourselves situated differently in relation to our homosexuality. In other words, it means something different for each of us to be gay. Yet *gay* is an important identity for each of us, and presumably, we each recognize the claim of the others to be gay however much the meanings we associate with our gayness may differ.

Returning to *The Hidden Law*, Henry's Mexican American identity differs from those of the straight Mexican American men he encounters because for all of them, sexuality is central to how they experience being Mexican American. Similarly, because part of what it means for Henry to be gay, unlike his white lover Josh, has to do with his Mexican American identity, their experiences of being gay differ. For Henry, *to be gay* means, in part, to deal with homophobia in a community (the Mexican American or Chicano community) to which he feels a tremendous degree of personal commitment. Conversely, another salient difference between Henry and Josh proves to be HIV status. Their conflicts over this difference result in the disintegration of their relationship by the book's conclusion, because Josh, being HIV positive, has a fundamentally different sense of *what it means to be gay* than does Henry—a sense that Henry ultimately fails to understand by the novel's close.

It is no coincidence that literary critics consistently interpret novels, plays, and poetry by women of color and gay men of color as challenging unitary, monolithic, or essentialist notions of identity.[14] Often, the portraits of multiplicity with which writers provide us are painful and heartrending, as in Cherríe Moraga's play *The Hungry Woman* or Randall Kenan's novel *A Visitation of Spirits*.[15] Rejection, homelessness, and suicide in these works serve not simply as metaphors for the consequences of a misunderstood and persecuted multiplicity. They also reflect lived realities.

The challenges posed by multiplicity in response to restrictive ways of understanding identity might seem to invalidate the category of identity completely. Accordingly, one might conclude that any claim to an identity can only be strategic or pragmatic. Such a conclusion contends that identity claims can never find strong justifications based in lived experience or social structures. In other words, if gay men have so little in common with one another, then perhaps we would be better off dismissing any attempt to account for a "gay" identity as such. I want to resist this extreme reaction to the challenge of multiplicity by considering an approach that is more *realistic* with regard to what makes identities *real* (rather than simply fictional or merely strategic) and to how people negotiate multiplicity.

Realism, Certainty, and Error (The First of Two Brief, Philosophical Digressions)

The pressing need to find a political language to deal with identity while at the same time articulating a sophisticated response to the challenge of multiplicity has increasingly led many academics to espouse a version of *realism*. These include theoretical physicist and feminist philosopher of science Karen Barad, literary theorist Satya Mohanty, Chicana feminist Paula Moya, education scholar Leslie Roman, and disability studies scholar Tobin Siebers.[16] Joining them have been numerous others, including literary critics Johnnella Butler, Esha Dé, Laurie Grobman, Carolyn Hau, Ernesto Martínez, José David Saldívar, Rosaura Sánchez, Susan Sánchez-Casal, Éva Tettenborn, Sean Teuton, and myself; historians Jack Tchen and John Zammito; performance studies scholar Carrie Sandahl; and philosophers Linda Martín Alcoff, Raja Halwani, Daniel Little, Amie Macdonald, and William Wilkerson.[17] Notably, most of these scholars work in the interdisciplinary fields of African American; Asian American; Chicana and Chicano and Latina and Latino; disability; feminist; gay, lesbian, and queer; Native American; and postcolonial studies. While they have sometimes drawn in part (and often with a critical eye) from the past forty years of work in the philosophy of knowledge and science studies, their influences are as varied as the fields in which they work. Realist theorists of identity have emerged concurrently with a number of other defenders of the political and social utility of identity. These other scholars come primarily from the social sciences, and have supplemented the theoretical work of realists with rich empirical accounts.[18]

Taken together, this body of scholarship builds a theoretical and philosophical base from which to understand how social entities, like identities, which are built out of a variety of shifting social determinants, can be studied with similar theoretical rigor (and uncertainty) as natural, scientific phenomena. Realism about identities, in other words, draws strength, on the one hand, from the acknowledgment of imprecision and the "mediation" of knowledge by theories and background assumptions within the sciences. On the other hand, it takes instruction from the ways that scientists deal with this imprecision and mediation—that is to say, by acknowledging uncertainty and mediation as the conditions that make good research possible rather than as interference that makes usable knowledge impossible.[19]

To be specific, the kind of realism that I (and most of the aforementioned scholars) have advocated is "postpositivist," which is to say that it differs from the tradition of positivism (or empiricism) in that it does not seek to find bedrock foundations for knowledge. The quest for foundations, in Western philosophy, is the attempt to find a basis for knowledge that can guarantee absolute certainty, to find something on which to base all of one's claims. Foundationalism takes two forms: inferential and premise. Inferential foundationalism seeks rules of inference that can guarantee certainty for all knowledge ("as long as you follow these logical rules, you cannot be led into error"). Premise foundationalism seeks the discovery of basic truths that cannot be doubted (for example, "I think, therefore I am") and that can therefore form the bedrock justification for all claims deduced from them (for example, "If I exist, then someone must have created me; therefore, there must be a God").

The will-o'-the-wisp for all questions of foundational knowledge is absolute, error- and presupposition-free certainty of knowledge (justified, true belief). Twentieth-century positivism (also called logical empiricism) sought to further its foundationalist project by discounting talk of anything "metaphysical" or "theoretical," that is, anything not verifiable empirically, anything that could not be seen, touched, heard, tasted, or smelled directly. If the existence of something had to be speculated about, then positivists wanted no part of it. Their approach, as with other positivist projects (for example, the early twentieth-century transcendental phenomenology of

Edmund Husserl that has been roundly critiqued by philosopher Jacques Derrida), involved searching for immediate experience—that is, experience of the world free of interference, or mediation, from presuppositions or theories about the world.

In contrast to positivism, a *post*positivist realism puts people in the world with nothing but theories and presuppositions to make sense of it. As many scholars have noted, the best scientific inquiry (especially new discovery) proceeds from an acknowledgment of the lack of absolute certainty for our current scientific beliefs, and of the possibility that they are in error. Many scientists and scholars of science have long accepted that knowledge is partly shaped by the theories with which one proceeds, by one's expectations, and even by the tools of one's inquiry.[20] If the best scientific knowledge about chemistry, physics, and biology need not be absolute or fixed in order to be sufficiently reliable and accurate to put out grease fires (regularly), to fly planes (most of the time), and to cure diseases (some of the time), then why set a higher bar for knowledge about culture and society?

Realism entails an account of how our beliefs about the social world can refer with some degree of reliability or accuracy to reality—and of how one can verify that reference. Realists about identity take from the study of science and from the philosophy of knowledge an acknowledgment that our beliefs and discoveries remain at least partly contingent on other beliefs, on our theoretical models, and on the tools of our inquiry. We do not seek to eliminate uncertainty or to fix any one identity forever, or to say that a particular identity is always better or correct. However, unlike versions of relativism that have permeated, if not dominated, humanistic inquiry in the United States over the past several decades, a realist approach commits one to the idea that a theory-independent social reality exists outside of our individual, subjective beliefs about it. Furthermore, it holds that theories of the social world can help us to understand that reality because they remain to some extent answerable to it.

Accounts of reference and verification have a long history in Western philosophy, but in the last decades of the twentieth century, a broad consensus emerged in humanities departments throughout U.S. universities *that accurate reference to an objective reality within the scope of inquiry about human beings and their societies is extremely dubious, if not impossible.* This consensus emerged primarily in literature departments but also, to a lesser extent, in art history, history, religion, philosophy, and in some of the humanistic social sciences like cultural anthropology, cultural geography, education, and qualitative sociology.[21] One of the most important questions to ask of this consensus, and one to which I shall return, is what one means by *objective*, and whether there might be multiple ways of understanding objectivity; for now, allow me to address the terms *accurate, reference,* and *reality.*

Instead of giving up on reference to reality, the kind of realism I advocate here replaces the quest for direct, or *immediate,* knowledge with an acknowledgment that all knowledge is subject to influence, or *mediation.* It understands both accuracy and uncertainty as relative. To take a simplified example, if I have a theory that water boils at 100 degrees Celsius, I might attempt to verify that theory. If the water does not boil, something independent of my theory (for example, altitude) has acted on my experiment. I would therefore revise my theory to take altitude into account. If altitude were not a theory-independent *causal* feature of the world (something that acts on other things, causing observable effects), I could not be forced to revise my theory to improve its accuracy and reliability. Unlike positivists, I need not directly observe altitude to believe in it. I infer its causal power through its effects, but I also acknowledge an element of uncertainty. Later experience or discovery might prove my inference wrong.

To take another kind of example, consider an intangible social force, like homophobia. I might sense that something acts on my life as I move through the world, but I cannot simply touch it and say, "This is homophobia." Rather, I must often infer its existence from cryptic comments by others, from hostile glances and words directed at my lovers and me as we hold hands in public, and so forth. (I am here leaving aside such tangible things as antigay legislation and physical violence.) Now, I could theorize that I am simply a paranoid person, distrustful of strangers. This theory of the world attempts to explain my experiences. However, another theory might claim that a social force called homophobia exists, so structuring my world as to bring about observable effects (glances and comments, as well as legislation and violence). Positing the existence of homophobia allows me to explain more reliably (and therefore, more accurately) my movement through the world and the kinds of responses I encounter. Importantly, it need not explain everything with complete certainty all the time in order to be a useful theory that refers to a real feature of the social world.

Realism, Causality, and Explanation (The Second Philosophical Digression)

Using what philosophers call a *causal theory of reference*, realists can avoid the pitfalls of theories of reference and verification that posit direct, one-to-one correspondences between our beliefs and the world. Whereas a correspondence theorist might claim that a given term corresponds to a given object out there in the world, a causal theorist might claim that the causal powers of that object (for example, homophobia) *condition the social use of the term*. This social use of language remains, therefore, at least partly conventional, and one must continually reconsider it, debating alternative usages, evaluating them within a social framework laden with unequal power relations, and considering how the social world itself changes over time.[22] Thus, a realist need not claim that people can have direct, unmediated knowledge of reality. Instead, one might claim that, through interpretation and the creation of theories to mediate the causal features of the world, people can more or less accurately grasp the complexity of the social processes and multiplicity of causes that make up the truth of experience.

At issue in realism's understanding of social identity specifically are the coherence and reliability with which theories about groups account for the causal social features of the systems of exploitation that give those groups their political significance in a particular society. Applying a realist analysis to social identity in a passage on feminist thought, Satya Mohanty writes, "The theoretical notion 'women's lives' refers not just to the experiences of women but also to a particular social arrangement of gender relations and hierarchies that can be analyzed and evaluated."[23] He goes on to argue that within such a framework, the political interests of women as a group can be "discovered by an explanatory empirical account of the nature of gender stratification, how it is reproduced and regulated, and the particular social groups and values it legitimates."[24]

An account of multiplicity would further complicate this explanation, but need not lead (as some impatient critics tend to fear) to an utter disintegration of the notion of women as a social group. To think of *women* as a category that is internally multiple, to believe that there are different kinds of women and different ways of being a woman, need not reduce all analysis to the level of individual characteristics. Nor, to be sure, does it inevitably lead to the conclusion that there is no such thing as *women* at all! Recognition of multiplicity may indeed require us to rethink our understanding of *women* as designating a unitary group, or to ask if it might be more useful to think about gender in a nondichotomous way, but I believe that more extreme conclusions are unwarranted.

A realist perspective recognizes causally significant aspects of the social world in which people live their identities and also holds that all knowledge depends on our theories of the world.[25] Realism can thus be *post*positivist and *non*foundational. An adequate account of causal features of the social world (such as ableism, class inequality, colonialism, heterosexism, homophobia, nativism, racism, sexism, structures of economic exploitation, and xenophobia) can yield accurate, reliable, and *revisable* understandings of the reality of experience and its construction in modern society. Because humans construct knowledge differently, realists about identity advocate an interpretation of experience in order to see how "theory-laden and socially constructed experiences can lead to a knowledge that is accurate and reliable" rather than seeking to discount experience altogether or assuming that the differences in human experience prevent any possibility of evaluation or interpretation across those differences.[26] Indeed, realists believe that interpretation of human experience and of causal features of the world like racism can lead to *better* knowledge than theories that fail to take adequate account of these features of the world. The last claim of mine (about *better* knowledge) distinguishes a realist position from many forms of relativism.[27]

Rather than fear mistakes and imprecision as insurmountable obstacles, realists view them as an inevitable and instructive presence.[28] For example, it has only been through an acknowledgment of error that feminists have been able increasingly to question the role of difference and multiplicity within the category of women. Related to this point, I should note that in responding to domination and exploitation, the objective knowledge on which realism bases its claims often arises out of oppositional political practice. Thus, awareness of the internal complexity of women as a social group has arisen from within struggles by those with opaque interests (women of color, working-class and Third World women, lesbian and bisexual women, disabled women, and transgender people) against domination and exclusion by women with more dominant positions in society (those with comparatively transparent interests). As Mohanty notes, citing feminist scholar Sandra Harding, without "alternative constructions and accounts . . . our capacity to interpret and understand the dominant ideologies and institutions [of society] is limited to those created or sanctioned by these very ideologies and institutions."[29] In contrast to a relativism based on a limited understanding of how knowledge can be discovered, verified, and evaluated, a sophisticated realism can more easily account for the need to revise our theoretical constructions (for example, understandings of identity) in response to the discovery of error and to challenges from competing theoretical or cultural claims.[30]

A restricted understanding of group membership fails to correspond accurately to the social features of the world, and its failure has something to tell us about the reality of how the world is organized. The apparent separation and fragmentation of identities result from the real relations of oppression and exploitation that structure our society. Fragmentation assumes a structure similar to that experienced by people with dissociative identity disorder (DID; formerly known as "multiple personality disorder"). However, whereas DID typically involves dissociation from traumatic experiences through the disruption of memory and sense of unified identity, fragmentation is a way that people come to be understood through the logic of oppression.[31] People who face multiple oppressions and have opaque interests may not have multiple identities, but processes of restriction can make them feel as if they do. Rather than having multiple identities, they are members of multiple identity groups in contexts in which the nature of oppression can make it difficult to see those groups as simultaneously salient.

Restriction and fragmentation are thus not *merely* illusions, nor are they accurate descriptions of how identities really are simply because those oppressive and exploitative relations attempt to make identities appear really separate and fragmented. The social processes of domination and exploitation become obscured by the "naturally" separate appearance that social groups take on within a social world organized according to a restrictive logic. Domination benefits from the naturalization of social identities as discrete groups that do not overlap; this process also makes relations of domination seem natural (such as the supposed "natural" inferiority of women). Consider, for example, former Harvard president Lawrence Summers's infamous and much-discussed gaff regarding "innate differences" as a possible explanation for the underrepresentation of women in top science and math positions.[32] This naturalization enables and benefits from everyday thinking that attempts to pass off justifications for inequality as commonsense conclusions about the way things naturally are. Better social theories help to move beyond the appearance of naturalness in human affairs in order to discover more accurate accounts of how this world has come to be the world it is.

Multiplicity Revisited

Given this realist account of identity, what might a theory of multiplicity look like? The early twentieth-century German philosopher Ludwig Wittgenstein, who began his career as a positivist before moving on to other theoretical commitments, once attempted to come up with a definition for what makes something a *game*. He almost immediately encountered a version of the challenge posed by multiplicity. Some games have one player (solitaire), others many (football); some have clear rules (chess), some do not (ring around the rosies). Yet, Wittgenstein notes, these many disparate things that hold "no one thing in common" do collectively entail enough sufficiently similar qualities that one can call them all games. He calls this phenomenon a family resemblance: "a complicated network of similarities overlapping and criss-crossing: sometimes overall similarities, sometimes similarities of detail."[33] Similarly, I would suggest that social group identities are also made up of relationships among people who, instead of sharing one thing in common, share various different kinds of commonalities and resemblances.

Philosophers of science sometimes refer to such a concept with the rather unwieldy phrase "homeostatic property cluster."[34] A classic example is a biological species. The Darwinian theory of the evolution and differentiation of species tells us that one *cannot determine* strict, invariable requirements for delineating the qualities that make up a given species. New species come into being through processes of variation and transformation. The theory of species development therefore predicts indeterminacy in species definitions in order to accommodate the process of evolution. Indeterminacy, however, does not prevent scientists from their unavoidable task of classifying species according to the kinds of overlapping and crisscrossing similarities noted by Wittgenstein. It simply means that species definitions remain necessarily imprecise, variable, and open—often the object of debate, disagreement, and revision. Attempts to impose overly exact boundaries on biological species, in turn, seem misguided insofar as they distort the reality of biological variation.

Similarly, definitions of identities and social groups need not entail absolute sameness or constancy. According to Lugones, "We have to constantly consider and reconsider the question: Who are our own people?"[35] Identities find themselves subject to a constant process of verification and revision.[36] To account for multiplicity, one can never view social identities as static entities neatly sutured at all ends. However, despite this emphasis on revision and transformation, one can justify claims and references to these identities insofar as the causal structures of the social world that give them their political significance (for example, ableism, economic exploitation, homophobia, racism, and sexism) seem neither arbitrary nor capricious. Forces of exploitation and oppression are discoverable and one can account for them in a theory of social identity even if the *exact* contours of a given identity must remain indeterminate, as in the case of a family resemblance. Verifiable accounts of how race or racism works, for example, enable the justification of claims on behalf of certain cultural, ethnic, and racial identities.

As I have argued elsewhere, one can similarly evaluate claims to moral truth in a secular society in terms of the adequacy and coherence of the theory of society that they invoke.[37] For example, the claim that slavery is not morally wrong entails, among other things, a view of what it means to be human that does not include freedom, self-ownership, and the capacity for self-realization (or it defines slaves as nonhuman). This claim does not account for the demonstrable fact that a person whose freedom rests on the enslavement of others limits that very freedom through fear of uprisings, mistrust of others, the necessary cultivation of cruelty or callousness, and so forth.[38] The theory of society that claims slavery is morally wrong, however, offers a fuller picture of what it means to be human—for example, that it includes freedom and self-ownership. It presents the premise that the freedom of one is connected to the freedom of all as a more adequate normative principle than the premise that one individual's freedom can be realized even if it rests on the enslavement of others. Such a theory more adequately accounts for the social features of the world and entails a more coherent and less contradictory conception of freedom. Similarly, some feminist and disability studies scholars have argued for understanding human beings as fundamentally dependent on others rather than as independent agents. Scholars and activists on behalf of people with cognitive disabilities (from Down's syndrome to schizophrenia), furthermore, have advocated for understanding the capacity to suffer as the defining feature of beings meriting ethical consideration rather than the more traditional philosophical criterion of rationality.[39]

This admittedly brief sketch provides an indication of how moral and political claims might receive justification without reference to absolute certainty or foundational beliefs. It also suggests how one might consider that justification objective. As long as the theory of society on which one bases them remains available to analysis, such claims remain open to verification, evaluation, and revision. This verification, evaluation, and revision necessitates a critical conception of objectivity that seems more subtle than the all-or-nothing idea that being objective means totally divesting oneself of one's humanity, making calculations like a logical automaton. According to feminist scholar Sandra Harding, one cannot separate a given knowledge claim from the process by which one arrived at it. In turn, one cannot extricate that process from its social context. Acknowledging how that process is situated in its social context, according to Harding, can enable strong objectivity rather than hindering it. By contrast, the false objectivity rightly criticized by many feminist and antiracist scholars most often results from taking partial perspectives (those of dominant social groups) to be universal, and from not examining the causes and results of their partiality.[40]

To return to my example from Nava's *The Hidden Law*, detective Henry Rios bases his insistence on inclusion within a Mexican American community on a moral sense of his right to participate in his community, due in part to his cultural upbringing and experience of racialization in the United States. He further supports his claim through a conception of gays and lesbians, not as detriments to community coherence and viability, but rather as assets. The novel argues for the accuracy of this conception through Henry's successful solving of the case of the senator's murder. Despite Nava's retention of notions of ethical truth and justification, however, there exists a sense in which the novel argues against moral truth as absolute. The detective novel typically presents justice as an absolute value that one can know with certainty. For example, in Dashiell Hammett's *The Maltese Falcon*, detective Sam Spade's integrity brings him to pursue the cause of justice whatever his personal feelings: the novel allows for no compromise, and the protagonist never doubts what is right. Although he hated his partner, he brings his partner's murderer to justice; although he loves the femme fatale, he turns her in; although he could have gotten away with a large sum of money, he hands it over to the police. Furthermore, detective novels historically reveal moral corruption through "abnormal" bodies: the villain in *The Maltese Falcon*, "the fat man," is both corrupt and obese; his accomplice, Cairo, has a body that the novel portrays as both racially and sexually ambiguous, and so on.[41]

The Hidden Law and other novels by Nava, however, present the non-white nonheterosexual as the enforcer of justice in a world in which moral corruption runs rampant among heterosexuals and white, middle- and upper-class communities.[42] Yet instead of merely reversing value hier-archies, Nava presents the issue of moral culpability as more dispersed throughout society, so that no one can really claim innocence in a cor-rupt world. In the world of *The Hidden Law*, this fact manifests itself in illness and addiction. Without exception, every major character, including Henry Rios and his lover, Josh, is either an alcoholic, or a drug addict, or HIV positive, or otherwise ill. At the same time, they all share guilt for the moral sickness of a violent society. This fact forces the main charac-ter, Henry, to retire from legal and detective work at the end of the novel. Rather than simply offering a strategic inversion of moral hierarchies or a quasi-relativist proposal for "alternative" values, Nava's work demands that we (all of us) take seriously the moral implications of Henry's expe-riences. It demands an acknowledgment of complicity in an unjust and immoral society. Furthermore, it demands that we consider Henry's claim to an internally multiple, constructed identity as having consequences not only for himself and others like him but also for others who are straight, not Mexican American, or neither. Nava asks of the reader not a one-way recognition merely granted to Henry but rather a two-way recognition that leaves the presumed unity of the onlooker forever altered.

The complexities of this process and its consequences for identity have not always received a full account in scholarly treatments of Nava's work. In an otherwise fine reading of another of the Henry Rios detective novels, *How Town*, literary critic Ricardo Ortiz seems to suggest that anything less than a complete suspicion of identity would be "utopian." He resolves the difficulty posed by Nava's recuperation of identity by distinguishing between the "importance for gay people, and for people of color, of achiev-ing a stable, resistant political identity," on the one hand, and "identity as such," on the other. For Ortiz, "identity as such" remains radically unsta-ble, "fundamentally an effect of the self's troubled relation to memory and desire, that is, to language."[43] It seems unclear how precisely the "stable, resistant political identity" embraced by Henry differs from "identity as such," however. In his reading of *The Hidden Law*, critic Ralph Rodríguez comes close to concluding that multiplicity in Henry's case proves identity to be an unstable fiction, but Rodríguez ultimately demonstrates how Henry "must return time and again to the space of the home and family to locate his identity."[44] Critics who resist the idea of identity thus have difficulty with Nava's books because of the need to account for Henry's desire for inclusion in an ethnic community (and, as Rodríguez observes, his need to revise and to recreate familial bonds).

Rather than casting Henry as an agent in the rejection of the bonds of social identity, *The Hidden Law* tries to demonstrate Henry's contributions to his community and to the pursuit of justice. The novel's project premises itself on a commitment to the preservation of identity categories, albeit in an expanded and revised form. Thus, the criticism of specific identities that comes through in the novel forms one step toward a positive reconstruction of a better vision of identity. Readings of such works as *The Hidden Law* that proceed from more relativist or anti-identitarian assumptions risk belittling or ignoring the substantive ethical and moral concerns that constitute their principle motivating forces and dominant themes.[45]

Who Our Own People Are

Attempts to answer Lugones's question, "Who are our own people?" inevitably run into concerns over exclusion through definition. If definition always implies exclusion, however, need exclusion always entail domination? Since some process of definition and categorization appears necessary for humans to cope with the world around them, I think that too easily collapsing definition with exclusion and exclusion with domination could effectively stymie any serious inquiry into how domination in a given society operates.[46] Being excluded or left out, in other words, seem to me not necessarily the same thing as being oppressed.

In other words, the claim, in and of itself, that identities are in some way exclusive does not provide evidence that identities themselves are oppressive or dominating. Indeed, as sociologist Manuel Castells argues, identities have proven to be among the most effective tools for challenging oppression in contemporary society.[47] Consider philosopher Linda Martín Alcoff's discussion of identity as a political position. Alcoff gives as an example "women who are not feminists" who "downplay their identity as women and who, on becoming feminists, then begin making an issue of their femaleness." According to Alcoff, "It is the claiming of their identity as women as a political point of departure that makes it possible to see, for instance, gender-biased language that in the absence of that departure point women often do not even notice."[48]

In this case, gender-biased language exists whether or not one notices it. Certain conceptions of identity, however, can help people to understand things such as gender-biased language more accurately in their struggles against domination. Alcoff goes on to describe a kind of politics in which "being a 'woman' is to take up a position within a moving historical context and to be able to choose what we make of this position and how we alter this context."[49] Rather than avoiding the act of classification that is entailed by theoretical generalities like "identity," this kind of political theory can self-consciously use general theories about the world in order to come to a better, revisable understanding of multiplicity and its wider social context.

Progressive social theory should enable the expansion of possibilities for solidarity across difference, but it must first account for multiplicity. In Lugones's account of multiplicity, she describes the act of separating people and groups into pure units as an act that facilitates domination.[50] By contrast, she champions "impurity," a lack of neat, distinct separateness, as a way of resisting the social forces of domination that try to freeze social reality, hiding the flux and indeterminacy of actual social existence. Under oppressive social relations, *separate* and *fragmented* become ways of seeing others and oneself that facilitate domination and exploitation. The logic of *purity* views people with opaque interests as split and fragmented rather than as whole and multiple. The reality of one's experiences, interests, and needs becomes obscured because "the interlocking of memberships in [multiple] oppressed groups is not seen as changing one's needs, interests, and ways qualitatively in any group." Instead, a person's "needs, interests, and ways are understood as the addition of those of the [dominant] members" of each group.[51]

Purity and separation thus distort opacity and multiplicity. People who reject identity completely often do so in an attempt to remedy and to avoid precisely this sort of miscomprehension of multiplicity by discrete, separate, and pure categories. However, rather than providing a solution to the distress of "walking from one of one's groups to another," a wholesale dismissal of identity increases the sense of homelessness for people with opaque interests.[52] It removes the ground on which people (like the character of Henry Rios in Nava's fiction) can claim that they "belong" in a group (or that others do not) and of making demands for inclusion, acknowledgment, and legitimacy. For Lugones, pure separation assumes that people's opaque "interests, needs, ways of seeing and valuing things, persons, and relations" do not differ qualitatively from those of the dominant members of the groups to which they belong.[53] Although such needs and interests arise socially, they do not result solely from the dominant ideas or beliefs of society. A theory of multiplicity must account for the experiences that generate opaque interests (without, of course, claiming to represent them "transparently") in order to justify the ethical and moral claims these interests make against dominating social relations.

Lugones's work, in part, attempts to reconceive identity, to go beyond, to resist, and to transform the very ways in which people imagine identities as separate and fragmented. As she points out, writing about lesbian separatism and being a Latina lesbian, "if we are to struggle against 'our' oppression, Latina Lesbian cannot be the name for a fragmented being. Our style cannot be outside the meaning of Latina and cannot be outside the meaning of Lesbian. *So, our struggle, the struggle of lesbians, goes beyond lesbians as a group.*"[54] Progressive social struggles and politics can only succeed when straight people of color and white lesbians and gay men come to see the interests of gay, lesbian, bisexual, and transgender people of color as *their own*. According to this prescription, dominant members of social groups must come to expand their sense of what their own interests are and who their own people are.[55]

Coalitions can thereby cease to constitute themselves as coalitions of people with different interests and the fragmentation within them can be healed. For this to happen, everyone must acknowledge opaque interests, reconceiving them as interests shared by all members of both groups (straight people of color on the one hand, and white lesbian, gay, bisexual, and transgender people on the other). In other words, fighting racism and homophobia must become a primary interest of all women and fighting sexism and homophobia must become a primary interest of all people of color within a given coalition.

This expansion of political interests can occur through attending to multiplicity and opaque interests. As I have already noted, Lugones urges everyone "to constantly consider and reconsider the question: Who are our own people?"[56] In other words, resisting domination and taking into account the experiences of those with opaque interests both require that we think beyond notions of group interests as tied simply to dominant group members, or of identity politics as expressive only of the interests of those with dominant identities. Lugones writes, "I don't think we can consider 'our own' only those who reject the same dichotomies we do"; instead, "we find our people as we make the threat [to domination] good, day to day, attentive to our company in our groups, across groups."[57]

House of Color Talks Back

Another example of resistance to restriction and of the affirmation of multiplicity through expanded interests is the work of the New York City–based video collective House of Color in the early 1990s. The members of House of Color included Robert García, Wellington Love, Robert Mignott, Jeff Nunokawa, Pamela Sneed, Jocelyn Taylor, and Julie Tolentino. The collective's members were bisexual, lesbian, and gay, and American Indian, Asian American, black, and Latino.[58] Its first video project, the 1991 short subject *I Object*, was followed by the collective's only other video, *Probe*.[59] These projects, like Nava's *The Hidden Law*, attempted to give voice to the reality of multiple interests, needs, and ways of being that have been obscured by forces of restriction and domination. *I Object* begins with a fast-paced, beat-driven pastiche of various white images of beauty, fashion, and erotica. The members of House of Color periodically interrupt these images by speaking out against the lack of representations of people of color. Next, the video presents a succession of stylized, exotic, or "whitewashed" images of people of color. One thing seems clear. Despite Pamela Sneed's demand in the video, "Mirror, mirror, answer me!" the House of Color members who appear and speak amid and against the pastiche of representations resemble none of the idealized or fetishized images. All the members speak their critiques of the portrayals of people of color in the media and in art (for example, the photographs of Robert Mapplethorpe). Wellington Love claims, "We just don't exist"; Julie Tolentino says, "I feel that this is something about exposing this big lie." Robert García asks, "What is it that determines it to be beautiful?" and answers himself that it is the penetration of white beliefs about beauty and exoticism. As the video makes clear, this penetration amounts to being "shafted."

In *I Object*, House of Color uncovers the reality of opaque experiences and interests. In an interview with the collective, Pamela Sneed describes the motivations behind the video this way: "While we wanted to give the world the message that we do exist, that we are not going to be spoken for by the White gay community, that we are going to take our own images into our own hands . . . we also wanted to pay attention to the fact that we are all individuals. We are Blacks, Latinos, Asians, who need to start a dialogue among ourselves."[60] Developing this dialogue, the second part of the video breaks down the distinctions between video makers and subjects by featuring all the members of House of Color in a kitchen. They interact with one another, first in friendly conversation and then in a more erotic series of images. Yet in contrast to the earlier images, produced by—and presumably for—white people, these are not highly stylized or idealized. Rather, they feature people of color as the subjects of their own desire, as intersubjective agents. They are also, as the voice-over states at one point, "the objects of [their] own desire." They are equal and reciprocal (although not symmetrical), respectful and respected.

House of Color developed a model for communication and solidarity across difference—through an appreciation of difference. Through the ambivalence of the title and the presence of all members of the collective both in front of and behind the camera, something important comes into being. As Sneed says, people of color reappropriate images of people of color. The members of House of Color can be objects, but they become their own objects as well as their own subjects. In one sense of the title of *I Object*, we see them speaking from the position of objects, as objectified individuals. The images in the video both demonstrate and challenge how cultural representations objectify people of African, Asian, Latino, and Native American descent. At the same time, however, one can detect the immense power of taking ownership of the objectified images of themselves: "I object." The forcefulness of the verb is arresting, stopping the proceedings of business as usual. The video signals an end to images of lesbian, gay, and bisexual people of color being made only by heterosexuals or by, in Sneed's words, "the White gay community." Indeed, the video attempts to destroy a tradition of excluding such images from representation altogether.

House of Color, however, did not seek merely to present "unmediated" images or to present any new images whatsoever. Instead, it sought to come up with a process of interpretation that allowed for the presentation of more accurate and more enabling images. This project, therefore, had a strong *normative*, or ethical, component. In a transcript of a conversation among several members of the collective that took place at the time they were planning *I Object*, Jocelyn Taylor described a need "to re-think our whole way of identifying beauty."[61] The video, to a certain extent, does pre-cisely this, and not only in the banal sense of portraying images of people who, because they are not white, might not conform to a Eurocentric stan-dard of beauty. Rather, people of color themselves label the images in this video as beautiful. In objecting to the traditional subject–object relation-ship in which people of color are objects of a white gaze, *I Object* speaks on behalf of objectified people of color telling themselves that they are beautiful. This reorientation does not merely *redefine* beauty by changing the role models who give definition to aesthetic standards (something a television series like *America's Next Top Model* might do through the rec-ognition of some women of color as beautiful).[62] Instead, House of Color urges people to rethink their whole way of *identifying* beauty. The subject–object relationship that grants one the ability, or agency, to call oneself or another beautiful is what *I Object* and House of Color seek to transform.

Solidarity and Expansion of Interests

The means of production for *I Object* play a central role in the artists' rethinking of representation. As an informally distributed video short produced by an independent artist collective, it came into existence under more activist impulses than more commercial representations of lesbian, gay, and bisexual people of color. Consider, by contrast, if a national toothpaste manufacturer were to begin producing television commercials that featured two women of color with minty-fresh breath kissing one another. In formulating an explanatory account for under-standing the position of the women in this commercial, one would want to ask about the mechanisms of production, ownership, and marketing that brought the commercial into being. With what theory of society do the manufacturer and the advertising agency operate? Has the commer-cial significantly altered or challenged the traditional conception of the subject if the toothpaste company uses underpaid workers in an unsafe workplace in a polluted county in North Carolina? If a wealthy group of international shareholders control the company? The women in the com-mercial may not become subjects in the eyes of the company or many viewers. The women's subjectivity, in turn, will probably not be under-stood in a complex, fluid way because their needs, interests, and ways will not have been acknowledged as "real," for and in themselves. Instead they will only exist *for others*, for the owners of the company as objects for the maximization of profit, for the viewers as objects of eroticization, identification, or shock. As "objects," they would have only the reality posited by a knowing "subject."

Viewer reception can be tricky and any analysis of popular culture can encounter complications in part because most people do not approach it statically. Viewers have multiple, sometimes contradictory, responses to television, for example. Often, one cannot predict their responses by looking only at the production of a given commercial or program. The television series *America's Next Top Model*, starring and produced by African American supermodel Tyra Banks, provides a good example.[63] The show, infused by Banks's own cultural politics, has consistently highlighted lesbian and bisexual women, women of color, women with disabilities, and "plus-sized" women as finalists and, sometimes, winners of its national modeling talent search. Banks regularly uses the show's platform to criticize the fashion industry for promoting eating disorders and unhealthy body images for young women, and often speaks out against racism and Eurocentric beauty standards, in support of sexual diversity, and for making the modeling industry accessible to women with disabilities. In addition, the show's regulars include several flamboyantly effeminate gay men of color in positions of authority. In these ways and others, the show attempts, with varying degrees of success and failure, to rethink U.S. attitudes toward beauty, body type, disability, gender, sexuality, and race. No doubt, the show's appeal among women and gay men of all races owes much to these attempts to reshape popular culture.

At the same time, however, the show adheres to most of the norms of the reality–competition genre, including an exploitation of contestants' personal tragedies and vices.[64] It also, ultimately, continues to feed a beauty industry that exists to sell products through the cultivation of a desire among women to "look better." Thus, when third-cycle winner Eva Pigford (the first African American winner of the show and the shortest winner, at 5'6") was announced, on December 15, 2004, she spoke about never having felt beautiful growing up and about still having difficulty thinking of herself as beautiful. Snapshots of her "tomboy" past accompanied this voiceover:

EVA: I am a Cover Girl. This little tomboy from L.A. that has never been beautiful. I was not the cute girl in school. I came here the shortest and the one that had the most insecurities inside of them. Now I'm America's next top model, and I get to represent all those little girls that feel the way I feel.

TYRA: Eva has vitality. She has sass and spunk that make her relatable to young girls everywhere. Eva is a true Cover Girl.[65]

Rather than valuing an unadorned, unaccessorized beauty that Pigford might have embodied as a child, the show narrates her triumph as that of an ugly duckling who has grown into her beauty—with some help from "Easy, Breezy, Beautiful CoverGirl® Cosmetics" (one of the show's sponsors); several thousand dollars in high fashion gowns and shoes; an expensive hair makeover; and a team of world-renowned stylists, photographers, personal trainers, and runway coaches. Finally, the value of Pigford's beauty comes from her talent at selling products with it. You, too, can be beautiful just as you are—so long as you buy enough things to bring out your true, inner beauty. Even Banks's liberal-pluralist identity politics cannot recover from such a contradictory tailspin.

Given these examples, I want to draw particular attention to the formation of House of Color itself. Writing in 1983, Chicana feminist Cherríe Moraga noted, "[We Latinas] have not been allowed to express ourselves in specifically female and Latina ways or even to explore what those ways are. As long as that is held in check, so much of the rest of our potential power is as well."[66] The project of House of Color held importance for precisely this reason. It sought to establish, from scratch, a way of being specifically queer and of color—without putting that identity in the service of corporate profit or the gaze and interest of others. The conversation within House of Color among queer, male and female Asians, African Americans, Latinos, and American Indians had few precedents. Furthermore, House of Color became a tremendous source of personal power. As Robert García noted, "Each time I speak as an individual . . . there is nothing. What fucks us up is that we wait for straight society to give us the models, the modalities for our existence, and we buy into it."[67] As a result of that conversation, House of Color produced some of the first autonomous representations of the lives of self-identified queer people of color in the United States.

As artistic works, I Object and Probe do not convey a sense of unmediated access to reality in their act of representation. The act of what García called creating new "modalities" for existence breaks with the assumption that such modalities might be obvious or simply available without the work of theorization and mediation. Instead, House of Color, especially in its second video, *Probe*, uses the concrete, lived experience of lesbian, gay, and bisexual people of color to elaborate commonalities and differences. This elaboration enables a mediated, fuller understanding of the forces of domination that act on gender-nonconforming people of color's lives. *Probe* intersperses short, experimental segments with longer, documentary-style interviews with lesbian, gay, and bisexual people of color. These interviews capture experiences both painful and liberatory, while the other segments mediate those experiences by providing an artistic, sociotheoretical context in which one can understand the importance of these experiences as insights into the nature and challenges of multiplicity.[68]

Writers, artists, and activists such as the members of House of Color, Michael Nava, and María Lugones do not take a racially unmarked sexuality and add to it considerations of race and ethnicity, understood separately but as intersecting. (Or vice versa.) Like Nava, House of Color's videos seek to describe the experiences of multiplicity that characterize the existence of gay and lesbian people of color. Its members thus transcend the "complex set of fictions" that have attempted to separate women, men, lesbians, gay men, African Americans, Asians, Latinas and Latinos, blacks, and American Indians into "pure," separate, and reified parts. In the process, artistic works like *The Hidden Law, I Object,* and *Probe* assert the multiplicity of queer people of color, expanding notions of social identity and group interests through the exploration of intra- and intergroup differences. This expansion, in turn, creates the possibility for solidarity across differences.

Using Tools Other than the Master's

Resistance to restriction requires that the self grow, transform, and expand. Resistance requires one to counter restriction with expansion, fragmentation with multiplicity, separation with solidarity, and exploitation with liberation. Thus, an understanding of identity that takes into account the social structures underlying domination must conceptualize identity beyond the limits imposed by restriction. In this sense, it must reject "the master's tools," the tools of purity and separation, and make connections between, among, and across groups.[69] Expansion of the self can only take place once we allow that groups truly *constitute* one another, constitute one another in such a way that the constitution of all groups is forever altered, enriched, and expanded—in other words, once "gay experience" can be understood in such a way as to include "Chicano experience." Only then can we expand the horizons of political action. This will not represent an end to identity politics, but an expansion of it and a growth of the self. In addition, it would need to engage in a project that could address not only the oppressed but also those who occupy more dominant positions within society.[70]

Most people can probably recall occasions on which their sense of who their own people were underwent a shift and became more encompassing. Many years ago, for example, I attended for the first time a meeting of an organization composed entirely of gays, bisexuals, and lesbians of color. Through my experiences as a member, and later cochair, of that organization, I came to understand my interests as more than just resistance to anti-Chicano racism and to homophobia and heterosexism. Once I came to understand "my own people" as black, Asian American, indigenous, Puerto Rican, male, female, and transgender, I was able to see the struggles against, for example, sexism and anti-Asian racism as my struggles. This is not to say that I came to see myself as sharing the experience of Asian women, for example, or as being able to identify as Asian or as female. Instead, as I came to think of myself as a queer person of color, I came to see myself as being part of a group that included Asian women and others. Although our experience was certainly not identical, there were similarities and commonalities, as well as connections, according to which I was able to see them as my people. Thus, whatever forces of domination and oppression they faced, they faced as my people. My interests came to expand beyond my own experience and beyond Chicanos, gay men, or Chicano gay men as discrete groups. It should be clear that this is not a rejection of identity or identity politics, broadly understood. Part of what made this expansion possible was understanding myself through a new identity category: queer people of color. At the same time, while this proved to be a necessary identity for me in expanding my sense of my own interests, I did not simply leave behind my identity as Chicano or as a man. All of these narrower and broader identities coexist within a complex multiplicity.

The challenges posed by multiplicity thus might also lead to a questioning of the desire to base solidarity on shared victimization. Not everyone occupies an oppressed location—and the overlapping structures of privilege and domination require more complex bases for solidarity. Expanding notions of shared interests and who our own people are can help to facilitate the kind of call made by feminist scholar Andrea Smith to ground alliances in an understanding of how "we are complicit in the victimization of others," rather grounding it in a notion of shared suffering.[71]

For example, nearly a decade after my involvement in the aforementioned organization, I underwent a more profound self-transformation. This time, it was a more academic encounter, although one with profound consequences for how I thought about the most intimate aspects of my life. Working together with such disability studies scholars as Tobin Siebers, Rosemarie Garland-Thomson, Carrie Sandahl, and Angel Miles under a general rubric of "minority studies," I had to come to terms with the significance of the ability–disability continuum for contemporary social life and with the assumptions about "normality" that have become constructed—literally—into our built environment.[72]

More importantly, however, I also had to deal with the consequences of my own status as what Garland-Thomson calls "normate," that is, an able-bodied person who largely matches my society's conception of what a normal body is like.[73] By this time, I had become accustomed to thinking about my maleness as a source of privilege, as something that preceded me into every room and followed behind me when I left, both opening doors for me and closing them again to others. The idea that I had a "normal" body, however, came to me as something new, and it raised troubling questions. How does my able-bodiedness relate me not only to individual disabled people (such as my cousin with Down's syndrome) but also to an entire regulatory system of knowledge, ethics, and aesthetics with dire consequences for bodies that do not fit its strictures as effortlessly as my own? What do I make of the contingency of that fit given the fragility of my body, like all bodies, my status as only temporarily able bodied? Perhaps more urgently, how might my own political and ethical commitments require alteration in light of, on the one hand, the historical links between ability and racial, gender, and sexual oppression, and, on the other hand, the frequent participation of liberation movements in justifying ability-based exclusions?[74]

These remain unanswered questions for me, and the project of answering them, importantly, is not an individual project. It remains the collective project of many in the disability community as well as those of us who do not share a disability identity but who remain concerned with overturning the social bases of disability oppressions. In other words, my solidarity with people with disabilities entails neither my own claiming of a disabled identity nor my sharing of a disabled experience. However, it does require me to rethink, in profound ways, my identities as gay, Chicano, male, and able bodied. True solidarity with others can never leave me unaltered because my complicity in the victimization of others always has implications for how I live and how I understand my life. Whether in coming to see myself as a queer person of color or as normate, I am transformed deeply and irrevocably.

Finally, I would like to invoke poet and essayist Audre Lorde's account of the role of difference in forging progressive politics:

> Advocating the mere tolerance of difference between women is the grossest reformism. It is a total denial of the creative function of difference in our lives. Difference must be not merely tolerated, but seen as a fund of necessary polarities between which our creativity can spark like a dialectic. Only then does the necessity for interdependency become unthreatening. Only within that interdependency of different strengths, acknowledged and equal, can the power to seek new ways of being in the world generate, as well as the courage and sustenance to act where there are no charters.[75]

Lorde's words call on women to use the resource of differences among them—intragroup, experiential differences—to create new ways of understanding the connections between women. These new ways of understanding must adequately accommodate the multiple ways of experiencing membership in the group "women." Her call does not discard "reality" or "identity politics," but recognizes the reality of different women's experiences and identities. This recognition can help create more accurate ways of accounting for the transparent and opaque interests of all women—a difficult, long-term, and transformational project.

Lorde predicates her words on the belief that differences among women (or among Chicanos or gay men for that matter) are neither incommensurable nor incomprehensible. While her emphasis falls on intragroup solidarity across difference, I find it compatible with Smith's vision of intergroup coalition. Lorde argues for the possibility and necessity of cross-cultural understanding and evaluation. In turn, her vision entails a theory of how group and individual interests can expand. Such a political commitment acknowledges the possibility of more and less objective knowledge of human needs and interests, like the need for self-determination and freedom from gender, racial, and economic slavery, or the interest in being a whole and multiple self. Precisely this kind of solidarity motivated my desire, first, to work with the men in the classes I offered at the prison, and second, to try to negotiate a sense of all the student-prisoners as "my own people," including not only those who seemed most similar to me as Latinos or as "queer" but also the straightest and most homophobic of these men. That desire for solidarity faces many obstacles, and might not always achieve full realization or reciprocation, but it has motivated many of the most brilliantly successful movements for progressive social change.

2

How Real Is Race?

The Abolition of Race

Few would deny that social identity has become a primary means for political action within liberal democracy. However, many bemoan this fact, and "identity politics" has become a pejorative, frequently denoting at best an unproductive approach to social change—as, for example, in Supreme Court Justice Sonia Sotomayor's 2009 confirmation hearings in the U.S. Senate.[1] Within the academy, furthermore, a strong body of work has emerged over the past two decades in opposition to the concept of identity.[2] Some critics argue that the multiplicity of identity vitiates any stable notion of the category, while others charge that many identities—and racial identity in particular—have no real referent, and therefore amount to nothing more than useless fictions. Indeed, race probably ranks among the most controversial social identities in the contemporary United States insofar as people often question its very legitimacy as a justifiable social distinction. Many in the United States cling to their own racial identity as a central part of their existence, while others consistently deny that they (or anyone else) even has a race because they see race as illusory. A quick read of Ward Connolly's so-called Racial Privacy Initiative (which would have eliminated California's use of race as a means of classification) reveals much about the contradictions in public discussions about race. Two clauses from the text of the failed ballot measure are worth singling out:

(a) The state shall not classify any individual by race, ethnicity, color or national origin. . . .

(g) Nothing in this section shall prevent law enforcement officers . . . from describing particular persons in otherwise lawful ways. Neither . . . the legislature nor any statewide agency shall require law enforcement officers to maintain records that track individuals on the basis of said classifications.[3]

Among other things, this initiative explicitly provides for the retention of racial profiling on the part of the police while freeing police departments from having to keep track of the race of the people they arrest or detain. The ballot measure, promoted using liberal, antiracist rhetoric, would thereby have frustrated all attempts to demonstrate discriminatory patterns of surveillance, arrest, or harassment by police. What ultimately swayed many white voters in California to oppose the measure, however, was not fear of police profiling, but fear of disease and a perceived need to use race to track harmful medical conditions popularly associated with biological conceptions of race.[4] Race clearly matters, and yet throughout its history as a concept, it has presumed the truth of various biological fictions that have not held up to contemporary scientific scrutiny. In this chapter, I explore some of the contradictions between social and biological conceptions of the reality of race and suggest that what is needed now is creative experimentation with racial identities rather than their abandonment. Furthermore, in shaping that experimentation, people must thoroughly engage with the mutual constitution of race with gender, sexuality, and other aspects of identity. In other words, we should measure the success of creative experiments with racial identities, at least in part, by their ability to evolve an understanding of the importance of race in relation to both the multiplicity of identity and the resistance to structural forms of discrimination, domination, exploitation, and oppression.

Despite notable challenges, a deep suspicion of identity in general and racial identity specifically has proven highly influential among many intellectuals in the humanities—and, as the Racial Privacy Initiative and Sotomayor hearings demonstrate, among many outside of the academy as well. (Within the field of philosophy, for example, a highly vigorous debate has taken place, primarily within African American philosophy, regarding the reality of race and its desirability as a concept. That debate, however, has not been broadly influential outside of its home discipline and has rarely considered race as a category mutually constitutive with gender and sexuality, preferring to analyze it in a state of presumed isolation.[5]) Against the current of intellectual suspicion of identity generally and racial identity specifically, I argue that racial and other identities can prove useful, productive, and transformative, and that their progressive political potential can benefit from a substantive account of their material reality in contexts of mutual constitution.

If social identities—understood as related to but distinct from the "self"—make a significant difference to how people live their lives, the kinds of experiences they have, and how others treat them, surely progressive politics would benefit from a substantive account of what makes identities matter and how people can elaborate them. Instead, however, some theorists have sought to make identities go away, although usually by arguing that they should rather than by addressing the material conditions giving rise to and resulting from them. I would like to begin this chapter, therefore, by considering two examples of antirealist views that see social identity generally and racial identity specifically as obstacles to progressive politics and as not referring to anything substantively "real."

The first approach to rejecting identity sees any invocation of collective identity (other than social class) as a divisive impediment to progressive social struggle. The second singles out racial identity specifically as irretrievably founded on a biological fiction and therefore as an invalid category of social analysis. These two positions are not mutually exclusive, and critics often invoke them simultaneously. By way of illustration, I will try to emphasize each approach through the writings of two influential scholars, both of whom have risen to academic prominence in part on the basis of their rejection of social identities: political theorist Wendy Brown and literary critic Walter Benn Michaels.

Identity as Impediment

The first, more general, rejection of identity emerges in Wendy Brown's book *States of Injury*, which paints a pessimistic picture of identity politics. According to Brown, identity politics errs in one of two ways. Either it commits itself to the preservation of class inequality by distracting attention from economic issues, or it becomes caught up in an unproductive cycle of blame and resentment. Both outcomes circumvent radical, progressive transformation of society. Brown thus charges that either identity politics seeks inclusion into society without asking if the society is just or it remains incapable of getting over resentment at social exclusion.[6] In other words, she does not believe that a political framework centrally concerned with identity can ever question the terms of social access, inequality, and scarcity that generate exclusions in the first place. She asks, "[T]o what extent do identity politics require a standard internal to existing society against which to pitch their claims, a standard that not only preserves capitalism from critique, but sustains the invisibility and inarticulateness of class—*not accidentally, but endemically?* Could we have stumbled upon one reason why class is invariably named but rarely theorized or developed in the multiculturalist mantra, 'race, class, gender, sexuality'?"[7]

In Brown's account, identity politics remains "a protest against exclusion" that seeks inclusion into what turns out to be a fictional communal ideal. She believes that, rather than seeking transformation of society, identity politics ultimately reinforces that fictional ideal and its various exclusions.[8] According to Brown's account of identity as pathological, advocates of identity politics seek "revenge" for their social exclusion.[9] They remain trapped, she believes, by their inability to get over the past (described variously as "a past injury" or a "history of suffering"), and they therefore locate a cause for past wrongs in the present. Basing their identity on a past injury or a history of suffering generates "an ethicizing politics . . . of recrimination that seeks to avenge the hurt even while it reaffirms it" and that cannot offer a "future—for itself or others—that triumphs over this pain."[10]

Conceding that one cannot simply do away with identity, however, Brown *does* offer a cure for what ails identity politics, in the form of two suggestions. First, she suggests something along the lines of a truth and reconciliation committee that would allow people to tell their pain, to be heard without seeking revenge, without asking for any remediation in the present to address past injuries (since to do so would inscribe the past in the present).[11] Second, she suggests that people should understand identity politics less in terms of "I am" and more in terms of "I want this for us," thus shifting emphasis away from an affirmation of identity in the present toward a focus on wants, needs, desires, and the future.[12]

Brown's account of identity politics, however, remains deliberately ahistorical and antimaterialist, and she casts her critique in the most abstract and general terms, implying that her account encompasses any kind of politics predicated on the affirmation of an identity. Absent from her account, however, is any specificity about *what* identity, *when*, and *in relation to* what other identities. Furthermore, she does not give an adequate account of either multiplicity or mutual constitution because she omits any specificity. Her critique could seem damning, except that she only offers a single example of identity politics in her discussion (an antidiscrimination ordinance in her local town), eschewing consideration of the *social movements* that have become the dominant expression of identity politics in the United States and elsewhere.

While her criticism of identity politics might hold validity for some examples of contemporary identity-based movements, it would require a significant amount of historical and ethnographic data to determine validity for all, or even most, of these movements. Such data are simply absent from her account. Ultimately, because Brown's work remains unengaged with the history of identity politics, even in the United States, I think she misses many of the ways in which that history demonstrates complex relationships among the affirmation of identity, the histories of oppression, and the articulation of freer, more egalitarian futures. Furthermore, identity-based political movements have often pursued socially transformative futures in more complex ways than even Brown's shift from "I am" to "I want this for us" can account for. This has been the case especially with regard to those movements that base themselves in a political recognition of the multiplicity of identity, such as women-of-color feminist movements.

Brown narrowly situates the origins of identity politics in a psychological need for recognition rather than in material, historical, and economic injustice, and understands identity politics as only seeking *recognition* within an unreconstructed social order. Consequently, her solution itself emerges as narrowly linguistic, rather than material, leaving unaddressed the material concerns that give identity its political salience to begin with. Rather than radical social transformation (something she criticizes identity politics for being unable to invoke), her solution amounts essentially to a change in political language.[13]

My objections to Brown's work do not entail a complete rejection of her core political commitments. Rather, it seems to me that she too narrowly circumscribes her conception of identity politics. Furthermore, she does not sufficiently acknowledge the limits of that conception (giving her work the tone of a definitive take on all that identity politics is or can be). Finally, she does all of this without empirical support, without any substantive engagement with (or even reference to) the long history of identity-based political struggles. This lack, in turn, prevents her from even beginning to consider the implications of intersectionality, multiplicity, or mutual constitution in the shaping of social identities and identity-based political movements. An examination of the history of identity politics would reveal that a goal of inclusion has often proved compatible with a goal of radical social transformation. Furthermore, many kinds of identity politics (from many versions of nationalism to lesbian separatism) quite simply do not seek social inclusion at all. While some identity-based movements might turn out to lack a future-oriented vision and might fail to move beyond an affirmation of identity, determining this to be the case would require careful, empirical consideration of each social movement. One cannot settle the issue in advance of the facts.

Racial Identity as Fiction

Another opponent of identity, Walter Benn Michaels, offers some objections similar to Brown's, but more specifically finds *race* an unjustifiable category of social classification. While many social constructionists claim that race is merely a social category with no basis in biology whatsoever, Michaels counters that this position makes little sense in light of how people actually act with regard to race. Every example of talk and action about race, he believes, relies consistently on reference to biology. Furthermore, race differs, Michaels claims, from other socially constructed identity categories, like class, primarily because of this reference to biology. However much social constructionists insist that they have rejected biological bases for race, Michaels argues that their arguments remain incoherent. If one rejects biological or other "essences" as the foundation for racial identity (as nearly all social constructionists believe one should), then Michaels claims that one must also absolutely reject race as a category. He puts his specific claim about race most sharply in a 1997 article:

> We cannot think of race as a social fact, like slavery or . . . like class. . . . I will argue that race is not like class, that it neither happens nor can be made to unhappen. And despite those who wish to "respect and preserve" rather than abolish race, I will argue it makes no more sense to respect racial difference than it does to try to abolish it. . . . [O]ur actual racial practices . . . however "antiessentialist," can be understood only as the expression of our commitment to the idea that race is *not* a social construction, and I want to insist that if we give up that commitment, we must give up the idea of race altogether. Either race is an essence or there is no such thing as race.[14]

He notes that for critical race theorists, "the claim that there are no races in nature—that race is a social construction—is not meant to deny that there is such a thing as race; it is meant to give us a better account of what race is."[15] That is, social constructionists about race, rather than arguing that race is merely a fiction, argue that it exists, only not as a natural or biological given outside of or before cultural meanings. For Michaels, however, race constitutes either a biological fact or a biological fiction; it forms neither a structural location within an economic system like class nor a mesh of cultural practices like ethnicity. (Of course, in his account these things—class, ethnicity, race—all appear separable rather than mutually constitutive.)

Indeed, one must concede that the central fact of biology has typically played the defining role in modern distinctions between race and ethnicity—a fact that would seem to support Michaels's claim that social constructionists' rejection of biological or natural facts results in some incoherence on their part. For example, while common ancestral lineage often figures centrally in defining both *race* and *ethnicity, race,* at least in the United States, typically carries with it more of an exclusive association with biologically inherited traits (for example, skin color, hair color and texture, nose and eye shape, height, or—most disturbingly— intellectual and moral capacity). This has remained true more or less since the nineteenth century. By contrast, *ethnicity* always includes—and has increasingly come to be limited to—cultural inheritance (for example, cuisine, customs, music, and folklore). Thus, Irish Americans, Russian Jews, Inuit, and Navajos might all constitute distinct ethnic groups, but in the contemporary United States, most would consider the first two racially white and the last two racially Native American. Furthermore, a Romanian infant adoptee in the United States would probably grow up both ethnically American and racially white, while Korean adoptees to white parents in the United States regularly grow up to think of themselves and to be perceived by others as ethnically American and racially Asian.[16]

For reasons I will discuss later in this chapter, many progressive social thinkers prefer to think of race as a social, rather than biological, phenomenon—or at the very least they consider it irreducible to simple, physical criteria (for example, skin color, descent, or genetic distance). Michaels holds that they must therefore believe that race comes about as a consequence of what one does, as an expression of actions and behaviors. He thus finds his (dis)analogy to class very important. While he agrees that social classes exist even though classes are not "natural," he denies that the same reasoning could apply to race (that it could be real without also being a fact about the natural world). For Michaels, class arises as a function of what someone does (for example, working or owning), not who a person is according to social categories or that person's self-conception. He understands class as a purely structural social location, in other words; either a person owns the means of production or one works for the person who does. (Of course, Michaels leaves unaddressed the difference that gender, sexuality, race, or ethnicity might make in *how* a person works for the person owning the means of production or their likelihood of occupying one class position rather than another.) In contrast to class, Michaels believes that race is "irreducible to action" because people can act in a way incompatible with their race. If a black person can "act white" without thereby becoming white, or a white person can "act black" without becoming black, in other words, then people must believe that race arises as a part of one's being rather than as a consequence of one's actions.[17]

If social constructionists do indeed argue that race comes about through one's actions, then Michaels has caught them in a contradiction—simultaneously upholding race as merely performance while believing in race as a part of one's being. Michaels thus levies his attack most successfully against those who appear to define race as strictly cultural rather than biological, since an account of race that refuses biological criteria cannot adequately explain the persistence of physical features, among other things, for determining racial identity. He goes further, however, and denies the possibility of a gray, "blurry" definition of race as something complexly arising out of the interactions of biology and culture—or, for that matter, out of the interactions of social class with biology and culture. Michaels insists that the "identity that is irreducible to action is essential, not socially constructed, and the identity that is identical to action is not really an identity—it's just the name of the action: worker, capitalist." This reasoning then leads him to conclude that if "we do not believe in racial identity as an essence, we cannot believe in racial identity as a social construction and we ought to give up the idea of racial identity altogether—we should . . . deny that there are such things as Jews, or blacks, or whites."[18]

Michaels's position ultimately proves too reductive, however. He bases his argument on the conviction that race must have only one meaning and only one determinate factor. Race, like most social concepts, however, means many different things and is not reducible to neat, orderly categories. As I argue in chapter 1, social identities, including race, have blurry boundaries, change over time and from place to place, and produce ambiguities and indeterminacies. Like Michaels, I would agree that one cannot reduce race to behavior, genes, or physiognomy alone. Race is not the same thing, furthermore, as class, color, culture, ethnicity, or nationality. This need not mean, however, that race has no relation to these things. Indeed, if, as some scholars suggest, racial categories originated as a way to assign places within a gendered labor market based on a calculus of physical appearance, genealogical descent, and geographical place of origin, then one need not deny the reality of those categories simply because the calculus usually proved vague and inconsistent or because one cannot easily separate race from class and gender. As I argued in chapter 1, the fact that one cannot easily define something—that it contains exceptions, ambiguities, and indeterminate boundaries—does not mean that it does not exist or that it makes no sense to speak of it.

The Stakes in Defining Race

Any adequate account of race must first entail a more subtle understanding of identity and experience. In making his general case against identity, Michaels seeks to replace political discussions of *being* with debates over *beliefs*. He elsewhere characterizes proponents of identity politics as claiming that "the things you do and the beliefs you hold can be *justified* by a description of who you are."[19] Like Brown, however, he assumes, rather than demonstrates, that this claim provides the basis of identity-based political movements. If, however, Michaels's statement were to read that the things one does and the beliefs one holds can be *explained*, in part, through a description of who one is and what one has experienced, then it would be a more accurate sense of the thinking behind much identity politics. Of course, in this formulation I do not see that Michaels's arguments provide a basis for opposition. After all, what *else* might lead people to hold particular beliefs *other than their experiences*?[20] This claim need not reduce all that a person is to ability, class, gender, race, sexuality, and so on. Furthermore, the claim that identity contributes to a person's beliefs need not imply that all people with similar identities will hold the same beliefs. Consider famed communist Angela Davis, who grew up as middle class, black, female, and intellectually gifted in Birmingham, Alabama, and famed anticommunist Condoleezza Rice, who grew up as middle class, black, female, and intellectually gifted in Birmingham, Alabama, a mere ten years later. The fact that they hold diametrically opposed political beliefs does not mean that their identities as black women had nothing to do with how they came to hold those beliefs. To argue otherwise would seem to border on obstinacy, or else to suggest that social identities cannot hold any significance unless they are absolutely bounded, uniform, deterministic, and foundational. Explaining either woman's political beliefs without reference *at least* to her gender, nationality, and race would be as absurd as arguing that the process by which Karl Marx came to his political beliefs had no relation to his being German or male or living in the nineteenth century.

What interests are served by polemics against race and other marginalized political identities? Studies of race demonstrate its power as a concept that has transformed repeatedly over the past five centuries. Race thus appears unlikely to go away any time soon. Rather than dismissing it, I believe that critical theorists should ask what possibilities exist for its further reinvention and how those possibilities might promote progressive social change. In a similar vein, Nobel laureate Toni Morrison writes,

> For three hundred years black Americans insisted that "race" was no usefully distinguishing factor in human relationships. During those same three centuries every academic discipline . . . insisted "race" was the determining factor in human development. When blacks discovered they had shaped or become a culturally formed race, and that it had specific and revered difference, suddenly they were told there is no such thing as "race," biological or cultural, that matters and that genuinely intellectual exchange cannot accommodate it. . . . It always seemed to me that the people who invented the hierarchy of "race" when it was convenient for them ought not to be the ones to explain it away, now that it does not suit their purposes for it to exist.[21]

Morrison's words might cause one to ask what critics have to gain by discounting identity and race. Cultural critic Carl Gutiérrez-Jones, for example, has noted commonalities between Michaels's rejection of collective identity and a larger "angry White male" cultural backlash in the United States in the 1990s.[22]

Of course, scholars of race can glean important insights from critics like Brown and Michaels. One might see Brown's work as an important caution against versions of identity politics that fall too easily into a liberal democratic framework without questioning the reproduction of economic inequality, as well as against those versions that fall into divisiveness and navel-gazing. Similarly, one might generously read Michaels's work as a caution against an overinvestment in racial language. Theorists and activists should not retain the language of race simply because we are attached to it, trying to make it do the work of culture, ethnicity, and class. Indeed, the mutual constitution of identities makes it even more important to consider the specific kinds of interactions among them. Thus, for example, defensiveness against attacks on affirmative action should not lead us to overlook the need for expanded access to higher education for lower socioeconomic status people of all races, as well as those from rural communities.[23] One should also guard against the lingering elements of nineteenth-century scientific racism in contemporary racial rhetoric, as well as against the collective tendency of the U.S. Left to conflate race with class and culture. I think that Michaels is wrong, however, in thinking that because people often conflate race with these other concepts, it does not describe any social reality at all. To be real, race needs neither to designate absolute, naturally given biological difference nor to conflate social categories with ways of acting. Rather than seriously asking what race means—whether or not it is useful, whether or not it actually obfuscates economic exploitation, and whether or not it refers to material contexts—Michaels, like Brown, opts for abstract, theoretical answers intended to transcend time and space. The empirical question remains of what race means and describes (or attempts to describe) in different times, places, and contexts and in relation to class, gender, nationality, religion, or sexuality. I will consider the consequences of this question in the remainder of this chapter.

The Power of Race and the Coloniality of Power

Social identity movements take many varied forms in contemporary society, and one must understand those forms in order to understand race. Sociologist Manuel Castells has emerged as one of the most influential empirical thinkers about identity in recent years. He offers a wide-ranging account of the new form of global social organization that he believes has quickly replaced both the industrial capitalist and state socialist forms of society at the end of the twentieth century: "the network society."[24] According to Castells, within the network society, collective identity movements have gained significance as the most powerful counterpoint to globalization. In other words, the contemporary destabilization of work and the increasing homogenization of ways of life and thinking have led political actors to embrace identity as the best way to organize themselves, both in resistance to and in support of a wide variety of political ends.

For Castells, identity-based political movements include what he calls "proactive movements" that seek to radically transform society and human relationships—movements such as feminism and environmentalism. They also include "reactive movements" that attempt to fight against the radical transformations of traditional ways of life being brought about by global capitalism as well as by other identity movements.[25] Castells does not use this dichotomy between proactive and reactive, however, as his primary way of categorizing identity movements. Instead, drawing from a broad array of examples from Africa, the Americas, Asia, and Europe, he argues for a three-part typology of social identities: legitimizing identities, resistance identities, and project identities.[26] *Legitimizing identities* arise through formal and informal, but "official," institutions, such as religious bodies, elections, schools, corporate and state media, and so on. Whether U.S. middle-class identity or citizen identities, they ultimately serve to reinforce and legitimate existing social structures and the often unequal relationships among people that these structures entail. *Resistance identities* come into existence through actions by people who believe they are dominated, excluded, exploited, or oppressed by existing social structures; they reject the institutions and norms of society, championing alternatives. *Project identities* attempt to redefine a group's position and role in society, but unlike resistance identities, they expand outward in the pursuit of radical transformation of society as a whole. In other words, their aim is not simply to redress the situation of one group, although they remain organized around identity. His typology, finally, is overlapping: some movements begin as resistance identities and later become project or legitimizing identities, or a mixture of some or all of the above.

Castells's account of project identities, specifically, makes accessible a whole range of possibilities that other accounts of identity foreclose, and raises serious challenges to the nostalgia of some on the Left for (allegedly) belief-based, as opposed to identity-based, political movements. According to Castells, project identities become part of a larger process of reinventing and reordering society. While the process of creating a project identity might begin through the affirmation of a denigrated identity, it has the potential to expand "toward the transformation of society as the prolongation of this project of identity, as in the . . . example of a post-patriarchal society, liberating women, men, and children, through the realization of women's identity."[27] While project identities need not necessarily prove politically progressive, Castells believes that they are, in the contemporary era, *necessary* for social change.[28] Castells does acknowledge that most contemporary identities do not become project identities, remaining caught in a reactive posture; however, despite the bad odds, he holds that identity remains the best hope for transforming the current global network society into a better and more humane world.[29]

Before turning to Castells's consideration of racial identity in the contemporary period, I want briefly to retrace some of the long history of race as a social category. I do so because I believe that social theorists discuss race without a full account of its history at their peril. In particular, I would like to turn to historical sociologist and world-systems theorist Aníbal Quijano's account of the origin and significance of race. I do so both because I find world-systems theory among the most powerful models for analyzing historical change on a global scale and because Quijano has been at the forefront of using that model to understand race. His use of world-systems theory, starting his analysis with the discovery of the Americas, offers a much longer and wider sense of the origins of race than do accounts that take the relatively recent scientific racism of the nineteenth century and legal classifications of the twentieth as the definitive examples of racial thinking. For Quijano, race emerges early in the sixteenth century, alongside a complex and global (re)organization of power around three interrelated and inseparable factors: "coloniality," capitalism, and Eurocentrism. The development of the concept of race occupied a central role in the shaping of a world system:

What is termed globalization is the culmination of a process that began with the constitution of America [the "discovery of the Americas"] and colonial/modern Eurocentered capitalism as a new global power. One of the fundamental axes of this model of power is the social classification of the world's population around the idea of race, a mental construction that expresses the basic experience of colonial domination and pervades the more important dimensions of global power, including its specific rationality: Eurocentrism. The racial axis has a colonial origin and character, but it has proven to be more durable and stable than the colonialism in whose matrix it was established. Therefore, the model of power that is globally hegemonic today presupposes an element of *coloniality*.[30]

Race has two crucial characteristics for Quijano. First, its origin presupposed the existence of biological differences from which followed a natural hierarchy among superior and inferior groups. Second, race enabled (and was enabled by) new social and economic relations; racial identities thus became "constitutive" of *unequal* roles, locations, beliefs, and practices.[31]

Thus, according to Quijano, race, in its origin, entailed a web of beliefs that served to legitimate domination and to naturalize inequality so that people understood them as inevitable and eternal rather than as contingent and produced. In the process, ideas about race "encroached on" already existing practices of gender domination, mutating and transforming them.[32] The encroachment of race on gender involved the mutual constitution of gender, race, and sexuality over the course of several centuries. (I consider this process of encroachment and mutual constitution at length in chapter 3.[33]) In short, emerging conceptions of gender, sexuality, sin, and perversion intermeshed thoroughly with the development of the colonial/modern racial regime outlined by Quijano, giving rise to what philosopher María Lugones calls the "colonial/modern gender system."[34] This process brought about a Eurocentric conception of gender and sexuality that eventually evolved into understandings of heterosexuality, homosexuality, and gender hierarchy that remain inseparable from the colonial encounter and that continue to influence modern practices of gender and sexuality today.

According to Quijano, race came into existence (separately from ethnicity or nation) as a marker of inherited, "natural," and hierarchically ranked differences in temperament, morality, intellectual ability, and aptitude for cultural and scientific achievement among geographically distinct populations. These supposed differences justified social relations of domination and made them seem "natural" to European colonizers. Race emerged both as a justification for social domination and as a basic way of assigning places within a labor market also segregated by gender.[35] In other words, it divided the world into inferior and superior populations, which then legitimated a racial and sexual division of labor. Wage labor became restricted to white males, while the racial-gender order assigned white females to paid and unpaid domestic labor and nonwhites (primarily Africans, Amerindians, and Asians) of all genders to various forms of hereditary serfdom and slavery. Quijano writes, "In this way, both race and the division of labor remained structurally linked and mutually reinforcing, in spite of the fact that neither of them were necessarily dependent on the other in order to exist or change."[36] His view of the relationship between race and labor marks a decisive departure from other social theorists, like Eric Wolf, who see race as essentially subordinate to the division of labor, and as not having structural independence.[37] The independence of race from the division of labor has significance for its continuing effects, what Quijano calls the "coloniality of power." Quijano, however, like Wolf, does not go far enough in considering the centrality of gender as a force shaping race and labor. He thus gives insufficient attention to, for example, how the complex relations among genteel, working-class white, peasant, and enslaved women differed from those among their male counterparts.

In addition to the material reorganization of the world, the classification of the world's population according to race also came to have intense effects on the ways in which people thought about how one can arrive at knowledge, what it means for something to be true, and what it means for cultural practices or objects to have value or significance:

> In the first place, they [Europeans] expropriated the cultural discoveries of the colonized peoples most apt for the development of capitalism to the profit of the European center. Second, they repressed as much as possible the colonized forms of knowledge production, the models of the production of meaning, their symbolic universe, the model of expression and of objectification and subjectivity. . . . Third, in different ways in each case, they forced the colonized to learn the dominant culture in any way that would be useful to the reproduction of domination. . . . All of those turbulent processes involved a long period of the colonization of cognitive perspectives, modes of producing and giving meaning, the results of material existence, the imaginary, the universe of intersubjective relations with the world: in short, the culture.[38]

Numerous scholars have studied this process at great length, especially over the past three decades.[39] *Eurocentrism*, for Quijano, names the cognitive and cultural dimension of the new model of global power dominant since the sixteenth century. It entails the imposition of a "racial, colonial, and negative" identity on non-Europeans, as well as the classification of their culture as "naturally" inferior and as historically antecedent to Europe (as premodern or primitive).[40] The well-discussed dichotomies of modern Western thought make up but one enduring legacy of the coloniality of power: civilized–primitive, culture–nature, male–female, mind–body, normal–abnormal, north–south, reason–passion, superior–inferior, white–black. The seventeenth-century separation of the body from the mind, and the identification of the body with nature (and female-ness, Indianness, and blackness), made possible, according to Quijano, the scientific racism of the nineteenth century.[41]

Based on the history of Eurocentric values that sedimented onto racial difference, one should not find it surprising that both Castells and Quijano cast race in almost exclusively negative terms. Quijano only discusses race as a means to facilitate oppression. For his part, Castells attempts to distinguish *race*, understood as a source of oppression and discrimination and as an externally imposed biological categorization, from *ethnicity*, understood as "a source of meaning and identity" that comes closer to *nationality*, although without the key features of language and territory.[42] After a lengthy consideration of the importance of race (in terms of oppression and discrimination) for African Americans, Castells finally holds that the concept of race (which he here conflates with ethnicity, despite his earlier distinction) can only take on significant communal meaning as it combines with broader categories (gender, nation, religion, class, and so on):[43] "[E]thnicity does not provide the basis for communal heavens in the network society, because it is based on primary bonds that lose signifi-cance, when cut from their historical context, as a basis for reconstruction of meaning in a world of flows and networks. . . . Ethnic materials are inte-grated into cultural communes that are more powerful, and more broadly defined than ethnicity, such as religion or nationalism, as statements of cultural autonomy in a world of symbols. . . . Race matters, but it hardly constructs meaning any longer."[44] The primary basis for this striking claim (striking because Castells does not make the same claim about nationality or religion) lies in the growing class polarization of blacks in the United States. In the case of race, Castells concludes that the fracturing of identity in one example prevents it from being a source of meaning in all cases (while the fracturing of some national identities does not preclude the cohesion of some other national identities for Castells). It seems ironic that Castells would argue that race in the contemporary era only provides meaning in combination with other categories of identity, since he introduces an artificial separation of race from gender, nation, sexuality, and so on in his analysis. Throughout his study, he conducts analyses on different religious, national, ethnic, linguistic, and gender identities, treating each in isolation from the others. Thus, he takes little notice of the extent to which Catalan nationalist movements might be shaped by gender and religion, or of how Islamic and Christian fundamentalist movements might emerge from core commitments to specific gender identities or to national, racial, linguistic, or tribal ones.

Is It Real? Is It Really Real?

If one understands race as different from culture, ethnicity, class, or nation, then I suggest that the claim that race is *real* could mean at least three different things: (1) race has a material-economic reality in the immediate effects and legacies of racism; (2) race has a social and psychological reality as an existing system of beliefs and attitudes with material effects (this would include certain effects on the production and acquisition of knowledge); or (3) race exists in a physical or biological form, as bodily matter. (In each case, of course, the reality and significance of race will be further shaped by gender and socioeconomic status, among other things.) Given Quijano's account of the origins of race as a concept tied to domination and exploitation, one can easily understand why people might want to argue against its biological reality—perhaps even more so in the wake of nineteenth- and twentieth-century versions of scientific racism.[45] Yet, as Castells notes, with a nod to Cornel West, "race matters a lot."[46] Determining what that mattering consists of, then, becomes an important task.

If one thinks of *race* as merely shorthand to reference the effects of racial classification and racism in contemporary society, then it is hard to deny its reality (although some might). Castells cites a host of studies on the impoverishment and imprisonment of blacks in the United States, for example.[47] As criminologist Coramae Richey Mann notes, "Racial minority suspects disproportionately become defendants [in court] and as defendants are disproportionately sent to prison or disproportionately executed."[48] A massive study of the death penalty in Georgia in the 1970s found that defendants were four times more likely to receive a death sentence for killing white victims than for killing black victims. Moreover,

— Reveals the stereotype threat.
Visible stereotypes will ~~become~~ have an effect on people affected by stereotype. —

blacks convicted of killing whites were twenty-two times more likely to receive a death sentence than blacks convicted of killing blacks. The study found race to have more influence than over two hundred other possible factors that affect sentencing (including various kinds and degrees of aggravation and motivation, whether victims were police officers or very young or female, and whether the defendant had a prior record).[49] Disparities in criminal justice have not diminished in the thirty years since. It is difficult to understand the unequal treatment of racial minorities in the United States as anything other than an effect and legacy of racism. At the very least, then, race remains important for understanding, explaining, and addressing the effects of contemporary and historical racism, a point that even most critics of racial identity concede in some form or another.[50]

Race might also matter as a set of beliefs with material effects. Put another way, ideas about race can have consequences for how people think and act. In 1995, for example, social psychologists Claude Steele and Joshua Aronson conducted a study in which researchers gave black and white college students difficult exams measuring advanced English language skills. When researchers told test-takers that the exam was diagnostic of verbal ability, blacks performed about half as well as whites. When the same exam was given and test-takers were told that it was not diagnostic of ability, but merely a way to study how people solve problems, blacks and whites performed roughly equivalently.[51]

Another group of researchers was able to produce similar results in the domain of physical performance, having black and white college athletes play ten holes of golf in a laboratory course. When athletes were told that the goal was to measure "natural athletic ability," the blacks outperformed the whites significantly; when they were told that the test measured "sport strategic intelligence," the outcome was the opposite.[52] Thus, setting aside the question of whether racism (intentional or structural) currently exists, race as a set of ideas exists and has significant material effects not only on people's thinking but also on their performance in a wide variety of mental and physical tasks. Furthermore, these effects are not arbitrary, but rather have clear connections to the long history of Eurocentrism and its attendant evaluative hierarchies (white–black, mind–body, and so on). Similar studies have explored the effects of gender, although it has proven difficult for such scientific studies to move beyond consideration of identity categories as separable units, combinable only on an additive model.

✱ Stereotypes in the edu. system impacts all students and their ability.

Verbal tests vs. athletic ability.
→ Stereotypes affect our beliefs, impacting our ability degree of self is impacted

Perhaps the most controversial meaning of the claim that race matters (or that race is real) would be the suggestion that race has a basis in biological or physical causal structures that, in turn, result in the social differences one finds between contemporary, socially defined racial groups. As I have just laid it out, this claim assumes an easy separability between biology and culture. Furthermore, it can easily play into historical and commonsense racist thinking. The belief in a biological basis for race lies at the core of what scholars call scientific racism, arguably the dominant form of racial thinking in the nineteenth and twentieth centuries.

Paleontologist and historian of science Stephen Jay Gould, among others, has meticulously documented the abuses of nineteenth-century scientific racism as an attempt to legitimate socially defined racial classifications and their attendant social inequality in terms of biological differences (for example, the idea that brain size or intellectual capacity has a direct connection to skin color).[53] More recently, evolutionary biologist Joseph L. Graves Jr. has compiled a range of scientific and social data to argue that contemporary categories of socially defined races in the United States usually prove unhelpful—and often harmful—for attempting to understand sexual behavior, health and medicine, athletics, and intelligence. While he also looks at considerations such as bone density and muscle mass, Graves mainly targets genetic explanations for social differences. He observes that humanity as a species has come into existence very recently, in evolutionary terms. The even more recent dispersal of human populations geographically and the relatively short time that populations have spent in geographical isolation have not sufficed for the development of different geographical races as scientists apply the term to other species. In other words, by contrast to many other mammals, humans seem remarkably alike when it comes to our genes. As he observes, "The genetic distances in humans are statistically about ten times lower (2 percent) than the 20 percent average in other organisms, even when comparing the most geographically separated populations within modern humans. There is greater genetic variability found within one tribe of western African chimpanzees than exists in the entire human species!"[54]

Furthermore, with regard to supposed racial genetic predispositions for disease, Graves shows that our current, socially defined races obscure the actual genetic commonalities and differences of various populations. Genes for sickle cells, for example, while prevalent in people from western Africa, the Mediterranean, the Arabian Peninsula, and India, are uncommon among people from eastern Africa. Similarly, while much has been made of a supposedly genetic predisposition among African Americans for high blood pressure, Nigerians have far lower rates of high blood pressure than do U.S. whites (the difference between Nigerians and U.S. whites being more than double the difference between U.S. whites and U.S. blacks).[55] As Graves observes, "Geographical distance does not necessarily equal genetic distance. In fact, assuming that two people are genetically different because they look like they came from different parts of the world can be really dangerous for their health . . . [b]ecause things like people's blood type or their ability to accept transplanted organs are dictated by how genetically close they are, not necessarily by where their ancestors came from geographically."[56]

Good reasons therefore exist for skepticism about attempts to link biology and race—especially given such familiar examples of racial biological determinism as Richard J. Herrnstein and Charles Murray's resoundingly refuted book, *The Bell Curve.*[57] However, I think there are important reasons not to eliminate all consideration of biology and the body from our discussions of race, provided we understand biology as mutually constituted with culture and as significantly less determinate than people often take it to be. In particular, an important dimension of what race is and how it functions results from the interaction of social practices and beliefs about race with visible human difference. To understand this dimension of racial experience, scholars must consider the physical matter of race. While such outward differences as skin color, hair texture, or eye shape may hold little or no meaning for our biological functioning as organisms or for our innate capacities, they can prove crucial, in Western societies at least, for our social functioning.

Racial Identity as "Intra-action"

It helps to understand physical or natural materiality as something that does not simply exist inertly and passively, waiting for culture to give it meaning and to act upon it. Theoretical physicist Karen Barad suggests that an adequate social theory of bodies needs to account for "*how the body's materiality*—for example, its anatomy and physiology—*and other material forces actively matter to the processes of materialization.*"[58] Drawing from the quantum theory of Niels Bohr, her view of bodies rejects the separation between observer and object, and therefore, also that between social and cultural forces and matter. If one understands the world as fundamentally a big soup of inseparable processes, with indeterminate boundaries and constantly in flux (which is easiest to do at the quantum level of atoms, particles, and waves), then one can begin to see the degree of mutual constitution at stake among observers and objects. Both the "observer" (which would include theoretical assumptions as well as instruments used to observe and measure) and the "observed matter" interact (or, as Barad insists, "intra-act") in order to produce an event or phenomenon. Both observer and matter are "agential," actively influencing one another. Barad's account does not understand the observer as neutral, nor matter as passive: "The world is a dynamic process of intra-activity in the ongoing reconfiguring of locally determinate causal structures with determinate boundaries, properties, meanings, and patterns of marks on bodies."[59] *Agency*, for Barad, describes a process through which the causal intra-actions of different parts of the world produce intelligible phenomena. As Bohr notes, indeterminacy becomes particularly salient in the study of quantum phenomena, so that accounting for a quantum event requires a thorough description "of all relevant features of the experimental arrangement."[60]

Extrapolating from Barad's and Bohr's ideas to the realm of social theory, I would argue that indeterminacy and mutual constitution play equally important roles in social, political, and historical phenomena as they do in quantum phenomena. In considering race, most biological reductionists tend to eschew histories of racism as irrelevant, while most attempts to debunk scientific racism tend to discount the importance of biologically superficial physical differences for understanding the reality of race. As Barad cautions, however, "explanations of various phenomena and events that do not take account of material, as well as discursive, constraints will fail to provide empirically adequate accounts (not any story will do)."[61] The temptation to eliminate race as a category of analysis in favor of culture, ethnicity, or class, furthermore, while well intentioned, can fail precisely by not accounting for the active role of otherwise superficial physical differences—as well as customs of assigning meaning to family descent—in shaping "racial formations," the broad processes that shape and reshape the cultural and structural meanings of race across history and geography.[62]

Unless we accept the causal role of matter in the formation of racial meanings and phenomena, our theories of society will prove incapable of explaining how and why people experience race as they do. To put it bluntly, how can I understand my ease at hailing a taxicab in New York City or Washington, D.C., in the face of countless stories from black friends about having to walk forty blocks without having one stop for them? Along similar lines, a 1991 study found that while African Americans identified as "very light" earned 80 percent of the average income for U.S. whites in 1980, "very black" African Americans earned 53 percent—with the incomes of "light brown," "medium brown," and "dark brown" African Americans forming a downward-sloping curve between the two extremes.[63] Other scholars have identified similar correlations to skin color in Brazil and among Mexican Americans and Puerto Ricans.[64] Another study among African Americans found slightly different data suggesting that while lighter-skinned blacks faced significantly less wage discrimination in relation to darker-skinned blacks, those identified as "medium-skinned" did not receive a significant preference from potential employers.[65]

In both studies, interviewers recorded skin tone shades of African American survey participants. The authors of the first study suggest that because of racism, darker-skinned blacks face (and have historically faced) greater discrimination than their lighter-skinned peers, resulting in both inherited and acquired income differences. Their explanation suggests the continuing effects at the end of the twentieth century in the United States of a racial division of labor that first emerged in the sixteenth century. In the more recent study, moreover, the authors suggest that the effects of skin color manifest in the decisions of employers, whose behavior reveals marked preferences in favor of lighter-skinned employees.

A theory of race that does not account for the intra-action of culture and body will prove inadequate to explain the data from these studies. Some of the social psychology studies discussed earlier also suggest the importance of considering the active participation of bodies in racial meanings. For example, when researchers administered a verbal ability test to black and white college students and described the test as culturally fair, whites did not outperform blacks. When they presented it as a normal diagnostic test, however, whites outperformed blacks—and blacks had dramatically higher blood pressure levels.[66] The biological body, it would seem, is not inert matter in the face of ideas and beliefs about race. Bodies respond to ideas as ideas respond in turn to physical bodies.

Race thus emerges as a phenomenon through the intra-action of a number of things, including human phenotypic differences such as eye and nose shape, skin tone, hair texture, height, and so on. These differences become salient in the ongoing process of racial formation. They become meaningful as components in the intra-active phenomenon of race, which in turn varies across time and space. While the significance of those bodily differences changes and is not always even present when the concept of race emerges, one cannot fully explain certain racial phenomena without reference to human bodies. For example, attempts to reconfigure race solely as culture or as legal fiction fall into absurdity if they cannot consider the significant role of bodily difference in the "whitening" of European immigrants in the United States (or the uneven ability of different Mexican Americans and Latinas and Latinos to "become" white).[67] Whiteness may not only result simply from a lack of melanin (there are many light-skinned people of color), but it certainly helps to be light skinned in order to qualify as white. Studies on the ambiguity of the category of whiteness in fact support the link between skin tone and social whiteness. After all, uncertainty about who qualified as white in U.S. history did not affect immigrants from Nigeria or Sweden. The very fact that U.S. case law determining the boundaries of racial identity focuses overwhelmingly on Arabs, Armenians, Asians, Latinas and Latinos, and people of mixed-race descent shows the extent to which physical appearance emerged as a causal, albeit not always determinate, factor in the materialization of race in the United States.[68]

Bodies do not have inherent meanings. Yet given the physical properties of bodies and the historical sediment of their intra-actions with cultural ideas and political-economic practices, one cannot attach just any meaning to any body. In other words, the body comprises something more than an inert, passive object on which people inscribe meaning. Bodies are agents with their own causal role in making meaning. Dark-skinned black people in the United States, for example, cannot become white simply through linguistic feats, because their body's production of melanin plays an indispensible role in racial production. Of course, race is not just color, but in some periods and places color becomes not merely an indispensable but a determinate component of race.

Race is a produced, intra-active phenomenon involving the colonial/modern gender system (itself a phenomenon with many intra-acting components) and individual bodily differences and histories of family descent, as well as social beliefs and practices (including those of courts, legislatures, police, and prisons). It consequently varies and changes across time and space, intra-acting significantly with practices related to gender and sexuality. That in the contemporary United States two people with very light pigmentation and known sub-Saharan African ancestry can be considered black, while in contemporary Brazil a brother and sister with different complexions but the same ancestry might be considered of different races, does not mean that race does not exist. Rather, such differences indicate that the social phenomenon of race emerges differently because of the different intra-actions among history, economics, law, sexuality, and human bodies in U.S. and Brazilian societies. Race, on this account, amounts to a social construction, but one in the emergence of which biology sometimes plays an important part.

Is Race All Bad? Racial Identity Projects

In the remainder of this chapter, I argue for considering the creative elaboration of racial standpoints as not just compatible with, but necessary for, radical social transformation. My position assumes the malleability of racial categories beyond what one might most often associate with *race*. It also assumes that racial meanings can transcend histories of racism. Given the more than three centuries of racial thinking that preceded the rise of scientific racism in the nineteenth century, it might seem odd to reduce race to the biological classifications of that period—even if the word *race* took on its sharpest definition at that time. It would seem considerably less odd, however, to view race as an inherently oppressive construction that legitimizes social inequality, domination, and exploitation. Such a view amounts to the assertion that *race* equals *racism*.

One can somewhat easily argue for the reality of race as a *social location* that one finds oneself placed in by racial classifications given the substantial empirical data on the effects of social ideas of race. It proves far more controversial, however, to defend race as a self-consciously chosen *standpoint* necessary to antiracist struggle—particularly given the persistent characterization of race as a negative construction, one that has had polarizing and destructive effects on human knowledge, morality, and aesthetics. In writing about standpoint and social location, I draw on a distinction developed within feminist philosophy. *Social location* names the part of one's identity defined by laws, customs, and practices quite apart from one's individual sense of self. Racial social location generally results in a person's experiencing or not experiencing the direct effects of racism, for example. *Standpoint* refers to the mediation, or interpretation, of social location. It generally reflects someone's decision to make a public and political issue of one's identity. In becoming a standpoint, an identity becomes rearticulated in the pursuit of social transformation, while remaining thoroughly bound up with one's individual and collective sense of self.[69]

Increasingly, a number of scholars have argued for identity's indispensability as a theoretical construct shaping one's cognitive access to the world. The clarity of this access remains an empirical issue, but that issue's resolution does not make socially constructed identities any more or less real. Even identities that obscure knowledge about the world can have substance to them. Furthermore, through active social struggle (or the elaboration of standpoints and project identities), one can both transform the world and generate new knowledge about what the world is and what it might become. In turn, social struggle can enable new social identities, and new social identities can give rise to social struggle. One might, therefore, understand some resistant and project identities as the elaboration of a standpoint from a social location in order to act in the world in such a way that forever alters that social location. However, people can have difficulty imagining imposed, negative identities as resources for hope and transformation.[70]

I offer two examples of racial project identities by way of concluding this chapter in order to suggest the possibilities for reimagining race and other stigmatized identities. Performance scholar Carrie Sandahl recounts one example of the potential for progressive project identities in her analysis of black and blind performance artist Lynn Manning's *Weights*. In her analysis of Manning's performance piece, she focuses centrally on his departure from the traditional "overcoming" narrative of disability, in which "disability experience becomes a generalized metaphor for psychological adjustment."[71] According to this traditional narrative (a narrative with no shortage of similarities to Brown's prescription for identity politics), newly disabled people first feel devastated by their disability and eventually learn to transcend it and to achieve a wiser, happier state because of the effort of overcoming.[72] The pivotal point at which *Weights* departs from the overcoming narrative occurs when Manning regains consciousness after being shot and learns that he has lost his sight. At this moment, he recalls, "Something akin to joy surges through me."[73] While his doctors see his response as "abnormal," Manning reveals that he feels not so much happy to be blind as happy to be blind and still alive. Later, however, he does begin to revel in his blindness and the vistas of opportunity and experience that it opens to him. As Sandahl notes, "[W]hat Manning learns could only be known through the biological configuration of his new body, or . . . the 'causal constraints' of the natural world. He discovers new dimensions, or new truths, about what he thought he had known."[74] These discoveries only become possible because of his experience of blindness.

Sandahl finds Manning's response to becoming blind significant because it reveals that his blindness, in conjunction with his blackness and maleness, provides him with an "interpretive framework" for understanding the world around him. Drawing from realist theories of identity, Sandahl argues that Manning's interpretive framework, rather than impeding objective knowledge about the world, makes it possible.[75] In order to obtain knowledge about the world from a blind person's standpoint, Manning must embrace his blindness and revel in his disability rather than seek to eliminate or overcome it. Manning's understanding of his gendered and racial identity as a black man, in turn, shapes this process. He must take the knowledge he has about what it means to be a black man and what it means to be blind and integrate the two standpoints. His integration of disability and black male identities calls forth a further reimagining of social struggles and categories, transforming the very elaboration of project identities.

The materiality of Manning's dark-skinned and blind body (his social location) occupies a causal, but not determinate, role in the process. His body comprises one of the agential factors in the emergent phenomenon of his blind man–black man standpoint. As Sandahl notes in conclusion, "Manning's performance makes clear that we need to spend more time exploring what disability *is* and *can be*, along with what blackness *is* and *can be*, in as many variations as possible."[76] (One might add, what manhood *is* and *can be*.) Not coincidentally, Sandahl's analysis addresses both race and disability. Disability activists and disability studies have occupied a position at the forefront of developing recent proactive identity projects. While emphasizing the constructed nature of reality, some leading scholars in disability studies have also pointed to the persistence of concrete physical bodies that remain irreducible to "culture" (understood as separate from rather than mutually constitutive with nature). For me personally, conversations with disability scholars and activists have greatly informed my thinking about creative racial identity projects. The connections between the two identities also enable one to recognize the historical inseparability of race and notions of ability and disability in the elaboration of modern conceptions of different and hierarchically ranked bodies.[77]

The project of reveling in minority identity remains necessary, not simply for the well-being of minorities, and not simply for its own sake, as if all identity projects will lead naturally to progressive social change.[78] Rather, by exploring identities and fostering communal resistance, one can reveal the social conflicts produced by modernity, coloniality, and patriarchy and begin to recognize possibilities that might lead to better ethical knowledge and progressive social change. Of course, people can often more easily grant the importance of embracing gender or cultural identity—which appear to have ready referents beyond domination, exploitation, and oppression—than disability or racial identity, which can appear exclusively negative. I believe this dwells at the heart of Castells's and Quijano's reservations about racial identity. One should note, however, Castells's account of the Zapatistas in Chiapas, Mexico. The Zapatistas comprise an indigenous resistance movement in Southern Mexico that for nearly two decades has existed in various levels of open conflict with the Mexican state. Castells finds the Zapatistas' identity formation remarkable and historically unprecedented, insofar as the indigenous communities of Chiapas have lived separated by ethnic and linguistic differences for centuries. Thus, "it does not seem that the defense of ethnic identity was a dominant element in the movement" because a "new Indian identity was constructed through their struggle and came to include various ethnic groups."[79]

Although Castells claims earlier to discount racial identity, one wonders what the Zapatistas' "new Indian identity" can be if not a racial identity. It seems based on neither ethnicity, nor culture, nor nation, nor language. Their "new" racial identity, in turn, does not make sense apart from the five hundred years of struggle against the coloniality of power, as described by Quijano. Yet Quijano, too, describes race in purely negative terms, as a "mental construction" that becomes mapped onto (passive) bodies and populations in order to naturalize social difference and a hierarchy of labor, knowledge, and value.[80] The Zapatistas' racial identity seems "new," however, precisely because it does not completely depend for its meaning on how race has taken shape within the colonial/modern

— Impose ethical knowledge

— Race has material impact on our lives. Use Identities to be able to explain social + historical experience of colonial + patriarchal oppression. Engaging ID also engages hists

gender system. While Eurocentrism as a standpoint for understanding meaning emerged from the birth of the colonial/modern gender system, Zapatismo emerged in the late twentieth century as a self-conscious indigenous standpoint seeking to criticize and transform that system.[81] As a critical standpoint, it does not advocate for the retention of racial categories and hierarchies as they currently exist (or, according to many of the Zapatistas' communiqués, gender and sexual hierarchies), but its birth in an analysis of a racially specific social location remains undeniable in the "First Declaration from the Lacandón Jungle": "We are the product of five hundred years of struggle."[82] Their radical, unprecedented, and transformational racial identity project aims to creatively reimagine the possibilities of existence not only for indigenous peoples in Southern Mexico but for all people.

The world needs identities more than it needs arguments against them—and I believe that it needs creative racial identity projects more than it needs philosophical arguments against race. Race is no more or less a fiction than nationality or ethnicity, and it is just as unlikely to go away. One cannot easily dismiss it as "only cultural" or "just ideological." It emerges from the intra-action of history, culture, economics, and human bodies. It has played a constitutive role in shaping the modern world, and it continues to shape people's most intimate and unconscious actions, behaviors, and beliefs. Race remains, moreover, an inseparable part of how most people experience gender, sexuality, and citizenship, among other things. Racial hierarchies and biological determinist assumptions about racial difference will not evaporate without a significant reorganization of cultural, economic, and political relations at the personal and societal levels, as well as an accounting for how different bodies intra-act with racial categories and ideas. That reorganization, in turn, must come in part from racial identity projects that do not simply reaffirm what race is and has been, but rather seek a transformation of race into something new.

There have been, and continue to be, many attempts at transforming racial identities, including that of the Zapatistas. Other creative and transformational racial identity projects include the Harlem Renaissance, the Negritude movement, Pan-Africanism, Pan-Indigenism, and the contemporary formations of Asian American and Chicana and Chicano identities. Writing in different contexts, both Linda Martín Alcoff and Walter Mignolo, for example, have noted the potential for some recent formations of U.S. Latino identity to challenge radically the meanings of race in both the United States and Latin America, perhaps pointing to less Eurocentric possibilities for racial formations in the Americas.[83] While internally heterogeneous and by no means perfect, these projects have begun *recently* (recently, that is, given that the present racial order took over five hundred years to occur) to imagine what race can mean beyond the facilitation of domination, exploitation, and oppression. To the extent that they have failed, it has often been due to their inability adequately to address race as one of many mutually constitutive aspects of identity formation. Still, I believe that only by encouraging racial project identities to flourish can we find possibilities for a more egalitarian future. Success, however, will require better theories about the interrelation of capitalism, class, coloniality, gender, race, and sexuality. The next chapter takes a step toward this goal.

3

Are Sexual Identities Desirable?

Federico Mérida and Falah Zaggam

On May 11, 2004, Federico Mérida, twenty-one, shot and killed Falah Zaggam, seventeen. According to newspaper reports, Mérida—a Mexican American from North Carolina, a husband and father, and a private in the U.S. National Guard—stood watch with Zaggam, a private in the Iraqi National Guard, on a military base near Tikrit, in northern Iraq. While on duty together, the two engaged in sexual activity, after which Mérida shot Zaggam eleven times, including one shot through the palm of his hand and one through his back. From there, accounts of what transpired that evening vary. Mérida's own story of what happened went through three versions. First, he said that Zaggam had tried to rob him. Next, he claimed that Zaggam had tried to rape him. Finally, he said that the two had engaged in consensual sex but that Zaggam had tried to blackmail him afterward. Mérida told military investigators that, in panic, he had shot Zaggam to death and thrown his body from the guard tower. Zaggam's family contends that Mérida attempted to rape the younger Zaggam and killed him when he resisted. After confessing and pleading guilty to murder and perjury charges, Mérida received a twenty-five-year prison sentence and a dishonorable discharge from a military court.[1]

Responses to Zaggam's murder came swiftly and varied widely. Once the story became public, the U.K.-based Islamic Human Rights Commission (IHRC), for example, linked the case to the abuses at the Abu Ghraib prison earlier that year and to several other murders of Iraqi civilians by U.S. soldiers in 2003 and 2004. The IHRC's press release asserts that Mérida raped Zaggam before killing him.[2] Meanwhile, the North Carolina–based Americans for Legal Immigration-Political Action Committee (ALI-PAC) offered, on its website, a detailed account of Zaggam's death, but eschewed much discussion of sex in favor of another politically charged issue. It observed that Mérida originally hailed from Veracruz,

Mexico, and implied that, despite membership in the U.S. National Guard, he may have entered the country without proper documentation. At the end of its account, the ALI-PAC website provides a link for readers who are interested in joining "the fight against illegal immigration."[3]

Since first reading about this incident, I have asked myself again and again whether the framework of identity has anything useful to contribute to understanding Mérida's actions or the numerous responses to Zaggam's death, including my own response. For example, while it seems certain that sexual activity took place between the men, neither man appears to have ever identified publicly or privately as gay or bisexual. At first glance, theories of sexual identity do not appear to help, other than to put Mérida's "homosexual panic" defense into a larger frame.[4] Theories that understand sexuality as intermeshed with race, ethnicity, and nation, however, can help to put IHRC's outrage into a long historical context of anticolonial responses to colonial sexual violence and to frame ALI-PAC's linking of homosexuality to immigration within an equally long history of sexually coded xenophobia and nativism. Even so, I am left wondering about my own response—as a person whose sympathies lie mostly with the slain Zaggam (despite knowing little of him), but whose own identity would seem closer to that of Mérida: a U.S. citizen at a time of war, a Mexican American in a country where many view us as potential threats to national security, and a man who sexually desires other men in a society that disapproves of expressions of sexual desire between men. Can one live in solidarity both with Mérida, possibly a victim of his society's homophobia and racism, and with Zaggam and his family, certainly victims of Mérida's homophobic violence as well as his country's jingoism and imperialism? I begin with this incident partly because the reactions it provoked and the questions it raises tug at a dense knot of beliefs, histories, and practices at the heart of what I am calling in this book the "colonial/modern gender system." One cannot untangle this knot without a broad sense of those beliefs, histories, and practices and the ways they shape modern identities and the social movements that emerge from them.

Homophobia and Sexual Identities

Sexual identities have political salience because of what they tell us about the organization of the social world, not what they tell us about the existence of particular desires or behaviors. Following from this claim, I assert that the status of identity, rather than the existence of homosexual desire or behavior, is central to understanding the political implications of modern homosexuality. Sexual desire and behavior have their own importance, of course, but I do not believe them to be definitive in the construction of a modern gay identity in the United States and Europe. Furthermore, gay, lesbian, and other sexual identities come into existence in the context of intermeshed social structures and personal experiences of ability–disability, class, culture, ethnicity, gender, nationality, race, religion, and sexuality. One can, therefore, never completely isolate sexual identities from those other structures and experiences. Identities thus offer both better and worse theoretical explanations about how intermeshed oppressions structure the world. Consequently, in considering sexual identities, one should ask how those identities take shape in resistance to and in complicity not only with homophobia but also with racism, colonialism, and capitalism.

Before addressing that question, I would like first to clear some conceptual ground to enable a more productive engagement with the notion of a "sexual identity." Discussions of sexual identities invariably stumble over questions of whether or not they exist across different times and places or whether certain ones, at least, like gay and lesbian identities, exist only in a particular epoch and culture. Attempts to address the issue of sexual *identity*, in turn, can spill over into nature–nurture debates over the origins of homosexual *desire*, even when theorists try to avoid them. In other words, discussions of the existence of gay and lesbian identities as social constructs relative to a given culture often end up sliding into discussions of the causes of same-sex sexual desire and behavior in human beings in general. For example, as numerous scholars have noted, the eighteenth and nineteenth centuries in Europe and North America saw a significant shift in how people viewed same-sex sexual behavior. Previously, people viewed it as deviant behavior of which just about anyone was capable and as therefore the object of penal and religious scrutiny. Later, same-sex sexual behavior came increasingly (although not universally) under the purview of medical and emergent psychiatric and psychoanalytic experts. Religious authorities before the nineteenth century saw little need to find causes within an individual's soul or personality for giving in to the temptations of the flesh; they understood the capacity to sin as intrinsic to human existence. For the new experts on sexuality, however, behavior had its sources in the individual— either in one's body or in one's mind, depending on the expert.[5] Historians have, of course, questioned to what extent changes in the beliefs of "experts" actually influenced transformations in how everyday people viewed their own sexual identities.[6] From the late nineteenth century onward, however, most official attempts to define homosexuality have simultaneously been discussions of its causes (and "cures")—of whether its origin lies in biology, psychology, society, or some combination thereof. Somewhat later, in the twentieth century, a new but related debate emerged, largely in the fields of historiography and philosophy. This debate concerned the status of homosexuality as something that exists or does not exist independently of cultural context or as something that can exist across different cultural contexts. Many readers will recognize this as a debate over "essentialism" versus "social constructionism."[7]

In writing about homosexuality and culture, one risks implying too much uniformity within cultures or implying that each culture has one, unique way of understanding sexuality. Empirical records show that people in numerous cultures and epochs have desired or engaged in significant sexual or emotional relationships with others whom their peers would recognize as members of the same sex or gender. Beyond this deliberately minimal description, matters vary widely. For example, in one society, most might consider such people "homosexuals" only when in a same-sex relationship, and not outside of such a relationship. Here, all homosexuality is situational. Another society might commonly hold that people remain "homosexuals" all throughout their lives, regardless of whether they ever enter into a same-sex relationship—or even despite having had "heterosexual" relationships. Here, one homosexual encounter or the mere presence of homosexual desire suffices to make one always and forever homosexual (a kind of gay "one-drop" rule).

In the first view, homosexuality is a kind of behavior and someone is a homosexual only when engaging in that behavior. In the second view, homosexuality is a kind of desire residing inside a person and a homosexual is the kind of person in whom this desire can be found, regardless of the person's behavior. Of course, most, if not all, societies actually include people who hold a range of views about homosexuality, such that, for example, both of the preceding views have adherents in the present-day United States. For the current discussion, I would like to remain agnostic with respect to these different views of what a homosexual might be, as well as to whether or not homosexuals are only people who think of themselves as having a homosexual identity. I will therefore use terms like *gay* and *lesbian* to refer to culturally specific identities, and *homosexual*, when necessary, as a way of minimally describing people who engage in or desire same-sex sexual or romantic activity without (I hope) implying anything about their personal or social identities. However, I contend that sexual identities, rather than behaviors or desires, hold the key to the politics of sexuality. To understand why, one must first ask to what, precisely, sexual identities refer.

The Politics of Sexual Identities

Sex researcher Alfred Kinsey declared in 1948 that "nearly half (46%) of the [U.S. male] population engages in both heterosexual and homosexual activities, or reacts to persons of both sexes, in the course of their adult lives."[8] Since significantly fewer than half of the U.S. male population identifies as gay, it follows that *gay identity* is something quite distinct from the same-sex desires or behaviors that might potentially lead one to identify as gay. Put another way, the fact that only a small percentage of men who have sex with men identify as gay or bisexual tells us that gay and straight male identities in the contemporary United States do something other than explain or predict a given man's sexual behavior. Consider when people behave differently from the manner that one might assume based on their self-proclaimed identity. For example, some straight men and some lesbians have sex with men. While these people's practices might lead a sex researcher to classify their *behavior* as bisexual, the identity that they use to make sense of themselves and their place in the world might remain *straight* or *lesbian* (respectively). These self-conscious, socially constructed identities do much more than attempt to transparently map a person's behavior or desires. It is not necessarily the case, therefore, that these identities are wrong and that a bisexual identity would be more accurate. Identities like *straight, lesbian,* and *gay* do not refer merely to sexual desire or behavior, although they certainly refer to these things in part.

Instead, these identities express a theoretical understanding of a person's relationship to the organization of the social world along the lines of gender, sexuality, and power. An exchange in U.S. playwright Tony Kushner's *Angels in America* illustrates some of what is at stake in naming identities. The exchange takes place between a fictionalized version of conservative lawyer Roy Cohn (at one time an assistant to U.S. Senator Joseph McCarthy) and Cohn's doctor sometime after Cohn has acquired AIDS in the 1980s:

ROY: Homosexual. Gay. Lesbian. You think these are names that
tell you who someone sleeps with, but they don't tell you that.
HENRY [HIS DOCTOR]: No?
ROY: No. Like all labels they tell you one thing and one thing
only: where does an individual so identified fit in the food
chain, in the pecking order? Not ideology, or sexual taste, but
something much simpler: clout. Not who I fuck or who fucks
me, but who will pick up the phone when I call, who owes me
favors. This is what a label refers to. Now to someone who does
not understand this, homosexual is what I am because I have
sex with men. But really this is wrong. Homosexuals are not
men who sleep with other men. Homosexuals are men who in
fifteen years of trying cannot get a pissant antidiscrimination
bill through City Council. Homosexuals are men who know
nobody and who nobody knows. Who have zero clout.[9]

What Roy articulates here is the conjunction between, on the one hand,
self-conception, sexual behavior, and how one is publically identified and,
on the other hand, *social power.*

To take a different example, for a woman who understands her sexual
desire as primarily oriented toward other women, to identify as a lesbian
while being in a sexual relationship with a man could be to acknowledge
the central structuring role of heterosexism, homophobia, and heteronor-
mativity in society. The identity *lesbian* in this case, rather than attempting a
neutral description of sexual orientation, would entail rejection of the social
injunction for women to downplay connections and identification with
other women in favor of heterosexual alliance with men. It would reject
both the idea that a woman's identity is defined by the presence or absence
of a man and the notion that a relationship with a man should matter more
in defining her than would relationships with women. It might be that some
other identity (for example, *bisexual*) would better describe her *behavior.*
However, in the absence of a politically salient and oppositional social role
for bisexuality or other alternatives, she might see a lesbian identity as best
bringing her public identity into line with her personal desires and behaviors, as well as her political and theoretical interpretation of the social world
in which those desires and behaviors take on meaning.

This example brings up the case of "political lesbianism," the belief
among many U.S. feminists in the 1970s that one needed to identify as a

lesbian because of what the figure of the lesbian represented politically, without any regard for one's sexual desires or behaviors.[10] I do not intend to endorse this kind of position, since I believe that a person adopts a social role and an identity within a context that includes preexisting, ongoing, and potential desires and practices. To choose an identity without regard for its ability to match up with one's desires and practices is to sidestep the hard work of elaborating a politically resistant identity from within the context in which one finds oneself.[11] That move can form a shortcut that avoids issues of privilege and power. In sum, how people self-consciously identify (their personal identities) within the socially intelligible roles available to them (social identities) says much about how they interpret their relation to structures of oppression.

One's sense of oneself as gay or lesbian (or queer or marimacha or same-gender loving) can therefore play a critical role in making possible the work of political coalition or collective resistance against oppression. Of course, contexts exist in which other ways of categorizing people (for example, according to behavior, without regard to identity) might be more immediately important. In HIV-prevention work, for example, the category "men who have sex with men" (MSM) has been crucial for identifying at-risk populations regardless of how they might understand their place within society.[12] However, people's sexual behaviors or desires say little about how they see themselves in relation to others. Men who have female partners but secretly engage in sex with men might exist alongside me in the category of "men who have sex with men," but quite possibly stand in a different relation than I and other jotos, gays, queens, and same-gender-loving men to the homophobia and heterosexism that structures our society. Their choice to have sex with men reflects desires that, in contemporary U.S. society, could have availed them of one of many gender-nonconforming sexual identities. In that context, their choice to continue to identify as straight or heterosexual might, in some cases, reflect a decision to retain the privileges of heterosexuality rather than to risk identification with women's oppression or with marginalized men who have assumed an identity in resistance to homophobia. Of course, I do not intend to privilege contemporary U.S. gay identity as the only or best antihomophobic identity possible or to head off the continued proliferation of alternatives, including the possible elaboration of antihomophobic identities for men whose primarily sexual desire is oriented toward women. There are, in fact, *many* antihomophobic identities available to men and women, including joto, gay, lesbian, queer, queen, marimacha, and same-gender-loving, to name but a few with salience in the contemporary United States.

Such antihomophobic identities, including gay and lesbian, reference theoretical understandings of the workings of oppression and resistance. Similarly, philosopher William S. Wilkerson holds that in coming out as gay or lesbian, a person "implicitly rejects homophobia and those parts and structures of society that maintain it," thereby condemning those social structures "as wrong."[13] Again, this is not to say that coming out as gay or lesbian is the only way to reject homophobia, or even the best. However, coming out does attempt to reject homophobia. The truth of a lesbian identity, therefore, lies less in its mapping of the behavior of a woman whose sexual desire is at least partly directed toward other women than in its interpretation of that woman's place within a given society, as well as her sense of that place given her desires.

My own color in Mexico and the United States is a similar example of how social identities are better understood as dependent on the available social roles and organization of a society than on some natural fact about a person. In Mexico, people have sometimes described me as moreno claro (roughly equivalent to "olive-skinned"), but no one would ever consider me moreno ("dark") or mestizo ("mixed-race"). The most politically salient racial categories, in turn, are indígena ("indigenous," marked not only by skin color but also by language, culture, and class), mestizo or moreno (not necessarily different from indigenous in complexion, but rather in the other factors), and claro ("light," an unmarked category of predominantly European-descent or mixed-descent Mexicans who speak Spanish as their first language). Although the middle and upper classes consist mostly of members of this last group, so do large sections of the working class and poor. In the United States, however, the same body (mine) is rarely taken for white, leading to sometimes comical efforts by strangers to "place" my race.

The category of brown, while not present in Mexico, has emerged among Mexican Americans who politically identify as Chicana or Chicano and among many U.S. Latinos. Brown follows a logic borrowed from black in the United States, unifying a large number of people who have a range of actual skin tones and socioeconomic statuses but who identify politically with similar racialized experiences. Claro and brown, here, are not labels whose truth or falsity lies in the melanin of my skin. My body can *look* claro in Mexico and brown in the United States because of how race functions in each society. I must therefore find ways to identify in each country that put me in resistance to racial oppression without shirking the responsibility of acknowledging racial privilege. Identities like *gay* and *brown* are therefore not arbitrary. While they have something to do with sexual desire and skin color, sexual desire and skin color alone cannot assess the truth or falsity of these identities. Furthermore, acknowledgment that sexual identities refer to political beliefs about the world, in addition to sexual practices and desires, should lead one to ask whether and in what ways these identities function in complicity with oppression, in resistance to it, or both. For example, how have gay and lesbian identities formed, or how can they form, in response to homophobia *understood as one of many intermeshed oppressions*?

The Colonial/Modern Gender System

If class, gender, race, and sexuality are mutually constitutive, then they have given shape to one another over many centuries. Following through with a similar claim, philosopher María Lugones rethinks historical sociologist Aníbal Quijano's account of coloniality, which I discussed at length in chapter 2. She argues that the elaboration of racial hierarchies and Eurocentrism occurred coextensively with a reorganization of gender roles and the elaboration of two sides to what she dubs the "colonial/modern gender system."[14] One side of this system understands white men and women as biologically dimorphic and adhering, respectively, to conceptions of activity and passivity, reason and emotion, publicity and privacy, and so on. By contrast, the other side of the colonial/modern gender system has historically constructed colonized peoples differently, according to Lugones. For example, Europeans did not always think of colonized peoples as biologically dimorphic and did not necessarily even accord them genders, the violence of colonialism having constructed them as bestial and outside of modernity, civilization, and *human* gender:

> Females excluded from [the category of women] were . . .
> understood to be animals in a sense that went further than the
> identification of white women with nature, infants, and small
> animals. They were understood as animals in the deep sense of
> "without gender," sexually marked as female, but without the

characteristics of femininity. Women racialized as inferior were turned from animals into various modified versions of "women" as it fit the processes of global, Eurocentered capitalism. Thus heterosexual rape of Indian or African slave women coexisted with concubinage, as well as with the imposition of the heterosexual understanding of gender relations among the colonized—when and as it suited global, Eurocentered capitalism, and heterosexual domination of white women.[15]

In other words, the elaboration of a colonial/modern world system entailed violent processes that sought to devalue and disenfranchise colonized women. This necessitated the wholesale redrawing of traditional gender roles in many cultures across Africa, the Americas, Asia, and the Pacific through "slow, discontinuous, and heterogeneous processes that violently inferiorized colonized women."[16] The dismantling of gender relations among colonized peoples and the imposition of new ones were central, according to Lugones and many other scholars, to "disintegrating" the relations, rituals, local economic structures, and forms of decision making that nourished resistance to European domination.[17]

Within the emerging colonial/modern gender system, sexual difference from Europeans became simultaneously a justification for imperial subjection and an explanation for the economic and political inferiority brought on by colonialism. The processes of establishing military and economic dominance in a region and of elaborating beliefs about racial supremacy, in other words, entailed the European colonizers' construal of the colonized as sexually deviant. They subsequently required the newly colonized peoples to model European ideals of sex and gender relations, often encouraging conformity by force. However, this system remained highly flexible, so that Europeans could envision colonial others as possessors of violent and barbaric sexualities or as developers of mysterious and libertine erotic arts, as hypersexual beasts in a state of nature or as asexual prudes caught up in overly repressive moral traditions. It all depended on who had the power to elaborate or to contest the rhetoric of gender, race, and sexuality in play and what they deemed necessary in a given time and place.

Teresia K. Teaiwa, for example, has studied how missionaries to the Pacific islands violently sought to convert the indigenous inhabitants, imposing "civilization" and modesty on people seen to be too naked and sexually libertine. However, the Pacific has more recently become a destination for Europeans, North Americans, Australians, and New Zealanders seeking a primitive state of relaxation, and "Islanders are increasingly exposed to sun-seeking and seminude 'First-Worlders.'"[18] This pattern took on different particulars in different parts of the world, but retained remarkable similarities in each instance. In an irony of history, the eventual success of many colonized people in conforming to Eurocentric ideals of gender and sexual morality would eventually become a justification for additional imperial interventions, this time in the name of liberating "their" women and defending freedom for sexual minorities.

Elsewhere, modern gay and lesbian identities began to emerge in resistance to homophobia in the twentieth century, but the sexual and gender relations of heterosexuality and homosexuality that gave birth to them arose as part of the colonial/modern gender system. The models of heterosexuality and homosexuality that crystallized in nineteenth-century Europe and North America composed but one stage in the long development of one side of that system. They came into existence alongside other, sometimes violently coerced and sometimes resistant, understandings of gender and sexuality among colonized peoples. As part of the *other* side of gender in colonial modernity, these alternative understandings continue to shape both colonial representations and postcolonial self-understandings of Africans, Asians, and indigenous peoples of the Americas and the Pacific, giving rise to several questions. Are gay and lesbian identities simply complicit with the coloniality of power, or do they demonstrate a strategy of resistance to it, parallel to other strategies enacted by colonized and formerly colonized peoples? Is the question too complex for an either–or? And what are the possibilities for developing sexual identities that reject not only homophobia but also the racism and Eurocentrism of the colonial/modern gender system?

A View from the Other Side

Such questions have emerged as central to understanding how gays and lesbians in the United States and Europe should respond to the wars in Iraq and Afghanistan. Just weeks after CBS's television newsmagazine *60 Minutes 2* aired photographs depicting the torture of Iraqi detainees by U.S. soldiers in the Abu Ghraib prison, gay British journalist Patrick Letellier reported that "300 Egyptian protestors rallied in front of a banner that read, 'Bring to justice the homosexual American executioners, their agents the traitors, their followers the enemies.'"[19] Although Letellier cites the *Kuwait Times*, this story originated from a wire report by Maggie Michael, an Egypt-based correspondent for the Associated Press, a U.S.-based news agency. According to Michael, the demonstration actually consisted of "about 50 Egyptian lawyers and journalists . . . surrounded by about 300 riot police."[20] While the protestors certainly expressed outrage at the unfolding tales of abuse by U.S. soldiers, the immediate target of the demonstration was David Welch, U.S. ambassador to Egypt. Welch had been critical of several Egyptian newspapers, accusing them of publishing doctored photographs, made to appear as pictures of U.S. soldiers raping Iraqi women. (At the time, U.S. officials were warning that additional, unreleased photographs showed forced same-gender sexual acts and images of Iraqi women forced to bare their breasts.[21])

According to Michael's report, many in Egypt perceived Ambassador Welch's criticisms of the newspapers as part of ongoing attempts to censor the Egyptian press and as "working against press freedom." Echoing the banner's sentiment, the editor of one of the newspapers criticized by Welch, Mustafa Bakri, stated, "Those gays forced our brothers in Iraq to practice homosexuality and filmed them. If we remain silent, we will be next." Michael does not indicate whether Bakri and the banner used the English words *gay, homosexual,* and *homosexuality,* or whether she is offering translations of Egyptian Arabic (in which case the original terms could have specified gay men, but more likely referenced sexual deviance generally). Regardless of the linguistic and conceptual fine points, however, many Arabs and Muslims in the wake of the Abu Ghraib revelations drew clear associations between Western homosexuality and Western colonialism and imperialism.

The logic of these associations informs, for example, an early 2005 recording issued by Ayman al-Zawahiri, the Egyptian surgeon and, at the time, the reputed second in command for the global militant Sunni Islamist network al-Qaeda. In the recording, al-Zawahiri takes aim at how U.S. officials define the concept of freedom and he champions an alternative based on Islamic law and Muslim (notably not Arab) independence from the United States, Israel, and the United Nations.[22] The Qatari television station Al Jazeera broadcast the audiotape on February 10, 2005, and the British Broadcasting Company (BBC) disseminated an English-language translation the same day:

The freedom we seek is not the freedom of the banks of usury, giant companies and misleading media. It is not the freedom of destroying others for material interests. It is not the freedom of AIDS, prostitution and same-sex marriage. It is not the freedom of using women as a commodity to lure customers, sign deals and draw in travellers. It is not the freedom of Hiroshima and Nagasaki. It is not the freedom in the trade of torture equipment and support to U.S. friends in the regimes of oppression. It is not the freedom of Israel to annihilate Muslims, destroy the Al-Aqsa Mosque and Judaize Palestine. It is not the freedom of Guantanamo or Abu-Ghurayb.

Our freedom is the freedom of monotheism, ethics and virtue. Accordingly, the reform that we seek is based on three foundations.

The first foundation is the rule of shari'ah Islamic law. . . .

The second foundation . . . is a branch of the first foundation, namely, the freedom of the Muslim lands and their liberation from every aggressor, thief and plunderer. . . .

The third foundation . . . is also a branch of the first foundation, namely, the liberation of the human being.

The nation must forcibly seize its right to choose the ruler, hold him accountable, criticize him and depose him. The nation should seize its right to promote virtue and prohibit vice. It should resist all forms of aggression against the people's sanctities, liberties and rights. It should resist oppression, tyranny, thievery, forgery, corruption and hereditary rule, a process that our rulers use with America's blessing and support.[23]

One might certainly debate whether and to what extent al-Qaeda actually operates according to the philosophy of freedom expounded here by al-Zawahiri. Leaving that question aside, however, one should note that much of the statement accords with standard leftist and progressive positions in Europe and the United States: its criticism of big business, the credit industry, and economic exploitation, for instance. Al-Zawahiri also expresses opposition to the commoditization of women, to tourism, to nuclear war, and to weapons dealing. He offers an alternative in pan-Muslim independence, thus tapping into rhetoric familiar from the Arab anticolonial movements of the mid-twentieth century. Rather than pan-Arab solidarity against European domination, however, al-Zawahiri calls for pan-Muslim solidarity against the United States and Israel (thus opposing a religious configuration to geopolitical ones). The importance of his move away from an ethnic, tribal, or national base buttresses his denunciation of the practice of hereditary rule in Arab states. Al-Zawahiri thus directs his recording toward Arabic speakers in predominantly Muslim countries and builds on a number of anticolonial, feminist, anti-authoritarian, and anticapitalist sentiments in order to garner sympathy for al-Qaeda's position. For the present discussion, however, his inclusion of "AIDS, prostitution, and same-sex marriage" among the supposed freedoms championed by the United States and Israel is striking.

At the simplest level, same-sex marriage functions here to link the perceived imposition of foreign cultural values about gender and sexual roles with the imperialist violence accompanying a purported imposition of "Western democracy." That violence, in turn, seems to be unmasked in the prison abuse scandal, with its obvious sexual character. The context for al-Zawahiri's association lies in a number of court decisions. In 2003, the Massachusetts Supreme Court, in the United States, ruled that the state could not deny same-sex couples the right to marriage and, in 2004, the Nazareth District Court, in Israel, ruled in favor of equal inheritance rights for same-sex couples (although to date, neither country recognizes same-sex marriages at the national level).[24]

Thus, at the time of al-Zawahiri's statement in early 2005 and in the wake of the 2004 Abu Ghraib abuse revelations, same-sex marriage served as a symbolic marker of difference in attitudes toward sexual morality between these two nations, on the one hand, and the predominantly Muslim nations of Northern Africa, the Arabian Peninsula, and Central and Southwestern Asia on the other. This marker had salience despite substantial domestic opposition to same-sex marriage at the time in both the United States and Israel. Al-Zawahiri concludes that U.S. forces of occupation in Iraq represent imperialist designs as well as sexual decadence, perversity, and the degradation of women. Social and sexual purity as well as national sovereignty remain impossible, in this view, until colonial and imperial impositions come to an end.

Sodomy and Empire

The message of al-Zawahiri resonates with many Muslims and the first part of his analysis rings familiar to many non-Muslims in formerly

colonized countries. To fully understand why, one must grasp how coloniality, modernity, and sexuality have worked together in the shaping of
the colonial/modern gender system. In the case of former British colonies,
one of the clearest examples of this process is the introduction by the English of antisodomy laws throughout Asia, Africa, and the Middle East. As
part of larger imperial penal codes, these laws attempted to introduce an
English understanding of "natural" and "unnatural" sex practices. In addition, they became a mechanism for allowing state regulation of personal
sexual and reproductive behavior among populations that, in many cases,
had previously not understood individual sexual preference and behavior
as an object of state interest—even if they had religious proscriptions or
cultural taboos against various sexual practices. This difference tended to
distinguish British sodomy laws within Europe as well, since the Napole-
onic Code that formed a legal basis for much of continental Europe in the
nineteenth century did not criminalize sodomy. Of course, Britain was not
alone in imposing sodomy laws on its colonies, as one can see from the
early imposition of Roman Dutch law by Holland in South Africa in the
seventeenth century and by the writing of antisodomy laws into the Leba-
nese penal code by the French (who did not themselves have them) in the
twentieth century. The British, however, played a particularly central role in
relation to the criminalization of sodomy throughout much of the world.[25]

As a result, official policies in formerly colonized countries bear an
imprint of European-imposed views on gender and sexuality. To make this
point, the Singaporean blogger Yawning Bread (Au Waipang) juxtaposes
two maps.[26] The first map shows the possessions of the British Empire
during the early twentieth century colored in red: the present-day areas
of Pakistan, India, Sri Lanka, the Maldives, Nepal, Bhutan, Bangladesh,
Burma/Myanmar, Malaysia, Brunei Darussalam, and Hong Kong. Other
European colonies appear in different colors: Indochina, the Philippines,
Indonesia, and East Timor. The independent nations of Mongolia, China,
Thailand, Korea, and Japan are uncolored. The second map shows in red
those countries that criminalized consensual sexual acts among adults
of the same gender as of 2004. With the exception of Hong Kong, every
former colony of Britain on the second map is colored red. Furthermore,
only these countries are red, so that the red in both maps covers the same
area.[27] Thus, regardless of religious tradition, only those East, South, and
Southeast Asian countries with histories of British colonialism criminalized same-sex sexual practices at the dawn of the twenty-first century.[28]

Britain achieved this remarkable influence on colonial and postcolonial morality largely through Chapter XVI, Section 377 of the Indian Penal Code (IPC), drafted by Lord Macaulay in 1860:[29] "Unnatural sexual offences: Whoever voluntarily has carnal intercourse against the order of nature with any man, woman or animal, shall be punished with imprisonment for life or with imprisonment of either description for a term which may extend to ten years, and shall also be liable to fine."[30] The IPC formed a major part of the British effort to consolidate their rule in the region, imposing a uniform criminal code to replace the disparate civil and religious codes that had previously applied throughout the territories unified under British India. Notably, these indigenous codes did not, for the most part, view same-sex sexual acts as punishable by law, and did not have a similar concept of sexual offenses against nature. The IPC later served as a model for other British possessions, and versions of Section 377 found their way into the colonial legal structures of much of Africa and Asia.[31] In Singapore and parts of what is now Malaysia, for example, Section 377 of the IPC became Section 377 of the Straits Settlements Penal Code.[32] Furthermore, in almost every case—from Hong Kong and Kuwait to Sudan and Jamaica—the legal codes of these nations retained criminal sanctions against sodomy after independence, although some countries with large Muslim populations later supplemented (for example, in Nigeria) or replaced (for example, in Afghanistan) their colonial-era laws with proscriptions based on various interpretations of sharia, or Islamic religious law. In any case, the inheritance of colonial/modern morality has left postcolonial nations in a double bind.

In an illuminating debate over Singapore's 2007 redrawing of its antisodomy laws, for example, members of parliament and the public considered the criminalization of anal and oral sex. The debate followed public shock at a man's two-year prison sentence under Section 377 for receiving oral sex from a young woman. The debate quickly recentered on the question of whether or not to legalize same-sex sexual practice among men. Some people cast homosexuality (and gay identity politics specifically) as a sign of Western influence and moral decadence, while others saw the law as a final vestige of British colonialism. Some adopted religious understandings of homosexual acts as sinful (usually according to Islam or Christianity) or not (often according to Taoism, but also citing Christian sources); others claimed that the law helped to prevent the spread of sexually transmitted diseases (like HIV and AIDS) or, conversely, that it inhibited adequate prevention strategies.[33] In the end, the parliament repealed Section 377, while retaining Section 377a, a more specific clause added to the Straits Settlements Penal Code in 1938 in the wake of a similar law in England: "Any male person who, in public or private, commits, or abets the commission of, or procures or attempts to procure the commission by any male person of, any act of gross indecency with another male person, shall be punished with imprisonment for a term which may extend to 2 years."[34]

While many supporters of Section 377a saw themselves as championing "traditional Asian values" or as resisting the imposition of "Western gay identity politics" in Singapore, the endorsement of the law might in fact have cemented a further "heterosexualization" and "homosexualization" of Singaporean society along the lines of the United States and Western Europe. In other words, the double action of repealing the broad Section 377 while retaining the narrow Section 377a signals, on the one hand, the victory of views that associate male homosexual acts and identity as incompatible with "Asian values" and as resulting from European and U.S. influence. On the other hand, however, the parliament's decision signals the solidification in Singapore of a Euro-American understanding of homosexuality as a specific kind of perversion, different from, for example, anal or oral sex among consenting adults of different sexes. The law's singling out of male homosexuality makes it even more likely that some men will rally around political identities based on homosexual desire.

Furthermore, throughout the debate over Section 377a, reformers opposing the law characterized their position as *modern* and *progressive*, and the law itself as *archaic* or *premodern*. This characterization inverted the rhetoric originally used by the imperial powers to enforce sexual prohibitions on colonized peoples, whom they frequently viewed as sexually licentious because of being uncivilized and premodern. The new inversion of the colonial rhetoric, however, merely casts the colonized as lacking enlightened sexual freedom rather than Victorian sexual restraint. Unfortunately, the rhetoric of civilization and modernity thus perpetuates a logic in which the former colonies lag eternally behind the colonial powers.

Modernity and Sexuality

Even in countries that managed to avoid direct colonial rule by Europe, such as Iran and Thailand, coloniality has profoundly shaped conceptions of both modernity and sexuality. Historian Afsaneh Najmabadi, for example, has meticulously documented the radical transformation of Iranian gender and sexual relations in the nineteenth and early twentieth centuries (roughly the period of the Qajar dynasty, 1794–1925). Iran avoided direct colonization by European powers, at least until the invasion of British and Soviet forces in 1941, but Najmabadi convincingly argues that Iranian reformers in the Qajar period often responded directly and indirectly to European judgments about modernity, sexuality, and civilization. These reformers, furthermore, pursued the development of a "modern"—understood to a certain extent to mean *secular*—society in part by self-consciously restructuring relationships among beauty, desire, gender, love, and sex. According to Najmabadi, the transformations that ensued entailed a profound reorientation of Iranian domestic and erotic life, including the introduction of a homosexual–heterosexual binary where one had not existed before.[35]

Specifically, two related characteristics of Iranian society came to mark it as "backward" in the eyes of both European observers and Iranian reformers: sex segregation and the veiling of women, on the one hand, and on the other, homoeroticism and same-sex practices (real or imagined) among both men and women. For Europeans during this period, according to Najmabadi, Iranian literary and artistic expressions of male homoeroticism between adult men and young boys, observations of physical affection among adult Iranian men in sex-segregated public space, and speculative or fictional accounts of sexual "perversion" among women in harems became either evidence of a lack of "civilization" in Iran or evidence of a "decadent" civilization in decline. (This network of associations and valuations among civilization, perversion, decadence, and modernity also ensnared reformers in the Ottoman Empire and the countries that emerged from its dissolution.[36]) Iranians, according to Najmabadi, responded in a complex manner to these charges. She writes, "[A]nger at European readings of Iranian social and sexual mores began to reconfigure structures of desire by introducing a demarcation to distinguish homosociality from homosexuality." Responding to the imposition of European categories on Iranian practices and beliefs, "Iranians began to find themselves 'explaining' to European visitors that at least some of the practices that the latter read as homosexuality, such as men holding hands, embracing, and kissing each other in public, were not so: the Europeans were misreading homosociality for homosexuality."[37]

She notes that the project of "achieving modernity" in Iran thus required the transformation of love and sexual desire into things that existed only together and only between men and women. Before the adoption of concepts of homosexuality and heterosexuality, Najmabadi argues, Iranians did not view beauty, sex, love, and gender as necessarily bundled. Anyone was capable of appreciating the beauty of a young boy, and many did not see sexual desire or sexual practices as necessarily tethered to a binary between masculine and feminine. Although gender had importance for structuring power in other spheres, it simply did not definitively structure sexual desire by itself. This changed through interactions with European concepts. As heterosexuality emerged and became the "natural" form of sexual desire, homosexuality became understood as an "unnatural" imitation of heterosexuality. Thus, the male homosexual also became scripted as exclusively passive and feminine, a new restriction caused by the introduced rigid linking of sexual practice to gender roles. As Najmabadi notes, "[A]ccepted 'typologies' of male homosexuality in Islamicate cultures assume the hypermasculinity of 'active' and the femininity of 'passive' males involved in homosexual practices." However, "This typology is itself a consequence of the modernist heterosexualization of love." While "the nineteenth century began with male and female beauties as desirable objects of male eroticism," the changes accompanying modernization required that "all objects of male erotic desire . . . become feminized. It is this momentum that created feminized passivity as the only position for the male homosexual object in modernist imagination."[38] Although he does not go as far in his claims as Najmabadi, historian Khaled el-Rouayheb's analysis of Ottoman culture before 1800 complements her work. He suggests that, depending on context, time period, and local region, factors such as age and social status could be at least as important as gender, if not more so, in structuring meanings around "active" and "passive" roles in penetrative sex among men and between men and boys before the (colonial) "modernization" of sexuality.[39]

In Iran, reformers articulated the initial modernization of sex and gender through the embracing of European-style heterosexuality—and its attendant bundling together of gender, beauty, eroticism, and sex—in resistance to colonialist charges of decadent sexuality. There followed a related reconfiguration of family life such that the family—previously a mere contractual relationship of duty, property, and procreation—became for the first time the place where love and sexual desire should coexist and where they should reside exclusively. At the same time, modernization required the transformation of public space from a sex-segregated (or "homosocial") one to a sex-integrated (or "heterosocial") one.[40] The articulation of gender, sex, love, and marriage ultimately bears an ironic relationship to later defenses of "traditional" heterosexual gender and sexual roles in Iran and elsewhere against demands from political actors in the United States and Europe for global recognition of sexual freedom and the rights of sexual minorities.

The irony of accusations of ethnocentrism and cultural imperialism against such demands lies in the fact that the supposedly traditional roles themselves in many cases result from a previous era of ethnocentric and imperialist demands. As Najmabadi observes, secular modernists in Iran viewed "erotic desire" as "self-evidently heterosexual" so they concluded that homosexual practices must arise when the "veiling and segregation of women did not allow its [erotic desire's] natural fulfillment." She further argues that the "modern Islamist attitude toward homoeroticism" in the late twentieth and twenty-first centuries takes its impetus from "similar moves of denial, disavowal, sanction, and approbation" as in the modern secularist attitude of the nineteenth and early twentieth centuries. Both locate the origin of homosexual practices outside of the natural sphere of erotic life, but while "secular modernists have located the 'vice' in the domain of Arabo-Islamic backwardness, contemporary Islamists locate it in the domain of Western secular corruption."[41] Thus, although conservatives present the sexual politics of the Islamic Republic of Iran after its 1979 revolution as rooted in Islamic law and traditional Iranian culture, the "traditional" views of masculinity, femininity, sex, and perversion that accompanied it have in fact evolved recently, over two centuries, in articulation with the development of a global colonial/modern gender system.

Orientalist Fantasies and the Imperial Gays

Given the legacies of the colonial/modern gender system, the struggle to tell the story of how people have conceived of sex and eroticism outside of Europe and North America confronts many difficulties and pitfalls that have plagued both academics and human rights advocates. Drawing from the research of historians and anthropologists, most academic researchers now acknowledge that the specific identity concepts of *homosexual, gay,* and *lesbian* have not existed—at least until very recently—in Iran or in

Arab societies. One could say the same of Western Europe and the United States, of course, but the emergence of numerous antecedent identities connected to same-sex desires, acts, and relationships since at least the nineteenth century now has a well-documented history in Europe and the Americas. So even if contemporary gay and lesbian identities differ substantially from early twentieth-century sexual identities in Europe, the United States, and Canada (for example, *invert, Uranian,* or *Sapphist*), one can at least trace their evolution with relative ease.

The pitfalls of the colonial/modern gender system make both the history of sex, gender, and identity and the telling of that history more fraught endeavors in relation to other parts of the world. Attempts to tell it have included, for example, the extreme Orientalist fantasies of French philosopher Michel Foucault in his *History of Sexuality*.[42] As theorized by Palestinian literary critic Edward Said, Orientalism typically uses a fictional description of radical cultural difference in the "East" in order to define the distinctiveness of the "West." In such cases, both constructs form part of a self-understanding of the "West," rather than saying anything "real" about the "East."[43] This is exactly what Foucault does with his portrait of a mysterious "Eastern" "erotic art" that he uses to highlight the distinctiveness of the "West's" invention of "sexuality" as a scientific, identity-based understanding of the self. More recently, scholars have argued that a variety of different ways of understanding eroticism and gender have existed throughout Arab, Iranian, North African, and Turkish societies at different times. These *sometimes* coalesced around identity categories, although when they have, they have typically differed from the homosexual, gay, and lesbian identities now common throughout contemporary Australia, Europe, and North America.[44]

Despite research showing the multiple ways that people have thought about sex, gender, and eroticism in various cultures, many anthropologists from the United States and Europe continue to reduce that multiplicity to simply binaries. The most common contemporary Orientalist fantasy of Arab sexual difference, for example, describes a culture in which the gender of sexual object choice for a man does not matter, and where significance attaches instead to the role a man plays in sexual penetration—that is, whether he penetrates another body (female or male) with his penis, or whether he submits to being penetrated.[45] (Anthropologists often also peddle this fantasy about Latin Americans and Mediterranean Europeans.[46]) The role one plays in penetration probably does matter to many men in

Arab societies. However, as with all Orientalist fantasies, the accuracy of this portrait of the "other" should interest one less than the European or North American anthropologist's motive in finding and describing sexual difference among other cultures in the first place.

Typically, I suspect the motivation lies in a desire to distinguish more clearly one's own cultural distinctiveness. In this case, of course, the fantasy implies that men in North America and Northern Europe attach less meaning to their role in penetration. It seems unlikely, however, that distinctions concerning a man's role in penetration hold no importance for European and North American sexual cultures. Just to pick some obvious examples in the United States, the culture of male hustlers, a cursory scan of gay personal ads, and the twenty-first-century phenomenon of "gay for pay" porn actors all suggest that a penetration-based binary operates centrally in how many men in the so-called West understand sexuality. In each of the cases I just listed, men consider the role of penetrator in same-sex encounters to be a "straighter," more masculine role, and in many cases see it as compatible with one's remaining heterosexual. Yet anthropologists have consistently presented all of these beliefs as distinctive of Latin America, Arab countries, or the Mediterranean, depending on where the anthropologist's fieldwork is located. I suspect that the attribution of such a distinction as central to *other* cultures—accurately or not—works mostly as a way to disavow its centrality to one's own culture. However, at the same time, it serves to make the "other" seem more distanced from civilization, reason, and modernity. It becomes an instance of using culture as "the essential tool for making other," to quote anthropologist Lila Abu-Lughod.[47]

Recently, these otherwise academic debates have entered the arena of global human rights activism. One skirmish began with a 2002 article by political theorist Joseph Massad.[48] Massad argues that international gay and lesbian human rights organizations have taken the lack of a clearly defined homosexual identity in predominantly Arab or Muslim countries as evidence of identity-based repression by government and religious bodies in those countries. In turn, these organizations have fought to liberate the presumed, but invisible, identity group, thereby inciting religious and state resistance in the form of both denunciations of "Western" decadence and an increased regulation of sexual activity domestically. Although this back-and-forth process might result, or might have resulted, in the development of gay and lesbian identities, particularly among the upper and middle classes, Massad argues that such identities emerge in response to both new domestic regulation of sexuality and European and U.S. cultural and political intervention. In other words, these new identities have not evolved organically from within Arab cultures and do not preexist "Western" (that is, European and North American) intervention. Massad condemns this entire process of advocacy, intervention, and response. For him, the process initiated by "Western" human rights advocates actually results in a restriction on sexual possibilities for Arab men, and he sees it as one step in an even larger process of assimilation, heterosexualization, and "Westernization"—in other words, the loss of Arab cultural, economic, erotic, and political autonomy and distinctiveness.[49]

Among the responses to Massad's position, one of the most compelling comes from Brian Whitaker, Middle East editor for the U.K.-based newspaper *The Guardian*.[50] Whitaker ardently defends the idea of rights for Arabs who choose to identify as gay or lesbian. On the political question of the desirability of gay and lesbian identities—as opposed to the anthropological question of the existence of homosexual behaviors and desires—Whitaker charges Massad with unfairly dismissing those Arabs who have embraced these identities, and with not addressing whether or not they "have a right to identify themselves as gay, lesbian, etc., if they so wish."[51] Indeed, Massad does rather vituperatively deride Arabs who identify as gay or lesbian as "Westernized" and "wealthy," and as "upper-class" "native informants" who consort with European and U.S. tourists and support the cultural imperialism of foreign interventionists.[52] Whitaker, by contrast, seeks to defend self-identified lesbian and gay Arabs against a false binary between "cultural authenticity" and the "adoption of all things Western":

> [N]either is a realistic proposition. Exposure to foreign ideas and influences cannot be prevented, but nor are Arabs incapable of making critical judgments about them. Equally, Arab culture cannot be treated as a fossil; it is a culture in which real people lead real lives and it must be allowed to evolve to meet their needs. The issue, then, is not whether concepts such as "gay" and "sexual orientation" are foreign imports but whether they serve a useful purpose. For Arabs who grow up disturbed by an inexplicable attraction towards members of their own sex, they can provide a framework for understanding. For families—puzzled, troubled and uninformed by their own society—they offer a sensible alternative to regarding sons and daughters as sinful or mad.[53]

Whitaker's views on culture here bear similarities to my own.[54] However, he takes "openness" and "publicity" about sexuality (same-sex or otherwise) as self-evidently desirable and good, ignoring claims by Massad and others that European and U.S. intervention has foisted specifically *public* sexual identities on Arab society.[55] More importantly, Whitaker leaves unaddressed the role of historically unequal colonial relationships between Arab countries and the United States and Europe in shaping governmental and religious responses to sexuality. Instead, he sees sexual reform as self-evidently necessary (apparently regardless of the means) and understands a distinctively Arab regard for the opinions of others and sense of familial obligation as primary obstacles to that sexual reform (rather than, say, cultural imperialism from elsewhere). Thus, he believes that traits specific to Arab cultures restrict public expressions of individuality, which he believes, in turn, to be necessary for sexual liberation.[56] Unfortunately, Whitaker thereby ends up portraying Arab cultures as monolithic—one of the very practices that he seeks to avoid. His failure to address colonial legacies and neocolonial economic policies, furthermore, prevents him from seeing Arab sexual politics as anything other than a question of cultural mores. Whitaker's position thus becomes a version of what philosopher Uma Narayan has called "death by culture," wherein laws or practices disfavored in Europe and North America become conflated with the "culture" of another country.[57]

Although Massad criticizes this phenomenon of "death by culture" and the strength of his analysis lies in his attention to the larger geopolitical and global economic relations surrounding human rights rhetoric about sexual minorities in Arab countries, his own argument sometimes also tends toward an overly deterministic and hermetic view of culture as generating wholly different "sexual epistemologies."[58] While not using Narayan's phrase, Massad points to an example of "death by culture" in comparing domestic violence in the United States to "honor killings" in Jordan. He observes the fervor that erupted in the U.S. media over reports that "honor" crimes were responsible for a quarter of murders of women in Jordan. At the same time, the media virtually ignored (and made no comparisons to) news "that at least one-third of all women murdered in the United States are murdered by their boyfriends or husbands."[59]

Despite this observation, however, Massad still tends to attribute too many things to culture and in too deterministic a way. Unlike Whitaker, Massad usually values cultural difference from the "West" as good, rather than as bad, but the emphasis for both men is on *cultures* and the opposition between cultures seems equally unbridgeable.[60] Massad's larger political point in his work, however, is one with which I concur: "[T]he very same discourse that calls for the 'liberation' of Arabs from dictators and 'defends' them against human rights violations is what allows both imperial ventures and human rights activism. Even the data on the Arabs necessary for imperial conquest and human rights activism derives from the same anthropological and Orientalist sources. The epistemic collusion is total, even though the political implications are articulated differently."[61] The "collusion" between human rights activists and imperial conquest typifies the vexed nature of gender and sexuality in the wake of the colonial/modern gender system.

Highjack This, Fags!

One need not look further for evidence of that collusion and the profound contradictions that sustain it than to the build up to the U.S. war in Afghanistan. U.S.-based anti-imperialist and transgender activist Leslie Feinberg observes, in *Lavender & Red*, that the U.S. State Department began as early as 2000 to disseminate reports about the execution of "gay men" by the Taliban, the ruling faction in Afghanistan from 1996 to 2001. After the September 11, 2001 al-Qaeda attacks on the U.S. Pentagon in Washington, D.C., and the World Trade Center in New York City, the State Department reports found their way into popular newspapers and gay and lesbian media outlets.[62] In the weeks leading up to the U.S. invasion of Afghanistan on October 7, 2001, stories about the Taliban's restrictions on women's freedom and its treatment of sexual minorities reverberated through the U.S. media in a feedback loop. This marked phase one: Afghanistan as repressive human rights violator. Later, reports emerged throughout the winter and spring of 2002 that attempted to explain to British, U.S., and Australian audiences the traditional male same-sex erotic practices (particularly cross-generational relationships) among some ethnic groups in Afghanistan, as well as the homosociality of its sex-segregated culture under the Taliban.[63] As with the earlier State Department reports, these journalistic ones typically imposed "gay" and "homosexual" identities on the men who participate in same-sex sexual practices, and many of the descriptions characterized them as predatory.

Despite contradicting some of the tenets of phase one (for example, it now appeared that at least one of those allegedly executed for "homosexuality" had, in fact, kidnapped, raped, and killed a boy), these journalists managed to craft a second phase tailored to suit U.S. foreign policy: Afghanistan as perverse and sexually uncivilized.[64] Within the space of less than a year, Afghanistan had gone in the U.S. and British popular imaginations from a persecutor of gay men to a nation of gay men for the United States to persecute.

Feinberg notes two particularly disturbing incidents in late 2001 and early 2002. The first was a widely circulated photograph by Associated Press photographer Jockel Fink of a bomb with the words "HIGHJACK THIS FAGS" scrawled on its side.[65] The photograph shows the bomb already mounted on a U.S. fighter plane aboard the aircraft carrier USS Enterprise. More disturbing still was the reaction of lesbian, gay, bisexual, transgender, and intersex (LGBTI) organizations in the United States. Feinberg notes that only one of the many U.S.-based LGBTI organizations that responded to the incident took the opportunity also to question U.S. foreign policy in Afghanistan. The responses of the others failed to take issue with the war. For example, a *Washington Post* article quotes Cathy Renna, the New York spokesperson for the Gay and Lesbian Alliance Against Defamation (GLAAD): "[The photograph] gets to something we need to discuss, which is that it's okay to be in the Navy and to write 'fag' on a bomb and drop it on a terrorist. That word is still okay with some people, and these are the kinds of things you might see if you happened to be gay and were serving in the military. It exemplifies every single reason why our work is as relevant as it was on September 10."[66]

Renna's concern turns immediately not to the Afghanis who might be killed by the bomb but to a closeted sailor who might be offended by the slur written on it. In the process, she uses her own slur, the twenty-first-century equivalent of *commie* or *red: terrorist.* Once she has declared with supreme confidence that the bomb will drop "on a terrorist" (with apparent precision accuracy), she need not consider that person to be a person anymore. The word obliterates the Afghanis in advance of the bombs. (Coincidentally, the *Washington Post* reported the same day that the Pentagon had confirmed bombing a Red Cross facility in Afghanistan for the second time in less than two weeks; the article goes on to discuss the "growing list of mistakes by U.S. aircraft or the smart 'bombs' they drop."[67])

The second incident chronicled by Feinberg is an account in *The Scotsman* of British marines in Afghanistan recounting their horror at "being propositioned by swarms of gay local farmers."[68] Reporter Chris Stephen offers an extensive account of this cross-cultural encounter, echoing the fascination and repulsion found in centuries of European anthropological accounts from Africa, the Americas, Asia, and the Pacific: "An Arbroath marine, James Fletcher, said: 'They were more terrifying than the al-Qaeda. One bloke who had painted toenails was offering to paint ours. They go about hand in hand, mincing around the village.'" Stephen's account continues, noting that the marines, "their faces covered in camouflage cream," entered villages to search for al-Qaeda operatives, only to be "confronted with Afghans wanting to stroke their hair." "'It was hell,' said Corporal Paul Richard, 20. 'Every village we went into we got a group of men wearing make-up coming up, stroking our hair and cheeks and making kissing noises.'"[69] These U.K. marines do not hesitate to label this behavior as "homosexuality," or at least as sexual perversion. Of course, it may very well be that the Pashtun villagers interpreted the soldiers—young men for the most part and themselves wearing "makeup"—within an indigenous man-boy erotic schema. It seems quite as plausible to me, however, that their "affection" functioned as a way of harassing and distracting the soldiers, possibly feminizing them out of derision and resentment at their presence or even in an attempt to provide cover to al-Qaeda or Taliban agents in the area.

As Feinberg astutely observes, sexual difference and gender equality never played a central part in the war effort in Afghanistan. Rather, activists, governments, and the media used gender, erotic practices, and sexual identities strategically in the service of many other political projects: inclusion into the U.S. mainstream for domestic sexual minorities, legitimation of the regime change abroad, maintenance of discipline in the military, and resistance to invasion and occupation. In the process, U.S. and European perceptions of gender and sexuality in Afghanistan shifted with ease from one distorted and incomplete understanding to its equally distorted and incomplete opposite. Such inversions of meaning, as in the case of sodomy statues in Singapore or the history of gender and eroticism in Iran, buttress the contention that configurations of gender, race, and sexuality within the colonial/modern gender system transform in relation to colonial domination and capitalist exploitation rather than permanently taking on one meaning or another.

Identity Flux

The struggles of people to transform their own society's attitudes toward sexuality and to enable more humane possibilities for everyone within that society cannot afford to take the meaning of sexual identities for granted. Setting aside the anthropological claims of how people do or do not identify, I am most interested in two questions. First, are sexual identities desirable in any given sociocultural context and toward what end? Second, if they are, then what identities might be most useful for attaining that end? The cluster of organizations and individuals advocating international recognition of sexual minority rights tends for the most part not to ask either question, simply assuming the necessity and desirability of Euro-American gay and lesbian identities. Massad asks the first question about the desirability of sexual identities and answers negatively; he therefore does not go on explicitly to ask the second question about which identities.[70] Whitaker asks the first question and responds affirmatively, but does not bother asking the second. Instead, he takes gay and lesbian identities as self-evidently the best available. Like many other social theorists, I believe that identity configurations provide highly useful and versatile strategies for political mobilization in the contemporary world.[71] However, this form of political mobilization in Arab and Muslim contexts has tended historically to focus on religious, ethnic, tribal, and national identities rather than on gender, sexuality, ability, or the other political identities common in North America, Western Europe, Australia, and, increasingly, across some parts of Africa, Asia, and Latin America.

Few agree, furthermore, on what advocacy of sexual identity politics might mean in an Arab context. Syrian literature scholar Iman al-Ghafari argues, for example, that lesbianism, as desire, practice, and self-conception, exists in Arab countries, albeit without codification in a public identity:

> In the Arab world, however, the lesbian identity doesn't seem to
> exist, not because there are no lesbians, but because practices,
> which might be termed as lesbian in Western culture are left
> nameless in the Arab culture. . . . [M]ost lesbians avoid any public
> assertion of their identities. Besides, it is quite easy for Arab
> lesbians to deprive their emotional and physical intimacies of
> their lesbian connotations, because it is common in a conserva-
> tive Arab culture that advocates separation between the sexes to

find intimate relations among members of the same sex, without having to call such relations homosexual. Therefore, homosexuals can really manage to go with the mainstream, unless they decide to openly state their homosexual tendencies.[72]

One goal of al-Ghafari's article is to distinguish between at least three different possible meanings of *lesbian identity*. The first is an essential, transhistorical description of homosexual desire among women, specifically inhering in some women as their own, "inborn" and "natural" form of sexual desire. The next is a "political" or "feminist" understanding of lesbian identity as a protest against men. The final is one she defines less clearly, but describes as "a transsexual and transgendered lesbian."[73] Massad would certainly take issue with al-Ghafari's decision to characterize women across history and culture with erotic feelings toward other women as "lesbians," regardless of whether or not they embrace that identity themselves, as well as with her understanding of "lesbian visibility" as a "problem" that makes a lesbian identity "impossible."[74] In any case, al-Ghafari, while explicitly rejecting the feminist lesbian identity based in politics in favor of one based on desire, ends her essay with a call for "the creation of a body politics and a new lifestyle that springs from [a positive] understanding of lesbian sexuality" and "a new way of perceiving the dominant norms, laws and regulations."[75] Thus, while retaining the term *lesbian*, al-Ghafari advocates an Arab sexual identity politics that departs from the lesbian identity politics of the United States and Europe.

It bears noting, however, that the meaning of gay and lesbian identities in the United States and Europe also remains a matter of debate and struggle. As I have argued earlier in this chapter, gay and lesbian identities have an important political component in the United States insofar as they take shape in resistance to homophobia, but they are by no means the only possible identities to do so. Massad seems to assume that a very narrow understanding of sexuality is dominant throughout the "West": sexuality as divided between two possible identities (homosexual and heterosexual). Within this schema, to which all must conform, everyone must take on one identity or the other, unifying self-understanding, sexual practice, and public identity.

I think one could debate whether or not this understanding of sexuality really is dominant, at least in the United States, much less across something called "the West." If so, then few conform perfectly to it, but, more importantly, I believe that Massad's picture of the "West" overlooks a tremendous amount of resistance to such a binary—resistance that would actually support his larger claims. Gay and lesbian identities—due to their origins in the European side of the colonial/modern gender system and the history of colonialist sexual exploitation—might never stand apart in non-Euro-American societies from associations with imperialist intervention. This could constitute one reason for rejecting them. One might also question how useful they have proven even in Europe and the United States for resisting intermeshed and mutually constitutive oppressions. This could constitute a second reason to reject them. In other words, has their narrow focus on sexuality, apart from class, race, and gender, too often led to their complicity with oppression?

Homosexual, heterosexual, gay, lesbian, and *straight* have never stood as the only sexual identities available in Europe and North America, and some of the others have challenged these specifically as overly restrictive, politically conservative, or both. Alternatives in the United States have ranged from those linking sexual desire to gender identity (butch, femme, invert, queen, two-spirit, Uranian) and those emphasizing sexual fluidity or indeterminacy (bisexual, DL [down low], queer, questioning, sex radical) to those claiming cultural or class specificity (AG [aggressive], bulldagger, butcha, desi dyke, joto, queen, same-gender loving, two-spirit) and political opposition (dyke, fag, joto, queer, radical faerie, woman-identified woman). In each case, these identities have often sought not only to express the specificity of sexual style and desire but also to structure people's sense of self and place in the organization of their society. They have also sometimes helped to organize opposition to the perceived politics of gay and lesbian identities, most often portrayed as accommodating a status quo that is neither egalitarian nor just. Examples include radical queer indictments of the class politics often associated with U.S. urban gay identities (for example, recent queer antigentrification movements against gay-led gentrification processes in San Francisco and New York City).[76]

Other colonial and postcolonial contexts have also yielded questions about the necessity of U.S.- and Western European-style identities as the only or the best way to promote sexual minority political agendas. In India, for example, much of the debate over sexuality has centered not on the desirability of sexual identities but on which sexual identities are most desirable. Parmesh Shahani notes in his ethnography of men associated with the Indian organization Gay Bombay that he found contending accounts of what *gay* meant within the organization. Some members "wished to assimilate and appropriate the term within the Indian context, recognizing fully well the unique set of circumstances within which this would take place." Others "questioned terms like *gay* and deemed them Western imports and negative influences and preferred to use *gay* as just one term, alongside indigenous terminology such as *kothi* or functional terms like 'MSM' [men who have sex with men]."[77] He concludes, however, that regardless of their preference, most of the men he interviewed, "even those who had access to the El Dorado of *abroad*, still wanted to configure their gay experiences within an Indian matrix."[78]

Feminist scholar Suparna Bhaskaran makes a similar observation. She identifies four dominant responses to same-sex sexuality in India: first, an "official homophobic nationalist response"; second, a view of India as "historically accommodating fluid homoerotic spaces" so that "being straight in India is almost queer"; third, a narrative arguing "that the global-modern gay identity is an inevitable consequence of modernity, globalization, and the exchange and movements of ideas and persons"; and, fourth, a position holding "that indigenous same-sex/gender sexualities co-exist easily and uneasily with postcolonial modern forms of same sex sexualities" because sexual identities "in India are not always the same as in the 'west' but are always marked by it in uneven ways."[79]

Like Shahani, Bhaskaran believes that these positions overlap and form various coalitions and alliances at the same time that they compete for legitimacy in the public sphere. What she also notes, however, is that local players rarely hold the most power in these debates. Rather, they often must compete against powerful nongovernmental organizations (NGOs) and human rights organizations with financial backing from abroad. Most notably, Bhaskaran demonstrates the extent to which World Bank–funded NGOs have enabled sexual minority rights activism in India. These same NGOs took over health advocacy after India had to divest much of its public health spending in response to structural adjustment demands from the International Monetary Fund (IMF) in 1991. They are, therefore, not without their own political and economic agendas with which local sexual minority activists must contend.

One cannot easily separate, then, the choices of individuals to embrace a given sexual identity from the political, social, cultural, and economic contexts in which they encounter a given range of intelligible identity options. In an essay on globalization and the "international gay/lesbian movement," Australian activist and scholar Dennis Altman acknowledges that "the assertion of lesbian/gay identity can have neo-colonial implications" and that people "outside the West tend to be more aware of the difference between traditional homosexualities and contemporary gay identity politics" than do members of the "international lesbian/gay movement." Nonetheless, he insists that "[n]ew sexual identities mean a loss of certain traditional cultural comforts while offering new possibilities to those who adopt them."[80]

It is not clear, however, that everyone either wants those possibilities or believes them to be worth the risks. For example, one of Whitaker's informants, described as "an Egyptian activist," expresses skepticism about the emphasis of self-identified gay and lesbian rights advocates on "visibility," arguing instead that Arabs "need to identify and explore non-Western ways of being gay."[81] Any transformative sexual politics in a transnational context must therefore entail efforts to free sexual minority activists in economically developing and formerly colonized contexts from "human rights" intervention on behalf of ethnocentric and imperialist agendas from Europe and North America. A persuasive body of empirical work has demonstrated how frequently women's rights agendas supported from abroad, for example, become entangled with the destabilization of national economies and the loss of cultural and political autonomy.[82] For transformative sexual identities to flourish, unequal colonial and neocolonial relations must end. For that to happen, in turn, LGBTI organizations and individuals in Europe, the United States, and elsewhere must acknowledge and confront their complicity with the colonial/modern gender system.

Homophobia, Patriarchy, and the "West"

That the agents of imperialism do not really have the best interests of gays and lesbians in mind should not come as a surprise to anyone. They as often vilify them domestically as enlist their support abroad. Indeed, just as in the case of GLAAD's response to the "fag bomb," the vilification can ironically lead gays and lesbians to sign up for imperialist endeavors to prove their worthiness. The vilification continues unabated, however. Right-wing pundit Dinesh D'Souza, for example, has charged a "cultural left" in the United States with responsibility for the events of September 11, 2001. His argument is multipart: first, the "cultural left" has created "a decadent American culture that angers and repulses traditional societies"; second, it has engaged in "an aggressive global campaign to undermine the traditional patriarchal family and to promote secular values in non-Western cultures"; and third, it has undermined U.S. foreign policy (specifically that of President George W. Bush's administration).[83] The pillars of D'Souza's accusations against U.S. decadence are abortion, divorce, and gay marriage (which, one should note, remains legally prohibited throughout most of the United States), while the deeper source of this "gross depravity and immorality" lies specifically in the secularization of morality.[84] He advocates a strengthening of patriarchal families and patriarchal and religious values, both in the United States and elsewhere. According to D'Souza, "American conservatives should join the Muslims and others in condemning the global moral degeneracy that is produced by liberal values."[85] Furthermore, they "should stop insisting on radical secularism, stop promoting the feminist conception of the family, stop trying to promote abortion and 'sex education,' and should try to halt the export of the vulgar and corrupting elements of our popular culture."[86]

On the surface, D'Souza's manifesto for patriarchal values bears some similarities to the taped declaration of al-Zawahiri and to Massad's criticism of gay and lesbian human rights organizations. D'Souza sees the "cultural imperialism" of human rights organizations as based in liberalism rather than ethnocentrism, but his conclusions might seem similar to Massad's at first glance:

> When Osama bin Laden champions the veil and denounces America as morally corrupt, he is appealing not only to traditional Muslims but also to traditional people around the world who support the idea of the patriarchal family. When Americans attack the Muslim family for being hierarchical, backward, and oppressive, many traditional folk in Asia, Africa, and the Middle East view their cherished values and institutions as being attacked. A good deal of bin Laden's support comes from non-Western people who see him as defending a traditional social order. It is an article of faith on the cultural left that Bush's policies, such as his invasion of Iraq and the use of torture, are fueling Muslim hostility. The irony is that it is the cultural imperialism of human rights groups and the left that is the deeper source of Muslim rage. In attempting to "liberate" Muslim cultures from patriarchy, the cultural left has provoked a cultural blowback that has strengthened the hand of America's enemy.[87]

Scholars such as Massad, Najmabadi, El-Rouayheb, and Dror Ze'evi show, however, that the "traditional social order" defended by D'Souza and al-Zawahiri has a history. Rather than simply being "traditional," it has evolved over the course of centuries through interactions among different societies competing for power and cultural legitimacy during the emergence of the modern world.[88] Indeed, according to scholars like Bhaskaran and Shahani, debates in India over whether or not to trade "traditional" practices of gender and sexuality for "modern" ones have given way in some cases to debates about which "traditional" understandings of gender and sexuality might best resist cultural and economic imperialism while accommodating ongoing cultural transformation.[89] This may result in part from more readily available historical resources in India for rethinking gender and sexuality from within indigenous traditions. Massad explicitly expresses a hope that his recovery of historical archives accounting for how Arabs have thought about gender, sex, and eroticism might enable a broader conversation and open more possibilities for understanding the relationships among them, independently of "Western" interventions.[90] The historical studies of Massad, Najmabadi, and others complement work that shows how "traditional" understandings of family, gender, and sexuality also have a history of transformation in the "West," adapting to changing social structures as well as to the shifting demands of colonial priorities.[91]

While D'Souza claims that a "cultural left" in the United States has tried to undermine U.S. foreign policy objectives, the highest profile LGBTI campaigns in the past two decades have advocated for the inclusion of lesbians and gays in the military and for legal recognition of same-sex marriage. Both of these campaigns ultimately seek inclusion of marginalized communities into the mainstream of U.S. society, and, by extension, U.S. foreign policy. Thus, as Feinberg demonstrates, at the same time that U.S.-based LGBTI organizations were advocating for equality, they were supporting U.S. military interventions abroad. Indeed, many critics of the mainstream gay and lesbian rights movement have argued that same-sex marriage, like military participation, makes for a particularly conservative political platform and epitomizes the quest for normalcy among the largest LGBTI rights groups.

Cultural critic Michael Warner, among others, has argued that this pursuit of normalcy leaves many U.S. social institutions unquestioned.[92] In scrambling for marriage, for example, gays and lesbians leave unasked questions such as whether or not immigration, taxes, inheritance rights, hospital visitation, end-of-life care, and child custody ought to have a necessary connection to one's involvement in a romantic relationship. It also leaves unasked the question of whether or not romantic relationships ought to constitute an object of state interest in the first place. Furthermore, does the complicity of LGBTI normalcy in a U.S. context also entail the endorsement of the normalcy of the United States, and by extension, its power over other countries? If so, then same-sex marriage and military participation constitute a conservative move to bring marginalized sexual communities in line with interventionist U.S. foreign policy objectives. In this light, the linking by al-Zawahiri of same-sex marriage and U.S. intervention appears not without justification. In other words, to the extent that gays and lesbians want inclusion in "normal" society (especially through marriage and military service), they may find themselves actively signing up against the interests of the victims of U.S. interventionism and the *other* side of the colonial/modern gender system.[93]

Alliance or Disjuncture?

If their emergence from different sides of the colonial/modern gender system means that U.S. LGBTI activists and sexual minorities in colonial, neocolonial, and postcolonial contexts do not always share common ground, what of the defenders of so-called traditional values? Does a description (common in Western gay reactions to the Abu Ghraib abuses) of both the U.S. Army and radical Islamists as *homophobic* miss important ways in which homophobia differs due to different points of origin in the colonial/modern gender system? Put another way, if both right-wing U.S. pundits like D'Souza and anti-U.S. Egyptian protestors see the incidents at Abu Ghraib as perversely linked to Western homosexuality, does that mean that they share the same homophobia? How might anticolonial or anti-imperialist homophobia differ from homophobia within the colonial and imperial centers of Europe and North America? Extrapolating from these questions, I would like to pose another, quite different and deliberately provocative one: *What are the limits to thinking that alliance is possible between sexual liberation movements in the "West" and decolonial and anti-imperial movements elsewhere?*

The rhetoric of gay pride and sexual freedom articulated within dominant sectors of the colonial/modern gender system has an inseparable relationship to legacies of colonial sexual exploitation and domination. Those legacies, for colonized and formerly colonized peoples, include the denial of their humanity (and gender) as well as their construal as racially inferior. The rhetoric of sexual liberation in the United States and Western Europe, by contrast, has taken shape in response to *local* practices of sexual repression rather than colonial sexual exploitation. The modern vocabulary of sexual liberation and repression only expresses an opposition from within the dominant side of the colonial/modern gender system.

From the perspective of the colonized, sexual exploitation and sexualized colonial violence take both repressive and liberated forms. One cannot view resistant practices emerging from the other side of the colonial/modern gender system as simply repressive or liberationist within the exact same dichotomy as practices on the dominant side. People like Whitaker's skeptical "Egyptian activist," whose gender and sexual expression might make them dissidents in their home country, might still resist U.S. and European gay liberationist rhetoric with good reason after seeing, for example, how coloniality and neoliberalism have developed an exploitative gay sex tourism industry in Southeast Asia and elsewhere.[94] The same organizations that Massad accuses of fomenting interventionist impulses toward Arab countries seem strangely silent on the subject of gay-funded sex tourism in other parts of the world.

Abu Ghraib, within the context of the colonial/modern gender system, appears consistent with gender expression and sexual freedom as it has consistently been conceived by the dominant players in colonial relations: the sexual access by white men and women to anyone (else) in any form, at any time, with the support of the state. The homophobia of the Egyptian protestors therefore differs from the homophobia of the U.S. military, if for no other reason than because the former consists largely of a practice of resistance to sexual forms of colonial exploitation.

Understanding this difference also reveals the limitations of many progressive, feminist, and antihomophobic responses to U.S. imperialism. Columnist Barbara Ehrenreich, for example, in a 2004 *Los Angeles Times* editorial, expresses shock at the images from Abu Ghraib.[95] Much of Ehrenreich's column reveals the extent to which her understanding of gender emerges solely from the dominant side of the colonial/modern gender system: "[Prior to Abu Ghraib] [t]here seemed to be at least some evidence that male sexual sadism was connected to our species' tragic propensity for violence. That was before we had seen female sexual sadism in action . . . [T]he assumption of [women's] superiority, or at least a lesser inclination toward cruelty and violence, was more or less beyond debate."[96] Ehrenreich equally reveals her naïveté and her complicity with colonial portrayals of the racial other as premodern, primitive, and historically antecedent. For her, the backwardness of the other manifests in its failure to realize the supposed gender and sexual equality of the United States:

> If you were doing PR for Al Qaeda, you couldn't have staged a better picture to galvanize misogynist Islamic fundamentalists around the world.
> Here, in these photos from Abu Ghraib, you have everything that the Islamic fundamentalists believe characterizes Western culture, all nicely arranged in one hideous image—imperial arrogance, sexual depravity . . . and gender equality. . . . Although I opposed the 1991 Persian Gulf War, I was proud of our servicewomen and delighted that their presence irked their Saudi hosts.[97]

Ehrenreich's delight reveals a colonial sense of cultural, if not racial, superiority. For Ehrenreich, the United States needs to bring gender equality and sexual liberation to the Arab world in order to liberate it from its gender and sexual repression. Ehrenreich does not consider that the roots of gender and sexual repression in Saudi Arabia might lie in global interactions stretching across the history of modernity and coloniality rather than in Islamic and Arab tradition. In other words, she does not challenge the assumption that contemporary gender roles among Arabs result solely from the uninterrupted development of Islam and Arab civilization, rather than from centuries of unequal interaction between colonizers and colonized within a colonial/modern gender system intent on restructuring life worlds according to the necessities of global power flows.

One should note that, among other things, Ehrenreich seems oblivious to the five-hundred-year history of women's complicity with racist violence and imperial projects. For her, the participation of women in the abuse at Abu Ghraib is the result of the successes and limitations of liberal feminism in the twentieth century. However, Abu Ghraib showed us nothing new. White women have participated actively in the torture and murder of colonized peoples for centuries. No one familiar with the history of lynching in the United States would ever have supposed otherwise.[98] Moreover, sexual degradation has always formed a part of the violence against people construed as racially inferior. Thus, one can easily see echoes of Abu Ghraib in pictures taken immediately following the 1971 uprising at the Attica Correctional Facility in upstate New York, where state troopers engaged in systematic racial humiliation of naked prisoners.[99]

Transforming Colonial Modernity

The colonial/modern gender system reveals the extent to which the gender and sexual domination of racially subordinated peoples has roots in the legacies of modernity and coloniality. European and North American capitalism has consistently imposed both sexual repression and hypersexuality on racially marked others toward its own ends rather than in the interests of their own freedom and humanity. The sexual violence and exploitation of colonialism has taken the form of imposed and constructed sexual liberty as frequently as it has resulted in a self-imposed sexual repression in resistance to coloniality. In other words, ideas of sexual liberation that emerge from the colonizers and travel to the colonized parts of the world have historically construed the people there as sexual objects with fluid (or no) gender and libidinous sexualities as readily as they have construed them as subjects with rigid gender roles and repressed sexualities.

Resistance to coloniality, then, often rightly views Eurocentric ideas of gender and sexual liberation as inseparable from the degradation of the colonized by the colonial/modern gender system. The reclamation of gender (either masculinity or femininity) on the part of the colonized can thus become a form of the reclamation of dignity and humanity. Of course, as Lugones observes, the reclaimed genders can too easily resemble the masculine and feminine gender binary historically imposed on colonized peoples, and often violently so. The embracing of this binary has attractions to both men and women, but particularly to men who have the hope of gaining not only recognition as fully human but recognition as *men* and hence power over women. Ultimately, embracing the imposed Western binary can collude with colonial violence while seeming liberatory within the terms of modernity's oppositions between purity and impurity, reason and the body, heterosexuality and perversion. For men and women of color to reject both sides of the colonial/modern gender system, the call for that rejection must entail a critical reworking of the whole system, including Eurocentric understandings of gender and sexuality. In other words, sexual liberation—or emancipation from the effects of colonial modernity—must emerge from within a decolonial project rather than from within the colonial/modern project of sexual liberation that sees gender and sexuality in isolation from racism and coloniality.

Efforts in this direction exist in numerous contexts. Consider the work of Helem, a gay and lesbian organization based in Lebanon and the first LGBTI organization in an Arab country to gain legal recognition. Both Whitaker (positively) and Massad (negatively) discuss Helem. However, I think that both scholars underexamine some of Helem's most well-known actions. For example, Helem's first public event was its participation in a March 2003 demonstration in Beirut to protest the U.S. invasion of Iraq. Massad focuses on who organized and participated in the action.[100] Whitaker argues for understanding Helem's participation as a "struggle against homophobia through visibility."[101] Neither one makes any significance of the fact that Helem chose to make its first public action not a gay pride march, but a march against U.S. military intervention in the region. One Helem member, Rasha Moumneh, for example, argues that Helem at the time had "a strong leftist contingent as its core group, two of whom were founding members."[102] Massad credits Sofian Merabet, a German Algerian, as "one of the main (if not the main) organizers of the demonstration."[103] He thereby seeks to discredit Helem as a front for "Westernized" Arabs.

However, according to Moumneh, the participation of Helem would have taken place without Merabet, although he was present. More importantly, the protest formed a part of the larger politics of the core group of Helem members at the time, who also supported other forms of "non-LGBT politics" such as the Palestinian solidarity movement, although the question of whether and how to address LGBT issues and other issues less obviously connected to them did generate debate within the organization.[104] Furthermore, Moumneh agrees with much of Massad's larger argument against international activists and NGOs. Neither Massad nor Whitaker, however, allow for the complexity of on-the-ground organizing or acknowledge that many in Helem (though not all) saw their activism as much directed at fighting against imperialism as aimed at eliminating homophobia and heterosexism. In 2006, during the Israeli invasion of Lebanon, Helem dedicated its resources and facilities to humanitarian aid to those displaced by Israeli bombing. In a recorded message to the organizers of the 2006 OutGames in Montréal, Canada, Moumneh states,

"We do not accept democracy at the barrel of a gun. We do not accept to be liberated through war, if the price of that liberty is our lives, meted out in collateral terms."[105] She concludes her message by calling for a boycott of the 2006 World Pride event in Israel.

Other groups in other contexts have made similar stands, including a coalition of the Hawai'i Gay Liberation Program, the National Community Relation Division of the American Friends Service Committee's Hawai'i Area Program, No Mamo O Hawai'i, and the Urban-Rural Mission (USA). This coalition formed in the wake of a 1993 Hawai'i State Supreme Court decision, *Baehr v. Lewin*, which ruled that the state's refusal to grant same-sex marriages violated the state constitution and ordered the state to justify its discrimination.[106] This decision not only put same-sex marriage on the agenda nationally but also led to an amendment to the Hawaiian constitution allowing the state to limit marriage rights to "opposite-sex couples."[107] In a series of documents, the coalition of social justice groups sought to place both the struggle for same-sex marriage in Hawai'i and gay tourism (which increased in the wake of the court ruling) in the context of ongoing colonial devastation of Hawaiian lands and people. Arguing that "justice for all *is* a gay issue," the Hawai'i Gay Liberation Program's statement describes the conditions of native Hawaiians, who have "the worst health, the highest levels of incarceration and poverty, the lowest level of educational attainment, and the highest mortality rate of all groups in Hawai'i—and among the worst in the U.S."[108] They juxtapose this condition with the claim that "the LGBT movement must be rooted in something far deeper and more genuine than political marriages of convenience forged in crisis, in reaction to the initiatives of the religious right."[109]

Specifically vexing for activists such as those from Na Mamo O Hawai'i was the position among mainstream gay and lesbian rights organizations that tourism from gays and lesbians should form an incentive for the legalization of same-sex marriage in Hawai'i. The Hawaiian groups argue that U.S. gays and lesbians have something to learn from native Hawaiian understandings of sexuality. According to the "Open Letter to the LGBT Community" by Na Mamo O Hawai'i, an "example of the unique needs of our Kanaka Maoli [native Hawaiian] LGBT is seen in the difference between Kanaka Maoli sexuality and the gay movement in [the United States]. For instance, while the [U.S.] gay movement claims its roots from the Stonewall riots in New York, Kanaka Maoli sexuality is grounded in a person's relationship to the 'aina or land."[110]

One thus cannot separate the decolonization of land in Hawai'i from the decolonization of LGBT sexualities there. Sexual decolonization also necessitates, from a Kānaka Maoli perspective, a critical relationship to tourism: "Tourism . . . appropriates, caricatures, and degrades Kanaka Maoli culture and spirituality. Tourism promoters offer soft, alluring, exoticized images of the Hawaiian landscape and sexualized, racial stereotypes of Kanaka Maoli as commodities to be consumed by tourists—who, often without realizing it, participate in practices that are rapidly depleting the natural and cultural resources of the islands."[111] While dominant understandings of gay liberation see sexual autonomy as a preeminent value—thereby separating resistance to homophobia from practices of colonialism and racism—these Hawaiian activist organizations instead argue that "struggles to decolonize the nation, culture, spirituality, social relationships, the body, and the self, are deeply entwined."[112]

Organizations like these understand the important connections between anticolonial struggles and true sexual freedom—freedom as personal fulfillment and communal connection rather than merely the license to do what you want, when, where, how, and with whomever you want. Similar connections also exist in Mexico, where, for example, the muxe of Oaxaca have maintained long-standing indigenous conceptualizations of gender and sexual identity that challenge both sides of the colonial/modern gender system. The muxe in the town of Juchitán, people who would most likely be considered transsexuals in the United States, live as thoroughly integrated and accepted within the local culture.[113] Elsewhere in Mexico, blending enduring pre-Colombian understandings of gender and sexuality with postrevolutionary leftist political commitments, groups like the Ejército Zapatista de Liberación Nacional (EZLN), or Zapatistas, have sought recently to connect their insurgent indigenous movement to progressive and anticolonial sexual politics. The EZLN began an armed uprising against the Mexican state in 1994 that has since evolved into a low-intensity standoff, with Zapatistas and their supporters in control of numerous communities in "autonomous zones" throughout the southern Mexican state of Chiapas. Early in the conflict, EZLN spokesperson Subcomandante Marcos issued a statement expressing solidarity with gays and lesbians. The Zapatistas launched the latest stage in their movement in 2005, with the "Sixth Declaration from the Lacandón Jungle," again committing themselves to a broad range of intermeshed causes. Describing resistance to colonial modernity in the form of neoliberalism, the declaration states:

[I]t is not so easy for neoliberal globalization, because the exploited of each country become discontented, and they will not say well, too bad, instead they rebel. And those who remain and who are in the way resist, and they don't allow themselves to be eliminated. And that is why we see, all over the world, those who are being screwed over making resistances, not putting up with it, in other words, they rebel, and not just in one country but wherever they abound. And so, as there is a neoliberal globalization, there is a globalization of rebellion.

And it is not just the workers of the countryside and of the city who appear in this globalization of rebellion, but others also appear who are much persecuted and despised for the same reason, for not letting themselves be dominated, like women, young people, the indigenous, homosexuals, lesbians, transsexual persons, migrants and many other groups who exist all over the world but who we do not see until they shout ya basta [enough already] of being despised, and they [rise] up, and then we see them, we hear them, and we learn from them.

And then we see that all those groups of people are fighting against neoliberalism, against the capitalist globalization plan, and they are struggling for humanity.[114]

The Zapatistas' work has, among other things, included solidarity with the Oaxaca-based Sexual Diversity Collective, and reflects a deep rooting of struggle in the connections among economic, cultural, and bodily decolonization.

To return to some of the questions raised by my opening anecdote, the violence done to Falah Zaggam, to his family, and to his community makes sense as part of a legacy of centuries of European and U.S. interference in Iraq rather than as the result of an ahistorical and transcultural homophobia. Those of us who want to reject homophobia need to understand it as part of the larger violence of the colonial/modern gender system. As a gay Chicano in the United States, I should not think that my own struggle for freedom and equality automatically exempts me from implication in colonial violence. I should not seek inclusion in the national projects of the United States on terms similar to those offered to Federico Mérida. The guards at Abu Ghraib could easily have included Chicana and African American lesbians or Native American and Asian American gay men.

To think otherwise is to gravely disadvantage ourselves in attempting to understand and to undo the violence of the colonial/modern gender system. Gays and lesbians in the "West" ignore our complicity in the coloniality of power at our own peril. Furthermore, no conversation about gay and lesbian identities or sexual freedom or human rights—in Lebanon, Singapore, Mexico, the Pacific, or the United States—can be adequate without taking into account how these concepts have taken shape within both sides of this gender system as a result of unequal and ongoing cross-cultural exchange. The Zapatistas' declaration urges us (and the case of Zaggam and Mérida requires us) to understand how and why our own identities and desires are connected to other identities and other desires and to work toward conditions that permit broad-based solidarity to end the violence of a modern and colonial world order.

4

Do Prisons Make Better Men?

A Crisis Not Made for Television

Almost everyone in the United States has at one time or another either told or heard a joke about prison rape. No one doubts the presence of same-sex rape in men's prisons and many people accept it as inevitable. Television writers Aaron McGruder and Rodney Barnes even chose to make the fear of it an object of extended parody in the fifth episode of their animated television comedy *The Boondocks*.[1] They suggest that the fear of "being anally raped" in prison serves as the most powerful force in dictating the life choices of at least one major character, a black man who, ironically, works as a criminal prosecutor.

While such rape humor (and rape fear) reveals a nexus of racial, gender, and sexual anxieties, it also functions to hide the reality of the prison crisis in the United States. In fact, prisons have rapidly become perhaps the most impressive mechanism for mass repression in modern society. Yet cultural representations of prison seem to conceal more than they ever reveal about incarceration. For example, while same-sex rape among prisoners does occur all too commonly in men's prisons, women face sexual assault in prison at least as often. Women prisoners, however, are far more likely to be sexually assaulted by guards (either male or female) than by other prisoners—a fact that seems much less amenable to comedy.[2] Despite the limitations of cultural representations, however, mass cultural depictions of the prison constitute many people's only source of information about what prisons might, in fact, be like. Since writers, directors, and producers seem to create most such representations with a white audience in mind, however, one finds that, ironically, studying multiplicity and representations of the prison often tells us as much about white identities as about those of people of color.

The contemporary prison crisis in the United States has a foundation in the homophobia, racism, and sexism that emerge from the colonial/

modern gender system. In this chapter, I give an account of the recent history of the prison crisis and then turn to a reading of the Home Box Office (HBO) television series *Oz* (1997–2003) to help illuminate the prison's homophobic, racist, and sexist underpinnings and to consider the possibilities and limitations of mass cultural representation as a resistant strategy.[3] As an entertainment phenomenon, *Oz* stands out against the backdrop of a remarkable silence in the U.S. media about the prison crisis. Furthermore, I find *Oz* striking for its attention to the mutual constitution of masculinity, race, and sexuality. The creators of *Oz* clearly wanted to make something radical. It was one of very few—if not the only—popular shows of its time that addressed racism unflinchingly; it also seriously confronted the topic of homophobia. *Oz* included gay sex scenes before gay-themed television series like *Will & Grace* (1998–2006) or *Queer as Folk* (2000–2005) had debuted.[4] Furthermore, its cast included an astonishing number of people of color, including some former prisoners, at a time when the other major networks faced threats of a boycott from the National Association for the Advancement of Colored People (NAACP) for the dearth of people of color in acting, production, and executive roles.[5] Yet, despite its achievements, in many ways *Oz* fails, and fails devastatingly. I contend that the failures and contradictions of *Oz* help to illustrate the consequences of the colonial/modern gender system's legacies for the representation of racial and sexual identities in mass culture. As a cultural production centrally concerned with both race and nonheterosexual sexuality, *Oz*'s inability to bring the two together coherently also sheds some light on possibilities for antiracist, anticolonial, and antihomophobic identities, representation, and political coalition in the wake of the colonial/modern gender system.

Before embarking on an analysis of *Oz*, however, one must grapple with the scope and origins of the U.S. prison crisis—a crisis that, I argue, defies comparison. As of 2005, the United States held well over seven million people in prison, in jail, or on probation or parole. By the dawn of 2008, one in one hundred adults was imprisoned—one in thirty-six Hispanic men over age eighteen and one in fifteen black men over age eighteen.[6] Many observers have sought to find analogies to help make sense of the state of incarceration in the United States today. They regularly make comparisons to the race-based slavery of the eighteenth and nineteenth centuries, as well as to the Middle Passage—that period of confinement endured by Africans as Europeans kidnapped them and forcibly took them on ships to the Americas.[7] While dramatic and evocative, however, such analogies can unintentionally minimize the severity of the present crisis, since, as slavery goes, imprisonment never seems quite as bad as "real" slavery. In order truly to feel their enormity, one must, therefore, understand prisons and incarceration today on their own terms.

In particular, one should observe three points about imprisonment in the United States today. First, the present crisis is historically anomalous, arising only within the past two to three decades (Figure 4.1). Second, it is geographically anomalous, the scope and form being unique to a single country (Figure 4.2). Third, it has a high degree of correlation to race, affecting blacks most severely (Figure 4.3). Indeed, what seem like dramatically steep overall rates of increase in recent decades appear nearly flat in the context of racially specific incarceration rates. By any standard, the rate of African American imprisonment during the past twenty to thirty years places this crisis among the greatest mass persecutions in

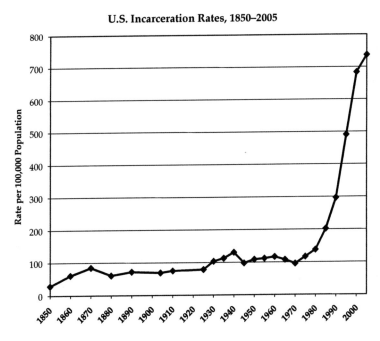

U.S. Incarceration Rates, 1850–2005

Figure 4.1. Combined federal and state incarceration rates in the United States, 1850–2005. Data compiled from Blomberg and Lucken, American Penology *and U.S. Department of Justice, Bureau of Justice Statistics,* Prisoners in 2005.

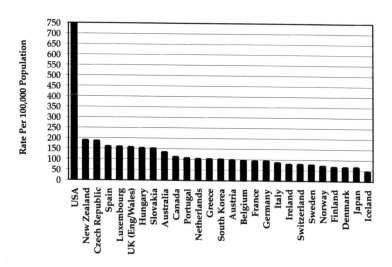

High-Income Country Incarceration Rates in 2007

Figure 4.2. Rates of incarceration for the 27 countries classified as "high income" by the World Bank in 2007. Incarceration rates obtained from the International Centre for Prison Studies at King's College, London (http://www.kcl.ac.uk).

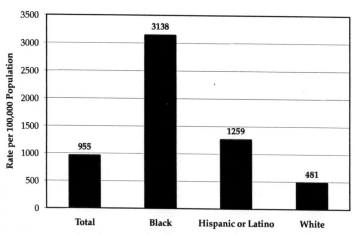

U.S. Imprisonment Rates for Men in 2007, by Race

Figure 4.3. Imprisonment rates (the number of state or federal sentenced prisoners under state or federal jurisdiction per 100,000 U.S. residents) for black, Hispanic or Latino, and white men in the United States in 2007. Data from U.S. Department of Justice, Bureau of Justice Statistics, Prisoners in 2007.

modern world history. Yet, shockingly, no one in the U.S. government or mainstream media seems particularly upset over this state of affairs. If anything, political rhetoric continues to demand more prisons, tougher laws, longer sentences, and more police. The mass detention of racial minorities quite simply does not have a place on the U.S. political agenda as a national crisis.

Data on the incarceration of Alaskan Natives, Asian Americans, Native Americans, and Pacific Islanders presents a striking complement to the better-known situation of blacks and Latinas and Latinos in prison.[8] In 2000, Native Americans had an incarceration rate of 709 per 100,000 for federal and state prisons and jails combined. Asians had a rate of 99 per 100,000, whites had a rate of 235, "Hispanics" a rate of 609, and blacks a rate of 1815. Native Hawaiians in Hawai'i, meanwhile, had a rate of 1,000 per 100,000 in 2000 (Figure 4.4).[9] While in most states, Asian Americans have lower incarceration rates than whites, the aggregation of the category *Asian American and Pacific Islander* makes the rates misleading. Something similar can happen with the categories *Hispanic* and *Latino*, although to a lesser degree because all major Latino populations in the United States have higher incarceration rates than Anglos.

Disaggregating these categories typically reveals higher incarceration rates for Pacific Islanders (including Native Hawaiians) and for Southeast Asians; by contrast, East Asians (including Filipinos) and South Asians typically have rates lower than whites. A recent study comparing foreign-born immigrants with U.S.-born Latinos and Asian Americans, for example, reports incarceration rates for U.S.-born Vietnamese, Laotian, and Cambodian men comparable to *or greater* than those for U.S.-born Mexican and Puerto Rican men. Indeed, the authors of the study point out that the incarceration rates for U.S.-born Laotian and Cambodian men are "the highest of any group except for native blacks."[10] The United States incarcerated a discouraging 7.26 percent of all U.S.-born Laotian and Cambodian men aged 18 to 39 in 2000. Of U.S.-born men within the same age range in other ethnic and racial groups, the nation incarcerated 11.61 percent of blacks (one in nine), 5.90 percent of Mexican Americans, 5.60 percent of Vietnamese, 5.06 percent of Puerto Ricans, 4.20 percent of Cubans, 3.71 percent of Dominicans, 3.01 percent of Salvadorans and Guatemalans, 1.71 percent of non-Hispanic whites, 1.22 percent of Filipinos, 0.99 percent of Asian Indians, 0.93 percent of Koreans, and 0.65 percent of Chinese and Taiwanese (Figure 4.5).[11]

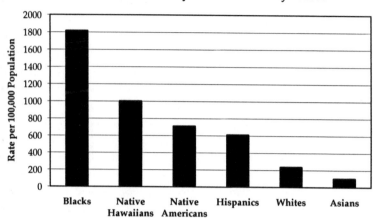

U.S. Incarceration by Race and Ethnicity in 2000

Figure 4.4. Incarceration rates in 2000 for blacks, Native Hawaiians, Native Americans, "Hispanics," whites, and Asians. Data compiled from several sources; see note 9.

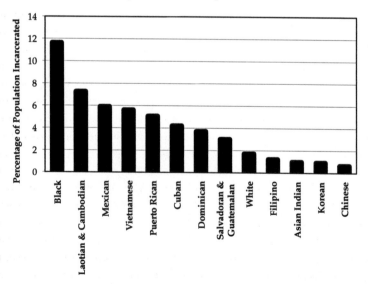

U.S.-born Men, 18-39, Incarcerated in 2000, by Race & Ethnicity

Figure 4.5. Percentages incarcerated in 2000 of U.S.-born men of African, Asian, white, and Latino origin between the ages of 18–39. Data from Rumbaut et al., "Debunking the Myth of Immigrant Criminality."

In most contexts, news that a nation had locked away one in nine members of a given population would incite outrage and talk of a humanitarian crisis, but the U.S. media has both ignored the dimensions of the crisis and even stoked the flames. I would think it obvious that a figure of one in nine for black men between the ages of eighteen and thirty-nine and one in eighty-two for white men in that same age range suggests that prisons function as something other than a mechanism for detaining violent or dangerous people (however true it may be that some violent and dangerous people are in prison). Yet addicted to endless reruns of television dramas like *Law & Order* (1990–present) and *CSI: Crime Scene Investigation* (2000–present) and reality-based programs like *America's Most Wanted* (1988–present) and *Cops* (1989–present), U.S. society has embraced a conception of streets flooded with murderers and the prison as the quintessential repository of violence.[12] Prison flickers across the television screen as the place where guilty evildoers go after a thorough investigation and fair trial, where noble law enforcers restrain them against their will for the safety of "the rest of us." Indeed, according to such propagandistic television fare, the greatest injustices occur not when the criminal justice system imprisons innocent or nonviolent people but rather when the guilty escape without punishment. (This thirst for punishing others through imprisonment reached its pinnacle of absurdity in the recent media circuses surrounding the locking up of white, female celebrities like media mogul Martha Stewart and hotel heiress Paris Hilton.)

Aside from the occasional investigative news report, the mainstream media and politicians rarely mention prison abolition, radical prison reform, prison moratoriums, large-scale decriminalization, or decarceration of nonviolent offenders as alternatives to the en masse detention of racial minorities.[13] Any public discussion of prisons inevitably downplays or ignores the fact that half of those incarcerated at the state level and over 90 percent of people in federal prisons have been convicted of *nonviolent* offenses (such as theft, prostitution, immigration violations, bad check writing, fraud, and drug use and possession).[14] The media raises few doubts about incarceration as the most appropriate way of responding to social ills like drug dependency, poverty, homelessness, and joblessness. Of course, the media has not created the present prison crisis by itself. It has undoubtedly played a role, however, in making acceptable the mass imprisonment of more than two million people (and the monitoring and temporary detention of five million more) in the United States—something that U.S. citizens do not see as a profound contradiction of their country's alleged commitments to democracy, justice, and freedom.

A Brief History of the Prison

Scholars often tell the narrative of U.S. prisons as a story of gradual reform and ever-increasing concern with the managing of populations on a large scale. Sometimes, histories focus on the creation of a controllable and serviceable industrial working class, and sometimes the dissemination of ideas and beliefs about individual responsibility in order to justify inequality. At other times, they focus on the gradual expansion of power throughout society by mechanisms of self-regulation and discipline. All of these narratives share an account of how the prison, in its nineteenth-century guise as penitentiary or reformatory, becomes something more (and more important and more central to society) than just a place for the detention of suspects before trial or the enactment of brutal punishments designed to enforce social order.[15] The story goes that in the wake of the Enlightenment and natural rights credos in the U.S. and French Revolutions, policymakers came to see liberty as something of which the state cannot deprive people without justification. They therefore immediately set about justifying inequality and unfreedom for various groups. Usually sex (femaleness) was sufficient justification, as was race (nonwhiteness). In the case of white men, the most widely accepted justifications for deprivation of rights included insanity (lack of reason to understand the meaning of rights) and law breaking (violation of the rights of others). As a corollary, the white male politicians, lawyers, and policy makers often justified sex and race as criteria for determining rights through a categorical association of women and nonwhites with a lack of reason and inherent tendencies for criminality.[16]

Since women and nonwhites at this time typically faced confinement and denial of rights through other legal mechanisms, society deemed the prison an institution most appropriate for the punishment of law-breaking white men, a penalty reserved for those privileged enough to have freedom that the state could take away.[17] In turn, the rhetoric of "reform" and "correction" that evolved in Europe and North America took as its task the rehabilitation of law-breaking white men with the aim of reintegrating them into society. Of course, "reintegration" meant something specific for poor and working-class white men, who made up most of the prison population in the United States before the Civil War. It meant that they should become good, obedient, and productive workers within the nation's emerging industrial-capitalist economy.[18] The efficiency of this new social task, in turn, took the form of a significant expansion of the mechanisms of punishment and their integration throughout society.[19]

The history of the prison in the United States cannot be told without accounting for the differential treatment of people of color, however. To be sure, free people of color were not exempt from the new regime of punishment and rehabilitation. Scholars have noted, for example, that the representation of blacks was grossly disproportionate in the nation's first modern prison, the Walnut Street Jail in Philadelphia.[20] (A black man was also the first prisoner admitted to Walnut Street's replacement, Pennsylvania's Eastern State Penitentiary.[21]) However, other scholars argue that the continued brutality of violence committed against people of color in the nineteenth century United States shows the extent to which whites mostly considered imprisonment as a particular kind of "enlightened" punishment for those at the top of the racial order. Whereas philosopher Michel Foucault asserts that prisons replaced the physical torturing of bodies with a disciplined training of bodies, political theorist Joy James makes a strong case that his narrative of the replacing of spectacular physical violence with incarceration overlooks the widespread violence inflicted on people of color in the United States well into the twentieth century.[22] One could include in this history of violence any number of massacres directly committed by or unofficially sanctioned by the state against African Americans, Asians, Mexicans, and Native Americans before and after the Civil War, the "Indian Wars," the Mexican–American War, and the Chinese Exclusion Acts. At least up until the end of the nineteenth century, the prison system, with its high-minded ideals of correction, penitence, and reform, did not exist with the primary purpose of targeting women and people disenfranchised due to race (a category that included Mexicans, even though the state often "legally" counted them as white).[23]

Histories of the prison in the United States before the twentieth century include several punctuating events.[24] The first of these is the Walnut Street Jail in Philadelphia which was converted to the nation's first modern prison in 1790. Lauded as an institution guided by "advanced" Quaker ideals, the jail introduced segregation among the inmates according to age, sex, and type of offense, separating men and women, children and adults, and violent and nonviolent offenders for the first time. It also emphasized penitence and self-examination, rather than merely confinement and corporal punishment. Constructed on a larger scale in 1816, the Auburn prison in upstate New York followed a similar model, but added contract labor in the belief that work would build character for the prisoners. The Eastern State Penitentiary in Pennsylvania followed that experiment in 1829, introducing complete solitary confinement and dispensing with contract labor. Its designers believed that total isolation would benefit the prisoners' reformation more than labor, since while working together they might have opportunities to conspire with other inmates. Over the course of the nineteenth century, the Auburn model became dominant, both because of the difficulty of keeping prisoners completely isolated for years on end and because of the economic benefits of providing cheap prison labor to state and private contractors.

The next major moment took place shortly after the end of the Civil War, again in New York. Following principles expounded at the National Congress on Penitentiary and Reformatory Discipline, held in Cincinnati, Ohio, in 1870, the Elmira Reformatory was constructed in 1876 in Elmira, New York. Reformers intended Elmira to herald a new rational age in the "science" of reform, or "penology." Elmira stressed individualized treatment and psychological reform rather than penitence through isolation or punishment through labor. In the wake of Elmira, prisons began to introduce experiments like parole, indeterminate sentencing, and educational programs, with the goal of tailoring the experience of imprisonment to the individual needs of the inmate, helping her or him to become a better-adjusted and more productive person.[25] A 1998 article on the history of Elmira from the Department of Corrections newsletter *DOC Today*, for example, opens with the claim that Elmira "rejected 19th-century penology's holy trinity of silence, obedience, and labor. Elmira's goal would be reform of the convict, and its methods would be psychological rather than physical. Instead of coercing with the lash, Elmira would encourage with rewards. Mass regimentation would yield to classification and individualized treatment. Instead of fixed sentences to fit the crime, the indeterminate sentence would be adjustable to fit the criminal. Rather than outright release after the offender 'paid his debt to society,' the new parole procedure would assure he did not begin running up a new tab."[26] Thus did Elmira seek to signal the completed evolution of rational correction and reform.

However persuasive one finds the account of Western European and U.S. prisons in the nineteenth century as institutions of reform, one can see, over the course of the 125 years from 1865 to 1990, a gradual transformation in the use and meaning of incarceration in the United States. This transformation has taken imprisonment from a practice aimed ostensibly at reforming low-status members of privileged racial and gender strata to one of controlling and repressing stigmatized and disempowered populations en masse—populations that society construes as racially inferior through the matrices of the colonial/modern gender system. In this sense, the latest stage in the life of the prison in the United States resembles more the nineteenth-century penitentiaries of Latin America than it does the designs of Enlightenment reformers.

Historians Ricardo Salvatore and Carlos Aguirre argue that Latin America's development of prisons differed importantly from the experiments in North America and Europe. In much of Latin America, reformers lauded the penitentiary in the nineteenth century as a sign of modernization. In fact, however, Salvatore and Aguirre argue that prisons functioned as more-or-less crude mechanisms for the repression of peasants, urban poor, slaves, blacks, indigenous people, and mestizos. Often, Latin American penal efforts lacked even the *rhetoric* of reform, of the disciplining of good citizenship, and of the social body—however imperfectly realized by prisons in England, France, and the northeastern United States. In place of this rhetoric of reform, Salvatore and Aguirre find an explicit interest in maintaining social and political hierarchies, supported by rhetoric of "unreformable" populations.[27] Similarly, while the change in direction for U.S. prisons after 1865 did not represent a new repression of racial minorities, it did mark an adaptation of this peculiar institution to take over from others. One should therefore note two key transition points in the U.S. carceral shift: first, the end of slavery and the Reconstruction period (1865–77), and second, the end of the civil rights movement (1948–72).[28]

Adapting a Peculiar Institution

As newly emancipated African Americans entered the political process during Reconstruction, whites immediately set out to regain sole control of the South. After the end of the U.S. Civil War, state legislatures controlled by Southern whites enacted a number of laws popularly known as Black Codes. The Black Codes criminalized massive numbers of newly freed slaves, forcing them back onto plantations via the "punishment" clause of the Thirteenth Amendment to the U.S. Constitution: "Neither slavery nor involuntary servitude, except as a punishment for crime whereof the party shall have been duly convicted, shall exist within the United States, or any place subject to their jurisdiction." Very shortly, federal intervention on behalf of the Civil Rights Act of 1866 and the Fourteenth and Fifteenth Amendments to the Constitution led to the suspension of the Black Codes. However, within a ten-year lag from the end of Reconstruction and the withdrawal of federal troops from the South, blacks again found themselves thoroughly disenfranchised by new "Jim Crow" laws, in conjunction with widespread acts of lynching and other forms of racist terrorism.

Alongside these new forms of control and violence came the transformation of Southern prisons.[29] Prison populations in the South rapidly shifted from mostly white to mostly black. During the 1850s, just before the Civil War, free blacks made up a scant one percent of state prison inmates in Alabama and Mississippi, while Georgia's state prison had no blacks.[30] However, in the Georgia Penitentiary during the years 1879–1909, the percentage of black prisoners ranged between 87.23 percent and 91.81 percent.[31] In Alabama, by the late 1880s, whites comprised only 3.3 percent of county convicts and approximately 15 percent of state prisoners.[32] The sudden demographic shift resulted in catastrophic consequences for the lives of African Americans ensnared in the newly reconfigured prisons. Prison abolitionist Angela Davis argues that, following Reconstruction, black convicts "could be subjected to . . . intense exploitation and . . . horrendous modes of punishment precisely because they continued to be perceived as slaves."[33] Blacks leased out as convict labor in Mississippi, for example, had an average death rate of 11.16 percent during the six years from 1880 to 1885—more than twice the death rate of whites (5.30 percent) in the convict lease system.[34]

In sum, the post-Reconstruction period witnessed the dawn of a regional experiment: the implementation of a new, caste-based model of imprisonment. This experiment adapted and expanded an existing institution to enforce a racial order that emancipation had put in serious jeopardy. In the process, the South began to bend the U.S. prison system so that it resembled more the "colonial" prison systems of Latin America than the "modern" prisons of Western Europe. In other words, the Southern prison system began to transform from a tool for reforming the undisciplined white poor to a tool for repressing the "unreformable" black poor. A wholesale transformation at the national level, however, was yet to come.

The changes that took place in incarceration at the end of the 1970s hold such enormous consequences that they suggest a generalization and expansion on a national scale of the use of prisons for the naked enforcement of racial hierarchy. Many critics of the U.S. prison system concur that a causal (if mediated) relationship exists between the civil rights movement and the dramatic rise in policing and imprisonment of racial minorities. As with Reconstruction, one can again see a lag of approximately ten years between the end of the movement and the beginning of the current incarceration upswing (Figure 4.1).[35] Throughout the twentieth century, American Indians, blacks, Native Alaskans and Hawaiians, Mexicans, Pacific Islanders, and Puerto Ricans have faced higher rates of incarceration than whites, and since the Vietnam War era, Southeast Asian Americans have also faced high incarceration rates (Figures 4.4 and 4.5). The escalation that began around 1980 took place in the wake of both the civil rights movement and the last great wave of liberal prison reform efforts in the 1960s, which saw the development of an expanded juvenile and family court system and the expansion of probation and counseling initiatives. Such liberal reforms, while championed by progressives at the time, have since faced criticism from some penologists for expanding the number of individuals under the purview of the criminal justice system, thereby increasing their chances for eventually ending up incarcerated, a phenomenon known as "net-widening."[36] The more recent, conservative reforms that emerged in the 1980s and 1990s (culminating in mandatory sentencing laws, California's 1994 "Three Strikes" ballot measure, and the Clinton crime bills of 1994 and 1996) have removed judicial discretion in sentencing, lengthened the time of sentences, restricted the use of parole, limited appeals measures, and increased the use of the death penalty. These reforms have *intentionally* exacerbated the *unintended* effects of the earlier wave of liberal reforms.

To understand how reform initiatives, public opinion, and policy decisions resulted in the current crisis, one must first understand the profound economic, political, and social forces at work in the 1970s and 1980s. According to geographer Ruth Wilson Gilmore, these forces came together in a perfect storm of multiple crises between 1968 and 1977 that set the stage for the massive prison buildup of the 1980s.[37] After World War II, in an attempt to guarantee financial and political stability, the countries of Western Europe and North America set up what became known as the Bretton Woods system of international monetary exchange. This system required all participating nations to link their currency to the U.S. dollar, which in turn became the international reserve currency, the only currency with a fixed rate of exchange with gold. The system gave the United States freedom (what French president Charles de Gaulle once called the "exorbitant privilege") to pursue its own interests internationally.[38] In exchange, the United States guaranteed the benefits of U.S. financing for postwar economic recovery and military protection in the Cold War with the Soviet Union to the economies of Western Europe and Japan.[39]

The Bretton Woods system faced significant strain in the 1960s, in part because its stability required the United States to run constant budget deficits. However, its deficits, increased by military spending in the 1960s, threatened to undermine confidence in the U.S. dollar as a world reserve currency that was as good as gold.[40] As people lost confidence in the value of the dollar, they sold dollars for gold, creating a run on the world's gold reserves, which, in turn, were insufficient to meet the number of dollars in circulation at the artificially fixed rate set by Bretton Woods. When U.S. president Richard Nixon unilaterally dissolved the system in 1971, he freed the dollar of its fixed rate of exchange with gold, leading to an inflationary spiral as the price of gold in U.S. dollars nearly doubled within a year. This monetary crisis and the effective devaluation of the dollar resulting from it coincided with a slowing of the world economy and sharp increases in the price of oil in the 1970s. The combination led U.S. economic elites to attack the welfare state that had grown out of twenty years of economic prosperity as well as forty years of concessions to the demands of organized labor and an economic philosophy of deficit spending. The subsequent cutting back in social services in the 1970s compounded the effects of high rates of unemployment and worsened the consequences of rapid inflation for members of the working and middle classes. All of this resulted in a surplus of dollars, abundant devalued rural land, and high numbers of unemployed persons in both urban and rural areas.

On the political front, widespread protests, social unrest, and prison reform movements in the late 1960s triggered a backlash leading to a highly charged and effective political platform advocating "law and order"—a platform that politicians could revive in the late 1970s and again in the 1980s and 1990s under the banner of "tough on crime" and that television networks and other mass media were quick to embrace. In the political arena throughout the 1970s, 1980s, and 1990s, anticrime and antidrug platforms alternated with antigay, anti–Affirmative Action,

anti-immigrant, and antiabortion platforms—thereby distracting public attention from stagnant real wages and growing wealth disparities.
On the economic front, resources that had expanded in the post–World
War II period became idled following a number of economic crises. These
included the recessions induced by the Federal Reserve Bank in the 1970s
and in the early 1980s in attempts to control inflation and cool down the
economy. To realize the law-and-order pledges of conservative politicians, state governments reinvested surplus resources in massive prison
construction and renovation during the 1980s, using abundant and now
devalued rural land.

Whether television simply mirrored law-and-order sentiments or
inflamed them, its programming throughout these decades seemed veri-
tably swamped with police officers, federal agents, and an assortment of
amateur and professional detectives. Early television crime dramas tended
toward staid action and investigative procedure—for example, *Perry
Mason* (1957–66) and the first incarnation of *Dragnet* (1951–59).[41] The wave
of police and federal agent programs that emerged in the wake of the civil
rights, antiwar, women's, gay and lesbian, and Black Power movements,
however, tapped into deep concerns about popular challenges to authority,
rising drug use, and antiauthoritarian sentiments among youth.[42] The proliferation of crime dramas that began in the late 1960s had no precedent
and it accelerated in the 1970s.[43] Then, with the coming of even more public concerns over crime and order, the trend continued unabated through
the 1980s.[44] Although some other programs throughout this period and
beyond continued to keep versions of the detective-mystery procedural
formula alive, often with a light comic, romantic, or nostalgic touch, these
usually only succeeded by targeting niche audiences and rarely climbed to
the top of the ratings heap.[45] "Serious" crime dramas, however, dominated
the public consciousness.

If one measures the success of a television series by its having survived
for three or more seasons, then more than thirty *successful* police-themed
television crime series debuted from 1965 to 1987. These chronicled the
work of protagonists that were overwhelmingly white and male (with the
occasional white female and the far more rare man or woman of color)
fighting to protect innocent middle-class victims (presumably like the
viewer) from an increasingly violent and chaotic world. Furthermore,
their debut dates cluster around political law-and-order campaigns,
with seven successful debuts in the four years from 1965 to 1968 (during

Lyndon B. Johnson's presidency), eight in the five years from 1972 to 1976 (spanning Richard Nixon's second presidential term and the presidency of Gerald R. Ford), and thirteen in the five years from 1981 to 1985 (covering Ronald Reagan's first presidential term). The deluge of the early 1980s constituted a veritable blitzkrieg of tough-on-crime, pro-police propaganda, and the police drama experienced an inevitable wane during the 1990s.[46] However, the genre—revitalized by advances in forensic science and sporting more diverse casts in terms of gender, race, and ethnicity—experienced a renaissance after the turn of the century, particularly in the years since the al-Qaeda attacks of September 11, 2001, with thirteen successful debuts from 1999 to 2005.[47] Two dramas stand out from the crowd during this period: *Cold Case* (2003–present) and the short-lived *In Justice* (2006).[48] These two series alone focused substantially on the correction of miscarriages of justice. *Cold Case* concerns both the resolution of unsolved crimes and the rectification of wrongful convictions, while the unsuccessful *In Justice* dealt solely with wrongful convictions. The shift in public sentiment that accompanied the conservative policy and media turns of the 1970s and 1980s, however, found its apotheosis not in shows about fictional police detectives, but in the "true crime" genre epitomized by two reality programs that debuted toward the end of the Reagan–Bush years and that have run continuously for two decades: *America's Most Wanted* (1988–present) and *Cops* (1989–present).[49]

In a book of breathtaking rigor and scope, investigative journalist Christian Parenti argues that political elites conceived of the changes in prison and policing policies in the 1970s and 1980s as a direct response to radical leftist activism and demands for civil rights among the poor and racial minorities: "[Nixon's] ultimate goal was to put the militant representatives of the urbanized poor in check. This required a generalized buildup of police power, hardware, and organization. As Nixon's Chief of Staff H. R. Haldeman had written in his diary: '[President Nixon] emphasized that you have to face the fact that the whole problem is really the blacks. The key is to devise a system that recognizes this while not appearing to.' That 'system' was the war on crime and criminal justice buildup."[50] Parenti's chronicle of the police and prison buildup during the 1970s, 1980s, and 1990s moves among ground-level changes in neighborhood policing, mayoral and police department initiatives in major cities, legislative changes at the federal level, and presidential policies under both Republican and Democratic administrations. He also ties these together with the widespread urban gentrification movements in the 1980s and 1990s that took advantage of the effects on urban communities of earlier phases of white flight and "urban renewal." In short, the redlining, blockbusting, and urban renewal of the 1950s, 1960s, and 1970s allowed property values in urban centers to plummet and gave rise to widespread unemployment, crime, and violence in urban communities. The militarization of police and the "war on drugs" enabled both the massive incarceration of urban people of color and the creation of "safe zones" in the downtown malls of cities like San Francisco and New York City. These safe zones, benefiting from both deflated property values and militarized policing, became prime opportunities for real estate speculators, sparking an urban development boom and introducing a new concept to the U.S. middle classes: the loft-style home.[51]

The U.S. Prison as a Patriarchal and Homophobic Institution

The account I have outlined so far explores the rise of the U.S. prison crisis in relation primarily to race and economics; however, race and class make up part of a larger matrix that includes multiple social identities and the mutual constitution of racism with homophobia and sexism. The U.S. prison complex, furthermore, is fundamentally a sexist and homophobic institution insofar as it reinforces destructive forms of masculinity while using the specter of same-sex rape as a tool for ostracizing and scapegoating poor men and men of color and unleashing a generalized sexual terror against poor women of color and sexual minorities. In particular, gender and sexuality bear crucial relationships to imprisonment, and the "ungendering" of both male and female prisoners offers one of the clearest illustrations of the violence committed by the colonial/modern gender system against subordinated people.

Women-of-color feminists have led the effort to understand the mutually constitutive roles of class, gender, race, and sexuality in the prison crisis. Feminist scholar Julia Sudbury, for example, argues for placing women of color at the center in any analysis of prisons.[52] In tandem with Sudbury's injunction, sociologist Beth Richie looks at the experiences of black lesbian prisoners and calls for a practice of "queer antiprison" work that would make sense of how police, prisons, and courts shape and control sexuality, "including but not limited to queer sexuality."[53] Sudbury and Richie draw inspiration from the activist interventions of movement organizations like

Critical Resistance and Incite! Women of Color Against Violence. Critical Resistance describes itself as "a national grassroots group that fights to end the prison industrial complex . . . by challenging the belief that policing, surveillance, imprisonment, and similar forms of control make our communities safer."[54] Incite! is "a national activist organization of radical feminists of color advancing a movement to end violence against women of color and their communities through direct action, critical dialogue, and grassroots organizing."[55] An oft-cited joint statement from the two organizations takes to task the antiprison movement for failing to center gender and sexuality in its analyses, thereby failing to respond to the needs of women of color, particularly survivors of sexual and gender violence. At the same time, it criticizes the mainstream antiviolence movement for relying on the criminal justice system for responses to domestic violence, thereby failing to see how that system continues to victimize women and communities of color. The statement calls for foregrounding the identities of poor women of color in campaigns against prisons and economic oppression. This move seeks ultimately to transform communities of color through a critical response to homophobia, sexism, and gender violence, while also bringing an end to state violence against them.[56]

Seeking similar goals, sociologist Juanita Díaz-Cotto illuminates the relationship of women of color to imprisonment while also exploring the extent to which the prison system entwines itself with other aspects of society. In her ethnography of Chicana prisoners in California, Díaz-Cotto introduces a wide range of issues as relevant to understanding these women's lives: U.S. and corporate policies in Latin America and the militarization of prisons and crime throughout the Americas, as well as gendered economic exploitation and the abuse of women within Chicano gangs, families, and the drug trade. She notes that 43 percent of women prisoners in 1999 were serving time for drug-related offenses in California, up from 13.2 percent in 1983, while the same percentages for men were 26.7 percent, up from the previous 7 percent.[57] Furthermore, Latinas arrested in California have a greater likelihood of receiving a prison sentence than either African American women or white women.[58] Scholarship like Sudbury's, Richie's, and Díaz-Cotto's suggests the inadequacy of frameworks that only look at class and race.

Indeed, the dramatic increase in the incarceration of women of color suggests the extent to which the institution of the prison has become further adapted into being a mechanism for the *general* repression of poor communities of color. Recent scholarship that focuses on masculinity in relation to race and class in the prison, by contrast, too often views men of color as the problem and fails to examine how the criminal justice system targets both men and women of color disproportionately without regard to either their actual rates of lawbreaking or their embodiment of masculine norms. Analyses of prisons that take *masculinity* as their central crux cannot explain, for example, the rapidly rising incarceration rates for *women*, particularly women of color. A significant amount of work on masculinity and prisons suggests that society criminalizes particular forms of masculinity, thus ensnaring men of color and poor men disproportionately in the criminal justice system.[59]

By explaining the incarceration rates of men of color through the criminalization of masculinity, this kind of analysis risks reducing the masculinity of men of color to an overly rigid stereotype and falsely implying higher rates of lawbreaking among men of color (incorrectly assuming, in other words, that because men of color have higher rates of imprisonment than white men, they must commit more crimes). Rates of imprisonment for both men and women of color, however, are vastly disproportionate to their rates of lawbreaking. People of color face higher rates of arrest, higher rates of prosecution after arrest, and higher rates of conviction as a result of prosecution than do whites. People of color also receive less leniency and longer sentences than whites under otherwise similar circumstances.[60]

Masculinity scholars who have attended to the prison have done well in explaining the role that imprisonment and debasement serve among men in the social regulation of masculinity and male gender identities, but their isolation of masculinity can sometimes simplify the effects of the colonial/modern gender system. According to Don Sabo, Terry Kupers, and Willie London, the masculinity of male prisoners serves as a scapegoat in U.S. society, deflecting attention from other violent masculine identities that function outside prison bars, in boardrooms and bedrooms: "The dark and hurtful sides of masculinity can be projected onto prisoners. They are the ones who have failed in life, and they deserve the horrors that await them in overcrowded and brutal correctional facilities. The darkest and most secret fear that straight heterosexist men harbor—being 'butt-fucked' and un-manned by a more dominant male—is deemed an appropriate fate for those at the bottom of the heap who have been disappeared and forgotten."[61] Of course, not just any men find themselves in the role of scapegoat. Overwhelmingly, these scapegoats include poor men of color from the populations that have historically faced some of the highest levels of U.S. state violence: blacks, Mexicans, Puerto Ricans, Native Hawaiians, Native Americans, Southeast Asians, Caribbean people, and Central Americans. Furthermore, as Angela Davis and others note, the incarceration rate for women in the United States in recent years has increased faster than the rate for men.[62]

The expansion of the prison system since 1980 to include greater numbers of women of color furthers the acceleration of its transformation into a mechanism of repression with an explicitly racial character. Thus, prisons do not simply seek to scapegoat subordinated men. Scholars of the early history of women's imprisonment have long observed how prison authorities perceived female prisoners as "failed" women for having fallen into a "life of crime."[63] This ungendering of women as female convicts parallels in some ways the ungendering of male convicts, as both become colonial scapegoats for modern society. As a colonial/modern institution for repression, the contemporary U.S. prison serves to further the degradation, social death, and communal casting out of men and women of color and the debasement of colonized and subordinated identities.[64] As in earlier colonial/modern periods, sexual violence and ungendering occupies a central place in the process of racial subordination.

Follow the Yellow Brick Road

In a context of virtual media silence about the staggering national and humanitarian crisis of mass incarceration as well as the widespread acceptance of sexual violence in prisons, Oz (1997–2003) offered viewers a rare attempt at antihomophobic and antiracist representation of the prison crisis.[65] In doing so, it unflinchingly explored voluntary and coercive same-sex sexual relationships in prison and put racism front and center in its portrayals of prisoner's lives. As a cultural critic interested in the intersections of homophobia, racism, and sexism and their effects on the possibilities for mobilizing transformational identity projects, I therefore find Oz to provide an exceptional point of entry for this project, although I ultimately do not seek merely to provide an interpretation of that series. By situating Oz within the context of the political economy of U.S. prisons at the turn of the twenty-first century, I hope to understand its representational crises as illustrative of some of the barriers to imagining racial, gender, and sexual identities beyond homophobic, racist, and sexist limits.

I begin with the pilot episode of *Oz*, emphasizing the interrelation of race, masculinity, homophobia, and same-sex sexuality—including the mapping of perversion onto white supremacists and "predatory" black characters. I then consider how the portrayal of same-sex sexuality in the pilot episode differs from the presentation of a sexual relationship later in the series between two white characters. In doing so, I specifically ask how the possibilities differ for representing white men and black men in relation to sexual indeterminacy in *Oz*. I also briefly contrast these possibilities with the presentation of the sole Latino male lead character. Ultimately, I argue that despite itself, *Oz* only successfully imagines a liberated *white male identity*—one that frees itself of sexual and racial limits through its proximity to racial others. The possibilities for sexually empowered, antihomophobic, and transformational identities for men of color remain, unfortunately, outside of the series' ken.

I consider *Oz* an important place from which to begin thinking about multiplicity in relation to the U.S. prison crisis. I first felt compelled to watch the show shortly after it premiered because students in my classes on prison literature made constant reference to it, but I found it too difficult for sustained viewing, both because, as a gay man, I found it homophobic and because, as a prison scholar, I found its portrayal of prison life unrealistic and sensationalist.[66] As a result, I quickly gave up on it. My eventual second look at the series reflected an effort to flesh out my discomfort with it and to understand its complex interweaving of race, gender, sexuality, and imprisonment. The first hour-long HBO original series, *Oz* established the gritty, realist tone that would become the hallmark of later series like *The Sopranos* (1999–2007), but the two things that most set it apart from earlier television are its graphic violence and its frequent (even gratuitous) portrayal of male nudity and same-sex sexuality.[67] *Oz* also broke ground as one of very few hour-long dramas in the history of television to feature nonwhite actors in at least half of its leading roles. Only a handful of hour-long primetime dramatic series on major networks had previously attained this level of racial diversity and avoided cancellation in their first season; these have nearly always focused on crime and policing, and include *Miami Vice* (1984–90), *21 Jump Street* (1987–91), *Homicide: Life on the Street* (1993–99), and *New York Undercover* (1994–98).[68] After its debut in 1997, *Oz* received frequent praise from critics, who often hailed it as groundbreaking television.[69] Surprisingly, however, *Oz* has received little attention from scholars—even (or perhaps, especially) from those who study prisons. Despite that lack of attention, it remains one of the few venues in popular culture to engage seriously not only with incarceration but also with race, masculinity, and homosexuality.

Despite its attempts to integrate gender, race, and sexuality in its depiction of the prison, the series tends to characterize black men within a stark dichotomy between asexual, moral virtuousness and perverse, moral degeneracy, participating in the gendered and sexualized logic of colonial modernity. This tendency says much about the limits of the liberal, antiracist rhetoric that informs the critical view of prison that the series creators attempt to present through *Oz*. The codes of racial representation inherited from the colonial/modern gender system tend to associate any sexual legibility among men and women of color with bestiality and perversity, with the result that the ideals of white masculinity and femininity lie consistently outside the reach of colonized and nonwhite people. To approximate these ideals, men and women of color find themselves required to repudiate any intimation of sexuality that might cling to their racially stigmatized bodies. With regard to its black characters, *Oz* replicates this dilemma and the mind–body, white–black, normal–perverse, and human–bestial dichotomies that work against possibilities for humanized sexual expression among people of color. It does so, however, with significant modifications that have important consequences for its presentation of whiteness and of antiracist and "queer" white male sexual identities. Furthermore, in its localization of sexual violence within the prison, the series replicates a vision of prison and prisoners (rather than social structures of oppression and exploitation) as the source of that violence. The resultant personalization of violence deflects attention away from institutions and the state as generators of violence, and further prevents an identification of the sexual and racial dynamics of the show as having an origin external to the prison in the long history of the colonial/modern gender system.[70]

Oz has a distinctive setting and large cast. The show takes place in the fictional Oswald Correctional Facility, nicknamed "Oz" and located in upstate New York. The series creators' decision to thus name the prison invokes multiple referents, including, through a number of allusions, the Attica Correctional Facility in Attica, New York. (Characters in the show explicitly compare *Oz* and Attica in a conversation in the final episode of the first season, during the show's first prison riot, and the New York prison system at the time of the 1971 Attica rebellion was overseen by Corrections Commissioner Russell *Oswald*.[71]) The name also refers, of course, to L. Frank Baum's 1900 novel *The Wizard of Oz*, with its suggestions of dream, escape, removal from everyday life, and rebellion against authority, as well as its associations with gay camp.[72] The show centers on the staff and prisoners of an experimental unit in Oz, called "Em City," after Baum's fantastical Emerald City. The unit's staff seeks to improve the possibilities for rehabilitation through increased personal freedom and responsibility, although if series cocreator, writer, and executive producer Tom Fontana wanted to champion such alternative approaches to rehabilitation, the sensationalistic demands of television work against him. Em City ends up being the site of unrelenting violence over the run of the series.

Oz alternately focuses on the interpersonal relations and internal struggles of several individual prisoners and some of the staff of Em City and the general dynamics among different groups of prisoners, such as the Muslims, the Gangsters, the Aryan Brotherhood, the Italian Mafia, and so on. Some of the most notable prisoners in the series include the following: Augustus Hill (Harold Perrineau), a wheelchair-bound black man who doubles as the narrator for the series; Tobias Beecher (Lee Tergesen), a middle-class white man convicted of killing a young girl while driving drunk; Chris Keller (Christopher Meloni), a white murderer who joins Em City in season two and eventually becomes sexually involved with Beecher; Simon Adebisi (Adewale Akinnuoye-Agbaje), a charismatic Nigerian sociopath; Kareem Said (Eamonn Walker), a black Muslim leader; Vernon Schillinger (J. K. Simmons), the leader of the Aryan Brotherhood; and Miguel Alvarez (Kirk Acevedo), whose father and brother are also in *Oz* and who becomes a father himself shortly after his arrival. Effeminate, gay black man Billie Keane (Derrick Simmons) and homophobic Italian prisoner Dino Ortolani (Jon Seda) also figure into my discussion of the pilot episode.

Racial and Sexual Crisis in *Oz*

From the beginning, *Oz* concerned itself with depicting crises endangering whiteness, masculinity, and heterosexuality. Beecher and Ortolani, in the pilot episode, represent two versions of white male heterosexuality confronted by the threat of homosexuality. Tobias Beecher's is the first face seen in *Oz*—aside from series narrator Augustus Hill, who opens the episode. The viewer encounters Beecher at the moment of his introduction to Em City. Series creator Tom Fontana notes in the commentary accompanying the DVD release of the series that he envisioned the character as a stand-in for the viewer entering the world of the prison for the first time.[73] Beecher appears scared and disoriented. He markedly differs in class status from the other men and clearly lacks their air of urban lower-class masculinity. The camera soon contrasts his character with Dino Ortolani, his assigned "mentor." Ortolani, the incarnation of East Coast, working-class, Italian American masculinity, looks at Beecher with contempt and lets him know in no uncertain terms that he will not help him adjust to life in prison. On his own, the white Beecher soon finds himself sexually threatened by his black cellmate, Simon Adebisi. Beecher turns for protection to Vernon Schillinger, only to have his white savior turn on him as soon as the guards have rearranged the cell assignments and put Beecher and Schillinger together. Beecher responds to the sexual advances of Adebisi and Schillinger with paralysis and fear, culminating in his off-screen rape by Schillinger. Standing in for the actual rape—in a spectacular moment of televisual metonymy—is a scene in which Schillinger tattoos the image of a swastika onto Beecher's buttocks.[74] This moment marks the beginning of a long period of mental and sexual abuse and degradation for Beecher at the hands of Schillinger and other members of the Aryan Brotherhood. However, if Beecher represents the crisis of white heterosexual masculinity, Ortolani represents its defense.

Although *Oz* introduces and plays on many of the prison-rape conventions familiar to viewers from film, ultimately those prisoners demonstrating desire for same-sex sexual contact early in the series come across either as threatening (as in the case of Adebisi and Schillinger) or as perverse (as in the case of Billie Keane), or both.[75] Like Beecher, Ortolani finds himself the object of unwanted sexual interest—in this case from black gay inmate Keane—but he responds in a dramatically different fashion than Beecher. In addition, the characterization of Keane also differs distinctly from Beecher's "sexual predators." While Adebisi and Schillinger enjoy a sadistic, masculine role in tormenting Beecher, Keane behaves with overtly effeminate mannerisms and touches his own body in an attempt to seduce Ortolani. By contrast, both Adebisi and Schillinger make their intentions known by touching Beecher, not themselves. Indeed, it is difficult to imagine how threatening Keane might have been in the off-screen encounter that leads to the on-screen beating he receives from Ortolani. The camera catches Keane as he follows Ortolani to the shower, but it does not pursue them. By the time the scene cuts to the shower, we see a naked Ortolani brutally beating a naked Keane. The excessiveness of the violence, including the violence of Ortolani toward a guard who tries to stop him, disrupts the easy prison-genre dichotomy of sexual predator vs. sexual prey, making the scene seem more like an incident of gay bashing than an attempted rape. Nonetheless, Keane's explicit public and clearly unwanted solicitations of Ortolani earlier in the episode suggest a perversity in his character.[76] Keane, furthermore, never becomes a main character. His brother, Jefferson (Leon Robinson), quickly overshadows Billie in later episodes, as events focus on the fallout from Jefferson's murder of Ortolani and subsequent death sentence.[77]

The pilot episode and the ones following it introduce some complexity in the portrayal of black men's sexuality, particularly in the sympathy for Keane from his brother and from the prison administrators as they try to address Ortolani's homophobia. Indeed, film scholar Joe Wlodarz notes Keane's storyline as one of the few moments in which the series encourages viewers to identify positively with gay, bisexual, or transgender characters.[78] However, Jefferson's gentleness toward his brother Billie, and his compassion, in turn, serve more to mark Jefferson as good than to mark Billie as normal. Indeed, Billie Keane only appears in three episodes.[79] After his pilot episode encounter with Ortolani, he appears again only in relation to his brother's execution, and then disappears from *Oz*, although the actor who plays him continues to appear in the credits as a stuntman.

Sympathy for homosexuality over the course of the series occurs primarily through a separation of *white* queerness and homosexuality from both white and black sexual degeneracy, ultimately leaving little, if any, space for complex representations of same-sex sexuality among people of color. Indeed, identification with nonheterosexual characters in the series seems to go hand in hand with a shoring up of white masculinity. As Wlodarz observes, for example, Beecher's eventual independence from Schillinger coincides with a significant transformation in the masculinity of his character's portrayal.[80] Furthermore, while the series' first season appears ultimately to embrace a vilification of male same-sex sexuality and to map that sexuality onto degenerate black and white characters, the second season disrupts that mapping through the introduction of Beecher's relationship with fellow white prisoner Chris Keller, which continues on and off until the end of the series.[81] Their relationship stands in dramatic contrast to the sexual degeneracy of the Aryans, the unexplored subjectivity of Keane, and numerous incidents of sexual exploitation by Adebisi.

In a 2003 article in the gay news magazine *The Advocate*, gay journalist, filmmaker, and blogger Lawrence Ferber describes Beecher and Keller's relationship as a "twisted, tortured, yet deeply loving romance."[82] Ferber quotes heterosexual-identified actors Tergesen and Meloni, who play the roles of Beecher and Keller and who famously gave each other passionate kisses at the 2000 Gay and Lesbian Alliance Against Defamation (GLAAD) Media Awards:

> Meloni and Tergesen have had to push for even more explicitly gay content. While shooting a scene that ended with a show of affection, the director of that episode grew uncomfortable, calling "Cut!" early and giggling. "Finally we were like, 'Hey, can you just let it run for a minute?' which they always do on these scenes," Tergesen recalls. "And the director goes, 'Why, are you going to blow him?' The truth was a real moment was happening."
>
> "And you called him out," Meloni recalls proudly. "Lee [Tergesen] goes, 'Look, just because you're uncomfortable with the sexuality going on here doesn't mean you have to rain on our fucking parade.'"[83]

Wlodarz notes that *Oz* uses crosscutting shots to contrast the Beecher-Keller relationship to rapes committed by Adebisi and by Schillinger in order to "differentiate between rape and homosexuality. . . . [Beecher] describes his love for Keller to Sister Peter Marie (Rita Moreno) by distinguishing it from the 'unloving, brutal' sex forced on him by Schillinger. . . . Yet . . . the contrast set up between [a rape committed by Adebisi] and the Beecher–Keller relationship also serves to displace racial and ethnic tensions from expressions of queer desire."[84] In other words, according to Wlodarz, as the series increasingly focuses on exploring nonheterosexual relationships in complex ways, it does so with white characters, thus avoiding explicit treatment of the intersections between racism and homophobia and the mutual constitution of race and sexuality with regard to men of color. Indeed, I would go further and suggest that the juxtaposition of Beecher and Keller's humanized (if not romantic) relationship with Adebisi's and Schillinger's actions results in an equation of *both* black sexual aggression *and* white racism to rape and perversion.[85]

Strange Bedfellows

No simple account can do justice to the complexity of *Oz*'s representation of same-sex sexuality in conjunction with gender and race. In his treatment of the series, Wlodarz focuses on the formal structure of *Oz*—in particular its combination of the genres of soap opera, "slash fiction," and prison drama—in an attempt to explain its fraught explorations of race and sexuality. He argues that the constant deferment inherent in the serial form, together with soap operatic elements such as romantic conventionality, melodramatic betrayal, and heightened "emotional realism," combine to enhance what he calls the "queer potential" of the series.[86] Wlodarz further notes the complexity and diversity of portrayals of same-sex sexuality in the series, which range from the consistent association of the Aryan Brotherhood with acts of same-sex sexual degradation and perversity to the romantically coded (if abusive and dysfunctional) relationship of Beecher and Keller. Between these two poles lie Adebisi's sexually predatory behavior, numerous transgender characters played mostly by uncredited (albeit recurring) extras, and occasional other gay white characters who feature from time to time in minor supporting roles, like Richie Hanlon (Jordan Lage), a masculine and out man who features in a narrative subplot during the second season before his death early in the third.[87] Among the many treatments of sexuality in *Oz*, Wlodarz privileges what he describes as the queer indeterminacy of same-sex desire revealed in the Beecher–Keller narrative arc. With regard to the possibilities of this pairing, he writes, "What in fact makes *Oz* so deliciously compelling (and steamy) is the way that it consistently thwarts clear, coherent, and unambiguous expressions of gay desire and identification in favor of a more enticing erotic uncertainty."[88] He goes on to caution, however, that "the structural and formal transitions that took place in season 2 signaled a racial shift and contributed to a general Whitening of queer sexuality on the show."[89] In addition to studying cues in the actual filming of the series, Wlodarz analyzes fan discussion forums on the Internet, as well as examples of amateur fiction written by fans about *Oz*, in order to study viewer identification with different characters. The results reveal an increasing identification among fans with Beecher and Keller far in excess of levels of identification with other characters in the show.[90]

The relationship between race and sexuality in *Oz* does not make sense without an account of the history of how racial meanings have emerged with and through gender and sexuality. Thus, despite the fact that Wlodarz correctly *identifies* a separation in the series and among fans of *Oz* between same-sex sexuality and blackness (the dominant coding of non-white racial identity in the series), and despite his attentiveness to race and his dissatisfaction with the separation of race and sexuality in the series, his formal analysis seems inadequate *to explain* that separation. In other words, if the heightening of queer potential in the series were due simply to its generic shifts (for example, from TV drama to soap opera), then it does not necessarily follow that this shift should entail a simultaneous (apparent) separation of sexuality from race, or, to be more precise, a simultaneous *limiting* of same-sex sexuality that is not perverse to white men.

I believe that this phenomenon has deeper roots in received cultural codes that enable different meanings for white and nonwhite sexual variation and sexual identities. As I argued in chapter 3, the colonial/modern gender system has two sides. One side constructs European men and women as dimorphic, heterosexual, and human, corresponding to dominant and subordinate roles. Liberation from this perspective can plausibly exist in the transgression of boundaries between male and female, heterosexual and homosexual—in what Wlodarz calls "queer indeterminacy." The other side of the system, however, casts colonized men and women outside of "modern" gender roles and outside of human civilization. "Liberation" from this side thus becomes a much trickier issue for people of color. The assumption of rigid gender norms and a conformity to heterosexual ideals can come to represent escape from sexual exploitation and degradation rather than the imposition of sexual repression. At the same time, the liberatory effects of the rejection of coherent identities—of queer indeterminacy—can seem too much like the state of vulnerability imposed by colonialism for the purposes of exploitation. What can seem at first like liberation from either side thus turns out to enmesh colonized men and women further in the sexual double bind of the colonial/modern gender system.

I do not mean to suggest that *Oz* does not have its own critical commentary on race and sexuality. While same-sex sexuality among both the black men and the white supremacists in *Oz* rarely serves to foster viewer identification or to develop character complexity, it has a particular function for the members of the Aryan Brotherhood. In the case of the white supremacists, same-sex sexual activity serves precisely the opposite purpose, suggesting the degree to which these characters have departed from civilized human norms. Indeed, their sexual behavior serves to make their racism legible as perversity, both their sadistic sexual behavior and their racism combining to work against viewer identification. Their racism becomes legible as perversity to the extent that the series associates the white supremacists with a same-sex sexual economy in the prison more frequently than any other group; furthermore, that association is explicitly sadistic and perverse. Beecher and Keller's relationship, however, develops in such a way as to humanize both characters and, as Wlodarz shows, to encourage viewers to identify with them. In contrast, the sexuality of the Aryan Brotherhood does not humanize its members, but marks them as beyond the limits of the human—as monstrous.

In its origins, the colonial/modern gender system marked nonwhiteness and perversion as overlapping states. It thereby created a rhetorical and social framework in which deviation from an ideal of dyadic heterosexual coupling and strictly demarcated gender roles could mark a people as outside the norms of modern civilization. Despite (or, perhaps, because of) the projection of "perversity" onto colonized peoples, the actual practices of colonizers included brutal instances of sexual violence in all kinds of configurations. In *Oz*, notably, the terms for understanding civilization in relation to sexuality depend on the recognition of these legacies of sexualized violence. Thus, in a striking reversal of the terms of the colonial/modern gender system, *Oz* represents *white racism* as sexually perverse. This reversal identifies and makes visible the centrality of nonnormative sexual practices and sexual violence to the practices of the colonizers and creates a space for the colonized to lay claim to liberatory sexual identities. It thus resonates with many attempts to assert normative genders and sexualities on the part of colonized and racially subjugated peoples.[91]

At the same time, however, by specifically marking the white racists as inclined toward same-sex sexual acts and not fully developing the alternatives for men of color in the series, *Oz* risks closing off possibilities for a richer exploration of sexual variation among men of color. The series can only imagine nonwhite sexuality as absent, highly idealized, or brutal and perverse. The difference between the way in which the series presents sexual possibilities for white and black men starkly highlights the tension between the rhetoric of antiracist liberalism that informs the show, on the one hand, and the material consequences of coloniality, on the other. That tension also surfaces in the gap between how the series portrays the Beecher-Keller relationship (as approximating a "real," if abusive, relationship) and the possibilities it leaves unaddressed for understanding same-sex sexual relationships among men of color.

The Price of Moral Virtue

The series tends to desexualize those black men whom it presents as sympathetic objects of viewer identification, as, for example, in the case of the series narrator, paraplegic Augustus Hill. The second episode of the first season makes a point of his inability to fully participate in sexual activity. A flashback recounting what led him to prison (a standard device the series uses to establish its principal characters) finds Hill in the middle of passionate sexual intercourse with a woman. The scene is poorly lit and the sex appears intense and forceful. Police interrupt the couple's lovemaking as they force their way into the room, battering down the door in a rhythm synchronized with the banging of the lovers' bed against the wall. A naked Hill grabs a gun from the nightstand as the woman moves off screen, and he shoots at the police before leaving through an open window onto the roof of the building. While naked and pursued, Hill shoots one of the officers before another apprehends him. When the white officer hears that the officer who was shot has died, he says to Hill, "You're gonna pay," and then throws him, handcuffed, from the roof to the street below. Hill's own voiceover then tells the viewer that he received a lifetime prison sentence for possession of controlled substances and murder in the second degree. Presumably, the fall from the roof has resulted in his disability.

A scene in which Hill and Adebisi fill out forms for approval of their conjugal visits follows the flashback:

HILL: I'm fiending to see my wife.
ADEBISI: At least you'll get to see yours, eh?
HILL: What you mean?
ADEBISI: Fucking part.
HILL: What, you think because I can't walk, I can't fuck?

ADEBISI: So you can fuck?

HILL: Yeah!

ADEBISI: Are we talking getting hard, or licky-licky?

HILL: We're talking in and out, up and down. That's what we're talking about.

ADEBISI: (laughs) Who'd have thought a nigger could get hard in a wheelchair?

HILL: Yeah, well it's easier for some of us than others. Some people gotta use pumps, some niggers gotta use drugs, get a needle stuck in their dicks. Yo, the worst one is implants. They slice your dick open, and they lay in this kinda like a steel rod to keep the shit stiff.

ADEBISI: Please.

HILL: I get hard the old-fashioned way.

ADEBISI: Good for you.

HILL: The only problem is, I don't know it.

ADEBISI: You don't know what?

HILL: I don't know when I'm hard.

ADEBISI: You don't know when you're hard?

HILL: I ain't got no sensation down there, so I don't know when I'm hard, I don't know when I cum. My wife gotta tell me.

ADEBISI: You don't know when you're hard? You don't know if you've cum? You don't get any pleasure at all? Eh? What the fuck are you doing it for?

HILL: For her.[92]

After this exchange, the episode cuts to a brief scene showing Hill's conjugal visit. In a scene replete with romantic cues, Hill and his wife laugh together as she helps him remove his pants. Candles fill the room, and she slowly removes her top for him while his voiceover comments on the importance of love between a man and woman. The scene provides a sharp contrast to the earlier aggressive sex that the police interrupted. Through his disability, Hill thus transforms from a dangerous black man (having wild sex and wielding a gun) to a symbol of heterosexual feeling and fidelity, supposedly incapable of enjoying sexual intercourse except insofar as he enjoys making his wife happy. Hill's symbolic castration is incomplete, of course, but powerful nonetheless. Although flying in the face of disability activists' attempts to reclaim their sexual agency, Hill's disability functions within the context of the series to contain a potentially dangerous black masculinity.[93]

In the presentation of Hill, disability, heterosexuality, and a symbolic castration combine to enable the character to emerge as an unthreatening object of identification for a full range of viewers, despite the violence of his past. His position as narrator further centers him for viewers, as he alone has the opportunity to address the camera directly. The narrative process of Hill's transformation builds on established models of "disability masquerade" noted by literary scholar Tobin Siebers, in which disability facilitates a narcissistic self-satisfaction on the part of the able bodied. In losing his ability to walk, Hill gains what in the context of the other, heartless characters in the prison amounts to a super ability to feel compassion and love. His sex scenes, in fact, serve as the only examples in the entire first season of nonviolent, consensual lovemaking. Thus, only the paraplegic black man knows love.

Writing about the genre of the disability human-interest story, Siebers notes that it typically "represses disability by representing the able-body as the baseline in the definition of the human." He writes that, as a consequence, since "human-interest stories usually require their hero to be human, they are obliged, when the focus is disability, to give an account of their protagonist's metamorphosis from nonhuman to human being."[94] In *Oz*, Hill goes from being less than human to superhuman, with the white, able-bodied men (Beecher, for example) providing the baseline for normality—if not humanity. Furthermore, one cannot separate Hill's disability from a context of race and sexuality. For *Oz*'s triangulation of race, gender, and sexuality to work, the narrative must disable Hill's black, male heterosexuality, not his ability to walk. In other words, his supposedly disabled sexuality allows him to undergo the metamorphosis from inhuman cop killer to human being. The price of the ticket to moral virtue for black men in *Oz*, one might say, is their sexuality.

To understand fully the narrative consequences of Hill's sexual enervation, one should observe that the black men in the prison who receive the most sympathetic treatment besides him are members of the celibate Muslim Brotherhood. Their leader, Kareem Said notably condemns both homosexuality and homophobic violence.[95] Of all the main characters, only Said's backstory flashback does not actually show him committing a crime, lending credibility to his own claims of innocence and thereby making him another option for viewer empathy.[96] Throughout the series, he consistently faces difficult moral choices, always favoring his conscience, no matter the cost—even when this entails siding with white inmates. The third season most explicitly addresses Said's own sexuality, when he falls in love with a white woman, the sister of a murdered inmate. He first contacts her to enlist her support for a lawsuit against the prison, but after a couple of meetings, the two develop romantic feelings for one another.[97] Tellingly, however, their relationship must remain unconsummated. In contrast to Beecher and Keller's steamy and passionate affair, Said's is the paradigm of a tortured, platonic love, burdened by the necessity of hiding from his followers the truth of his feelings. The pair's courtship develops through a series of conversations, a brief touching of hands, and a hug; it ends because Said's followers make him end it. The scene in which he breaks the relationship off drips with repressed emotions and tears.[98] In a different way than Hill, Said's humanity and his role as a defender of the rights of all inmates reveals itself through his distancing from the raw sexuality that others in the prison (Adebisi, Schillinger, Beecher, and Keller) embrace.

Thus, while *Oz* remains remarkable as a television drama that reserves many of the most morally complex roles for black men, it does so in part by desexualizing them. The desexualization of Hill and Said, in turn, occurs in the context of a show famous for its unprecedented and raw portrayals of male nudity and same-sex sexuality. The show, for the most part, does not present those black men who willingly engage in sexual activity as objects of sympathetic identification. They much more often appear coded as sadistic and morally corrupt, as in the case of Adebisi, or perverse and pathetic, as in the case of Keane. While not villains in the vein of the Aryan Brotherhood, they remain far from the humanized, pseudoromantic coding that Beecher and Keller receive. By contrast with both the Aryans and the nonwhite characters, Beecher and Keller's sexuality entails a dangerous *indeterminacy* that can destabilize commonsense notions of masculinity, heterosexuality, and homosexuality. In other words, the sexuality of Beecher and Keller seems to promise something destabilizing, if not liberatory, because it resists consolidation within a coherent *identity*.[99] Seen from the perspective of the colonized, however, indeterminacy, ambiguity, and lack of identity appear less attractive. Precisely this state—lacking full subjectivity, identity, and gender—has historically left colonized peoples vulnerable to colonial degradation, abuse, and violence. One can thus understand the insistence on their manhood among the Attica prisoners in 1971: "We are men. We are not beasts, and we do not intend to be beaten or driven as such."[100] That rallying cry distills a fundamental need for recognition in the face of epistemic erasure and ontological obliteration.

Flexible White Masculinity

In reaching for commercial intelligibility, the series makes sacrifice after sacrifice, veering away after only a couple of episodes from a complex exploration of black men's sexuality and displacing that complexity to white characters. Despite its attempts to lay bare the evils of the U.S. prison system and to critically explore race, homosexuality, and disability as mutually constitutive, *Oz* ultimately fails. It does experiment with its presentation of masculinity, but the "unstable" model of masculinity that evolves over the course of *Oz* does not represent a fully viable alternative for men of color because the dominant representational codes of television seem to insist on their sexual legibility as either hypersexual beast or chastened eunuch. The show also succumbs to sensationalized portrayals of violence within the prison that ultimately convey a sense that these men are indeed the worst of the worst rather than contextualizing their lives within a much larger violent, racist, homophobic, and patriarchal society outside prison bars.

In the absence of alternative ways of framing its black protagonists, *Oz* partly succeeds in navigating a course around the Hollywood trope of the "Magic Negro," but it struggles to escape the trope's gravitational pull.[101] *Washington Post* movie reviewer Rita Kempley dates the phrase "Magic Negro" to 1950s Hollywood, but she observes that the figure has a longer history.[102] It refers to certain black roles that appear in films centered on white characters. Specifically, the "Magic Negro" fills a mostly functional role, facilitating positive change or redemption for the white characters. In recent years and with a shockingly improbable frequency, filmmakers have endowed these black characters with supernatural powers to accomplish their feats of white betterment.[103] However, characters need not necessarily possess magical properties in order to fulfill their functions of improving the lives of the white characters, and the stock figure of the saintly black helpmate abounds in Hollywood cinema, making whites into better people without the benefit of magical powers.[104] The characters' only magical power often lies in their ability to reassure whites that five centuries of racism does not really matter anymore or else that at least it can be overcome before the final credits roll, and that a black person might forgive them for being white.

So ubiquitous is this stock type that nearly half of the twelve Academy Awards for acting that have gone to black actors have been for portrayals of "Magic Negros," whether of the truly magical or merely saintly variety.[105] Other characters form variations on the trope, like the character portrayed by Samuel L. Jackson in M. Night Shyamalan's 2000 film *Unbreakable*.[106] In this case, the film's final twist depends on the audience's familiarity with the black helpmate convention and its consequent assurance that the magical black character must be good. Although he ultimately emerges as more demonic than saintly, Jackson's character still works to help the white protagonist find his purpose in life and to become a better man. Of course, helping white characters in and of itself is not necessarily a bad thing, but as Kempley notes, "It isn't that the actors or the roles aren't likable, valuable, or redemptive, but *they are without interior lives.*"[107]

In *Oz*, none of the black characters completely fits the traditional mold of a "Magical Negro." They mostly have well-developed interior lives, possess full personal histories, seem grounded in black communities, and, on an average day, could care less about improving the lives of white people. That said, they still tend to conform to a well-defined and racialized polarity of moral virtue and degeneracy—what film scholar Linda Williams calls the moral dialectic of Tom and Anti-Tom.[108] Furthermore, some of them, like Hill and Said, while remaining far from "Tom-like" in their behavior, still occupy a structural role in relation to Beecher and Keller—a structural role that remains difficult to see if one fixates on the representation of blackness rather than the representation of whiteness in relation to blackness. The structural relations among the characters allow Beecher and Keller to triangulate a white male identity that transcends both histories of racism and limits on sexual expression. The device that enables them to do this, however, is not a particular portrayal of blackness (like the Magic Negro), but rather a particular portrayal of whiteness that defines itself through a number of contrasts.

One possible starting place for a theory of this differentiated whiteness lies in disability studies scholar Robert McRuer's reading of the 1997 film *As Good as It Gets*, starring Jack Nicholson, Helen Hunt, Greg Kinnear, and Cuba Gooding Jr.[109] McRuer uses this film to elaborate a theory of what he calls "flexible able-bodied heterosexuality." According to McRuer, the flexibility of protagonist Melvin Udall (Nicholson) reveals itself through his interactions with the black, gay, and disabled characters. Through his responses to them and through his growing tolerance of them, he can embrace a new-and-improved heterosexual, able-bodied masculinity that culminates in his "getting the girl" in the end. According to McRuer's reading, Melvin makes himself worthy of the attention of his love interest, Carol Connelly (Hunt), by demonstrating that he can become a better man. He demonstrates this manly improvement, in turn, through a growing tolerance of his gay and temporarily disabled neighbor, Simon Bishop (Kinnear), and of Carol's seriously ill son, Spencer (Jesse James). His transformation into a better man, however, comes at the expense of the narrative subordination of the characters marked as "different" by their sexuality, race, or disability. What McRuer calls "flexible, able-bodied heterosexuality" thus becomes visible through its tolerance of and cooperation with social others, and it contrasts markedly with other models of heterosexual masculinity that become visible by demonstrating their *intolerance* of sexual and disabled others.[110] While McRuer's reading focuses principally on Melvin's relationships to Simon and Spencer, however, an analysis of the role of Simon's black friend Frank Sachs (Gooding) could further highlight the mutual constitution of race, sexuality, and dis/ability in this film. Despite the fact that he underemphasizes Frank in his analysis, I find valuable McRuer's decision to delineate the political importance of *Melvin's* identity (the flexible, heterosexual, able-bodied white man), rather than focusing on the merely functional identities of the others (for example, the Magic Negro, "Magic Queer," or "Magic Cripple").

I believe that a similar shift in attention can help to make sense of the reinvention of white masculinity and white male identity in *Oz*, although, within a framework of the colonial/modern gender system, I would recast McRuer's "flexible able-bodied heterosexuality" as a *flexible, able-bodied, white masculinity*. Among the many forms of masculinity present in *Oz*, Beecher and Keller's best fits this model. Both characters distance themselves from the racism of other white characters. Furthermore, their bisexuality marks them as sexually ambiguous, but unlike the gay and transgender characters, that sexual ambiguity does not jeopardize their masculinity. Their tolerance of the black and disabled Hill and the black and celibate Said, together with their apparent absence of malice toward gay and transgender characters in the prison, creates a contrast between their flexible masculinity and the inflexible masculinity embodied by most other prisoners in the show (for example, Ortolani).[111] Hill and Said can also tolerate and accept difference and diversity, but only at the price of themselves becoming asexual—a price that Beecher and Keller emphatically do not pay.

A part of the way in which flexible white identities come into play in *Oz* results from casting decisions that privilege white men throughout—and not only in the realm of sexuality. According to a Human Rights Watch report in 2003, blacks alone made up 54.3 percent of the New York prison population.[112] However, while *Oz* is significantly nonwhite in the context of television history, the show retains a cast of roughly 50 percent white men across its fifty-six episodes. In the second season, the staff of Em City divide the prisoners into groups based on affiliation. The groups include the Aryans, the Bikers, the Irish, the Italians, the Christians, the Gays, the Muslims, the Gangsters, the Latinos, and "the Others." Each group has four members. While the first four groups (the Aryans, Bikers, Irish, and Italians) are all white, the Christians, Gays, and "Others" (a group that includes Beecher, Keller, and Hill) are mostly white, each having one token black member. Two groups (the Muslims and the Gangsters) are all black, leaving one group for the few Latino inmates in Em City.[113] The series creators apparently perceived a need for a wide range of white characters, but, as a consequence, even though some of the men of color have complex personas, they cannot help becoming more "representative" of their groups than the white men. For example, the show's inmate roster includes only one developed Latino prisoner: Miguel Alvarez. While his character has emotional and moral complexity, he becomes more strongly associated with family loyalty than most other prisoners, a standard stereotype for Latinos in U.S. film and television.[114] He thus comes across as both a morally ambiguous character and well outside the sexual economy of *Oz*.

Theorists of the psychology of representation help to provide some rationale for why a television program with a largely white audience might benefit from offering diverse portrayals of whites and narrowly stereotypical portrayals of Latinos and others. A 2008 study, for example, exposed white television viewers to ambiguous (as opposed to stereotypical or counterstereotypical) portrayals of Latinos. Exposure to characters strongly identified as Latino in *morally ambiguous* storylines caused whites both to evaluate the characters negatively and to report higher levels of self-esteem.[115] In other words, the authors of the study propose that these portrayals of Latinos caused white viewers to feel worse about Latinos and to feel better about themselves. This study supports similar findings by social psychologists regarding the effects on whites of viewing Native American sports mascots.[116] Although television, as a highly complex narrative form, allows for any number of unpredictable viewer responses, the narrative displacement of viewer sympathy from blacks and Latinos to white men allows, or perhaps even encourages (white male) viewers to embrace a flexible white masculinity. This masculinity sees itself as working with blacks, Latinos, the disabled, and gays; it perhaps even embraces sexual ambiguity. Although itself a racialized masculinity, this flexible white masculinity thrives on the supposed dissolution of boundaries and identity categories to make its own race and gender seem inconsequential—and yet it relies fundamentally on the presence and compliance of "others" to put its own flexibility into relief. Meanwhile, the basic terms of the prison system and its racist and colonial origins remain intact. The new-and-improved masculinity closes a self-referential loop of white narcissism, transforming the prison into a temporary stop for coming into contact with "others" and for repudiating rigid models of white masculinity and bigotry.

The truth of the prison system in the United States as a racist and homophobic institution and the legacy of colonial modernity for black and Latino men's sexuality becomes secondary to the project of making whites—both straight and gay—into better men. Of course, antiracist activism has always struggled to overcome the challenge of getting whites to really care about the fate of people of color, and this challenge faces prison abolitionists as surely as it faced slavery abolitionists. In that sense, perhaps *Oz* does not differ all that much from Harriet Beecher Stowe's bestselling abolition novel, *Uncle Tom's Cabin.* Both narratives stand as testaments to the difficulty of telling an antiracist narrative without turning the stories of people of color into lessons for the betterment of whites and the shoring up of an enlightened white identity.[117] In any case, the actual connections between colonial legacies of sexual violence and the racial violence of the U.S. prison crisis so far remain beyond the limits of the imagination for both producers and consumers of U.S. mass culture. A show focusing largely on white men in prison produced at the very moment that U.S. prisons had become massive dumping grounds for black and brown men and women on a scale never before imagined can only serve to shield viewers from that awful truth.

Reflections on Identity in the Obama Era

In 2009, Barack Hussein Obama became the first president of African descent in the history of the United States. Like many left-leaning voters, I saw my own vote for Obama as largely symbolic. I did not expect him to pursue a political agenda significantly more progressive than that of President Clinton nor did I hold any particular faith in the power of U.S. presidential electoral democracy to bring about an end to oppression. Yet I suspect that precisely the symbolism of Obama's election has posed, in some ways, a significant challenge to progressive thinkers. A *New York Times*–CBS News poll taken just before the presidential election found that 68 percent of respondents believed that blacks had an equal or better chance of "getting ahead in today's society" compared to whites. Among black respondents, 44 percent agreed, while among whites it was 72 percent.[1] This kind of belief has echoes among progressives, whom I heard during the presidential campaign repeatedly saying things along the lines of "maybe once Obama is elected we can focus on class" or "maybe now it will become more clear how important class is." These views echo positions taken variously by Wendy Brown, Walter Benn Michaels, and Manuel Castells and discussed in chapter 2.

However, class (understood either as an identity category or as mere socioeconomic status) in the United States has always been and continues to be deeply influenced by race. For example, scholars of race know that the waves of foreclosures following the 2007 subprime mortgage crisis hit black and Latino homebuyers disproportionately hard. Even after controlling for neighborhood risk and individual homebuyer characteristics, researchers have found "that individual race, ethnicity, and income . . . are significant and positively related to the likelihood of subprime borrowing."[2] This pattern, in turn, has emerged as the latest stage in seventy years of unfair lending practices in mixed and predominantly nonwhite neighborhoods. U.S. Census data also show that in 2007, "non-Hispanic Whites" had a median income of $31,051, while blacks had a median income of $18,428 and "Hispanics" a mere $15,603.[3] Figures based on total wealth rather than simply on income paint an even starker picture.[4] As I have argued throughout this book, inequality and oppression have had and continue to have complex relationships to sexuality, race, and gender, as well as to class.

I wholeheartedly agree that an increased attention to class would behoove progressive intellectuals greatly. I find it striking, for example, that Obama proved, throughout his 2008 candidacy for president, seemingly incapable of mentioning the working class. His campaign cast all of his policies as improving the situation of the middle class alone. Yet, when given the option, 30 percent of respondents to the *New York Times*–CBS News poll self-identified as "working class" rather than "middle class" ("lower middle class" was unavailable as an option).[5] As we turn to class, however, we need to understand it as mutually constituted by race, religion, gender, sexuality, ability, and citizenship. We also need to continue to keep analyses of the United States situated within a large geographical perspective and a long historical sweep. The road ahead in the new world that the 2008 election brought about will require complex thinking about identity, about oppression, about privilege, about intersections, and about multiplicity.

A quick look over the first year and a half of Obama's presidency (the period before the wave of Republican congressional victories) reveals much about the new challenges that we face. Many things could be worth mentioning in the context of a book on identity and multiplicity. Obama took little action during this period regarding his promises to gay and lesbian constituents beyond a few, largely symbolic acts, seeming to betray a multiple and overlapping base that had come together in support of his election.[6] Similarly, he took little action during the first year and half regarding Latina and Latino voters' concerns over comprehensive immigration reform. Indeed, Obama chose early in his presidency to step up many of the objectionable immigration policies of his predecessor.[7] In the place of immigration reform, Obama chose to offer Latinas and Latinos a largely symbolic gesture: the nomination of Sonia Sotomayor for the U.S. Supreme Court. Finally, the president's most publicized gesture toward starting the conversation on race that he urged the nation to have in his 2008 primary campaign address in Philadelphia was to extend an invitation to Harvard Professor Henry Louis Gates Jr. and Cambridge, Massachusetts police sergeant James Crowley to have a beer at the White House.[8]

I would like to reflect briefly on these last two items—Sotomayor's nomination and Senate confirmation hearings and the incident that comedic television news commentator Jon Stewart dubbed "Henry Louis Gate" in an echo of Nixon's Watergate scandal—as they touch on the future of identity and identity politics. In the case of Sotomayor, Obama bypassed a number of more liberal, white, female candidates in order to nominate the first Latina candidate to the U.S. Supreme Court.[9] In doing so, he seemed to adhere to a philosophical commitment similar to that expressed by Sotomayor herself in a number of speeches she gave before her nomination. At the core of this commitment lies the belief that identity plays a meaningful and substantial role in the shaping of a person's opinions, values, judgments, moral convictions, and capacity for empathy. Having experience as a business owner can make a person more understanding of the stress that high wages and benefits can put on the long-term profitability of a company. The experience of serving in the U.S. Senate can make a president more sympathetic to the legislative process than a president whose experience lies solely in serving as a governor of a state, while experience in state politics might help a president better empathize with the plight of state legislatures when a recession hits. Alternatively, in Sotomayor's words, "Our gender and national origins may and will make a difference in our judging. . . . Hence, one must accept the proposition that a difference there will be by the presence of women and people of color on the bench. Personal experiences affect the facts that judges choose to see."[10] Sotomayor's position closely resembles a realist one about identity and knowledge. She does not suggest that Latinas always make better judgments than white men. Nor does she suggest that Latinas (or anyone else) only base their decisions on experiences specific to their ethnicity and gender. Nor does she suggest that when Latinas do make better judgments than white men, they do so automatically because they are Latina. Rather, she merely suggests that some Latinas might sometimes come to better conclusions than some white men—and that at least some of the time, this fact might have a relationship to their ethnic and gender difference from white men. Her identity politics, in other words, are a realist identity politics, pointing toward the importance of identity for understanding the world.

On its surface, I find her statement entirely unobjectionable and even unremarkable. It seems like a rather obvious statement of fact. Yet, undeniably, many whites found the statement highly objectionable, and even "racist."[11] To find the statement racist, however, would seem to suggest that these people either simply missed the statement's many qualifications or believed its opposite to be an obvious and unremarkable statement of fact—namely, that no Latinas could ever come to better conclusions than any white men could, and if they ever did, it could not have anything to do with their ethnicity or gender. This, apparently, would not constitute a racist statement, since its adherents felt entitled to make the charge of racism against their opponents. That so many whites in the United States could find it inconceivable (even objectionable) that a Latina might ever know something that a white man did not suggests a profound and unabated sense of white supremacy and male superiority. Further lost amid all the controversy over Sotomayor's "identity politics" is the fact that her court record—certainly on issues of crime and imprisonment—seemed more conservative to some observers than that of the white man she replaced, Justice David Souter.[12] Her confirmation therefore marked in some ways an additional step to the right for the U.S. Supreme Court, despite the historic opportunities presented by a black president and a Democratically controlled and filibuster-proof U.S. Senate.

Crime and prison policy should have constituted precisely the focus of debate following Henry Louis Gates Jr.'s arrest by police in his home on July 16, 2009.[13] Instead, all the major parties (Gates, Sergeant Crowley, Obama, 911 caller Lucia Whalen, and the media) chose to individualize the incident, focusing on the personalities of the people involved and on the details specific to the event. Very quickly, everyone lost sight of the role that police profiling and the disproportionate treatment of black suspects play in sustaining the U.S. prison crisis. No one asked whether Gates would have been released had he not been famous and wealthy, for example, and faced with unprecedented access to the national media, Gates himself seemed incapable of offering a cogent macroanalysis of the structures linking race, crime, policing, and imprisonment in the United States, focusing instead on his personal outrage and the injustice of what happened *to him*. Even more disturbingly, public debate focused very quickly on whether or not individual charges of racism against Crowley and Whalen (the white woman who called the police to report Gates's entry into his home) had any justification.[14]

This debate cemented a popular conflation of racism with personal prejudice and with malicious actions on the part of individuals. Much was made, for example, of the fact that Crowley conducted diversity trainings for his colleagues.[15] When Whalen identified herself as the person responsible for reporting Gates to police, she seemed indignant that anyone could have thought her to be racist. Indeed, it clearly pained her, and it seemed an important part of her self-concept that she saw herself as not racist.[16] Of course, there seemed no other explanation for why Whalen would call the police on her neighbor and his driver rather than offering to help them get into the house. There also seemed no explanation for why Crowley would arrest a man in his own home, no matter what that man said or did, as long as he posed no danger to himself or to others. The assumption over and over again held that these actions could only be understood as problematic if they were intentionally motivated by conscious racial hatred on the part of someone with a history of mistreating people of color. Anything else simply could not constitute racism and therefore could not be objectionable.

The mind-set that would see Sotomayor's statement as racist, but not the actions of Crowley and Whalen, suggests a profound confusion about the role that identity plays in shaping knowledge, beliefs, experiences, and actions, and about the nature of racism. As soon as the incident became individualized (thanks in no small part to Gates and Obama), the ground was lost for understanding how the actions of Crowley and Whalen might contribute to a racist system with racist outcomes. Instead, the debate moved from the single injustice done to Gates to the motivations of those he accused of racism. Of course, Crowley and Whalen probably do not go around wearing hoods and burning crosses on people's front lawns. However, when they acted as they did, they were not ignorant of Gates's race and of the negative meanings associated with his race in U.S. society. Furthermore, their actions resembled others that result every day in the disproportionate surveillance, arrest, and imprisonment of blacks and other people of color in the United States (see chapter 4). The fact that they can also hold a sense of self as nonracist only goes to show the extent to which the unjust treatment of people of color in the United States has become invisible and taken for granted. Injustice and inequality (of gender, of race, of sexuality, and of class) is the air that we breathe in this country. For this reason, it remains unremarkable and unrecognizable. Those who call attention to it appear to be speaking an unintelligible language, describing solid objects where others see only the wind.

It falls to scholars and activists to create a public space in which that language can become intelligible. In the case of Gates, an opportunity for immediate discussion clearly passed the nation by, but there may still emerge possibilities for deeper considerations of race, class, and policing. If nothing else—until media fixation with Gates's and Obama's gaffs crowded out other concerns—the incident brought to the attention of many in the United States, perhaps for the first time, the fact that people of color *are* vulnerable to abuse by the police at any time and in any place. More promisingly, the debate about Justice Sotomayor's wise words—despite the many stupidities of some Republican senators—opened up some room for rethinking the meaning and value of gender and ethnic identities. Popular left-leaning commentators Jon Stewart, Stephen Colbert, Maureen Dowd, and others, for example, had a field day making fun of conservatives' racial and gender insensitivity and backwardness during the confirmation hearings.[17] The incident also galvanized many Latinas and Latinos politically in a way that had arguably not happened since the mass immigration rallies of 2006.[18] However, Obama's failures early in his presidency to initiate a meaningful discussion on race, to address the concerns of sexual minorities and immigrants, or to bring to an end the nation's two, ongoing imperialistic wars, suggest a continuing relevance and fragmentation of racial, sexual, gender, and class identities in the United States despite the watershed election of a black man. They also suggest that the world we live in today requires a thorough understanding of identities both as negatively imposed limits to possibility and as resources for knowledge and transformation. Finally, that world requires an awareness of multiplicity and of the relations among overlapping identities. Of course, the world always required that of us, but the present historical moment perhaps makes its necessity more clearly apparent than ever before.[19]

Acknowledgments

This book has taken me fourteen years to write, and in many ways it constitutes an extended response to the questions I first went to graduate school seeking to address. Indeed, the first draft of the essay that became chapter 1 of this book began as a graduate seminar paper in 1995 for a class at Cornell University with Satya Mohanty and Richard Boyd. Having now finished it, I must reflect that no book really has a single author—and certainly not a book that has been fourteen years in the writing. Of course, all the errors are my own, but there are many people who helped to keep other, more egregious errors out. There are so many people to acknowledge that I will certainly overlook some.

First and foremost, I must acknowledge Ernesto Martínez for his intellectual engagement with the manuscript, his sharp criticisms, his unwavering support, and, above all, his emotional sustenance. I have been blessed to have him as a companion in my life and in my work.

This book as it now stands was finished at the University of Oregon but was enabled by my seven years at Binghamton University, during which time I had the good fortune to develop a long and sustaining intellectual companionship with María Lugones. María's role as interlocutor has played an integral role in my growth as a scholar.

A key part of my rewriting of chapter 1 was sparked by a question in 2006 by Kia Caldwell regarding intersectionality and multiplicity, followed by subsequent conversations on the topic with María Lugones. I also had a number of fun and useful interdisciplinary conversations about this chapter with Stephanie Fryberg, particularly regarding the notion of "mutual constitution" and other matters.

Chapter 2 benefited from important comments by Ernesto Martínez, Paula Moya, Stacy Alaimo, and Susan Hekman. It began, however, through conversations with Rosemarie Garland-Thomson, Satya Mohanty, Carrie Sandahl, and Tobin Siebers as part of a Future of Minority Studies Project symposium on "Disability Studies and the Realist Theory of Identity" at Cornell University in 2005. Some of the ideas in it were also presented as part of the "How Do Identities Matter?" workshop at the University of Michigan, Ann Arbor in 2006, at the invitation of Claire Decoteau and Roxana Galusca. Much of the chapter was completed while serving as the Barbara and Carlisle Moore Distinguished Visiting Professor in the Department of English at the University of Oregon; I am grateful to everyone in that department for their generosity, hospitality, and support.

My understanding of coloniality in chapters 2 and 3 would not be possible without a number of conversations over the past several years with Manuel Chávez-Jiménez, María Lugones, Ernesto Martínez, Walter Mignolo, Paula Moya, Pedro Di Pietro, Joshua Price, Shireen Roshanravan, José David Saldívar, Ramón Saldívar, Gabriel Soldatenko, and Gabriella Veronelli. A conversation over dinner with Omar Naim was also very useful, and I am further indebted to him for putting me in touch with Rasha Moumneh, whose help and insight were invaluable to me in completing chapter 3.

Portions of chapters 3 and 4 were presented and commented on in a variety of venues between 2006 and 2008 and I am grateful to the audiences and organizers who engaged with my work during that time. These have included the Department of English Lecture Series at the University of Albany, State University of New York, at the invitation of Rosemary Hennessy; a Future of Minority Studies Summer Colloquium at Stanford University; a presentation sponsored by the Ethnic Studies Program at the University of Nevada–Reno, at the invitation of Daniel Enrique Pérez; the "Empires in the 21st Century" conference of the Center for the Study of Women in Society (CSWS) at the University of Oregon, at the invitation of Sangita Gopal, Lamia Karim, and Sandra Morgen; a presentation at Pitzer College, at the invitation of María Soldatenko; and a keynote presentation for the second annual National Association of Chicana and Chicano Studies (NACCS) Joto Caucus Conference at the California State University, Los Angeles, at the invitation of the conference organizers, José "Pepe" Manuel Aguilar-Hernández and Emmanuelle "Neza" Leal. Some of my ideas from these chapters were also presented on panels at the 2006 American Studies Association meeting in Oakland, the 2008 "Race, Sex, Power: New Movements in Black and Latina/o Sexualities" conference in Chicago, and the 2008 LatCrit XII conference in Seattle.

A significant part of my research for chapter 4 was completed during a "Projects of Queer Studies Working Group" retreat sponsored by the Center for the Study of Women and Society (CSWS) at the University of Oregon and organized by Ernesto Martínez and Irmary Reyes-Santos in the summer of 2007, and a first draft was the focus of a workshop by that working group in early 2008. Many of the participants in that workshop helped my thinking, including Ernesto, Irmary, Lynn Fujiwara, Julia Heffernan, Julee Raiskin, and Lizzie Reis.

Kathleen Rowe Karlyn and Priscilla Peña Ovalle both kindly took time out of their schedules to read a draft of chapter 4 and their feedback vastly improved it. (Indeed, Priscilla's comments inspired me to go back and reorganize much of the rest of the manuscript as well!) Several of my students in a 2006 course on the prison industrial complex also provoked me to explore new questions and lines of thinking in relation to chapter 4, including Michael Brown, Oscar Guerra, Nate Gulley, Kyra Hayashi, Ronan Kelly, Sothreaksa Keo, Colin Kraus, Kira Lee, Amy Leikas, Jennifer Lleras, Diertra Lynn, Héctor Miramontes, Josué Peña-Juárez, Paloma Reza, Shalan Ryan, Nancy Muey Saechao, Chii-San SunOwen, Kenshi Toll, Margarita Wickham, and Dave Young. I also had numerous productive conversations about *Oz* with Michael Aronson, Sangita Gopal, and others.

I am extremely grateful to the participants in the 2006 Future of Minority Studies Summer Institute at Stanford University, which I co-led with Paula Moya: Deanna Blackwell, Kia Caldwell, Stephanie Fitzgerald, Stephanie Fryberg, Danielle Heard, Angel Miles, Nana Osei-Kofi, Daniel Enrique Pérez, Margaret Price, Jessi Quizar, John "Rio" Riofrio, Tyrone Simpson, and Tania Triana. Our conversations over the course of two weeks about realism, multiplicity, intersectionality, identity, sexuality, disability, race, transnational feminism, and the politics of the academy remain an inspiration to me.

In addition to those mentioned already, a few of the people whose comments, questions, disagreements, or offers of support stand out to me include the following: (at Oregon) Chad Allen, Karen Ford, Warren Ginsberg, Daniel Martínez HoSang, Shari Huhndorf, Brian Klopotek, Anne Leighton, David Li, Enrique Lima, Michelle McKinley, Dayo Nicole Mitchell, Sandra Morgen, Steve Morozumi, Jeffrey Ostler, Peggy Pascoe, Paul Peppis, Robert Reid-Pharr, Lynn Stephen, Martin Summers, Cynthia Tolentino, Mia Tuan, David Vázquez, and many others associated with the departments of English and Ethnic Studies and the Center for Race, Ethnicity, and Sexuality Studies; (outside Oregon) Eddy Álvarez, Mario

Barnes, Angela Davis, Juanita Díaz-Cotto, Gabriel Estrada, Mary Fan, Nisha Gupta, Zoe Hammer-Tomizuka, Joy James, Carlos Manuel, Margo Okazawa-Rey, Ben Olguín, Dylan Rodríguez, Ramón Saldívar, Ramsey Scott, and Julia Sudbury.

This book would still not be finished if it were not for the extraordinary support of Donella-Elizabeth Alston in the Department of Ethnic Studies at Oregon. Her patience, cooperation, and efficiency humble me and also make my life infinitely easier every day. I am also very thankful to the patience and support of the folks at the University of Minnesota Press, in particular my editor, Richard Morrison, as well as the production coordinator Rachel Moeller, copy editor Philip Culbertson, and project manager Sarah Breeding.

Last, but by no means least, I am indebted more than words can describe to the best research collective a scholar of multiplicity could ask for. I cannot acknowledge everyone, but I am grateful for the support of those who have been a part of the Future of Minority Studies Project, including, in addition to those already named, Samaa Abdurraqib, Linda Martín Alcoff, Johnnella Butler, Alice Cho, Elora Chowdhury, William "Sandy" Darity, Michele Elam, Beverly Guy-Sheftall, Jennifer Hartford-Vargas, Paulo Horta, Ogaga Ifowodo, Joseph Jordan, Sang Hea Kil, Amie Macdonald, Carol Moeller, Chandra Talpade Mohanty, Tamiko Nimura, Helen "H. Q." Quan, Susan Sánchez-Casal, John Su, Sean Teuton, Bill Wilkerson, Tiffany Willoughby-Herard, Cindy Wu, Kay Yandell, and many, many more. I apologize deeply to those I have undoubtedly, but unintentionally, overlooked.

Notes

Preface

1. Key examples of women-of-color feminist texts from this period would include the following: Anzaldúa, *Borderlands/La Frontera*; Anzaldúa, ed., *Making Face, Making Soul/Haciendo Caras*; Carby, *Reconstructing Womanhood*; Collins, *Black Feminist Thought*; Crenshaw, "Demarginalizing the Intersection of Race and Sex"; Crenshaw "Whose Story Is It, Anyway?"; Davis, *Women, Race, & Class*; hooks, *Ain't I a Woman*; hooks, *Talking Back*; Hull, Scott, and Smith, eds., *All the Women Are White, All the Blacks Are Men, but Some of Us Are Brave*; Lorde, *Sister Outsider*; Mohanty, Russo, and Torres, eds., *Third World Women and the Politics of Feminism*; Moraga, *Loving in the War Years*; Moraga and Anzaldúa, eds., *This Bridge Called My Back*; Smith, ed., *Home Girls*; and Williams, *The Alchemy of Race and Rights*.

2. People most often associate the term *intersectionality* with the work of legal scholar Kimberlé Williams Crenshaw. I discuss Crenshaw's work on this concept in chapter 1. See Crenshaw, "Demarginalizing the Intersection of Race and Sex" and "Mapping the Margins."

3. See, for example, Bhaskaran, *Made in India*; Eng and Hom, eds., *Q & A*; Ferguson, *Aberrations in Black*; Gaspar de Alba, ed., *Velvet Barrios*; Gopinath, *Impossible Desires*; Hames-García and Martínez, eds., *Gay Latino Studies*; Johnson, *Sweet Tea*; Johnson and Henderson, eds., *Black Queer Studies*; Lugones, *Pilgrimages/Peregrinajes*; Manalansan, *Global Divas*; Muñoz, *Disidentifications*; Quiroga, *Tropics of Desire*; Ramos, ed., *Compañeras*; Rodríguez, *Queer Latinidad*; Shahani, *Gay Bombay*; Srivastava, ed., *Sexual Sites, Seminal Attitudes*; and Yarbro-Bejarano, *The Wounded Heart*.

4. For such an intellectual history, see Hames-García, "Queer Theory Revisited."

5. Rosemary Hennessy first pressed me on the question of class as a social identity following a presentation of some of the arguments in this book in an earlier form for the English Department of the University of Albany, State University of New York in 2006. Her questions have stayed with me and this reflects my best effort at providing a coherent answer for why I do not include a specific focus on class as a social identity in this project.

6. For the development of an analysis of capitalism along the lines of a "world system," "modern world system," "modern/colonial world system," or "colonial/modern world system," see, among others, Abu-Lughod, *Before European Hegemony*; Frank, *ReOrient*; Frank and Gills, eds., *The World System*; Grosfoguel and Cervantes-Rodríguez, eds., *The Modern/Colonial/Capitalist World-System in the Twentieth Century*; Mignolo, *Local Histories/Global Designs*; Quijano, "Coloniality of Power, Eurocentrism, and Latin America"; Wallerstein, *The Modern World-System I*; Wallerstein, *The Modern World-System II*; Wallerstein, *The Modern World-System III*; Wallerstein, *World-Systems Analysis*; and Wolf, *Europe and the People without History*. See also Amin, *Eurocentrism*; Bello, Cunningham, and Rau, *Dark Victory*; Escobar, *Encountering Development*; Galeano, *Open Veins of Latin America*; Lugones, "Heterosexualism and the Colonial/Modern Gender System"; and Rodney, *How Europe Underdeveloped Africa*.

7. The first works by women-of-color feminists that I remember reading in college included Anzaldúa, *Borderlands/La Frontera*; Moraga, *Loving in the War Years*; and Moraga and Anzaldúa, eds., *This Bridge Called My Back*.

8. See Siebers, *Disability Theory*; Lugones, "Heterosexualism and the Colonial/Modern Gender System"; and Lugones, *Pilgrimages/Peregrinajes*.

9. See Massad, "Re-Orienting Desire"; Massad, *Desiring Arabs*; Mignolo, *Local Histories/Global Designs*; and Mignolo, *The Idea of Latin America*.

10. Hames-García, "'Who Are Our Own People?'"

11. This question reprises that asked in Hames-García, "How Real Is Race?"

12. Lugones, "Heterosexualism and the Colonial/Modern Gender System."

13. This question reflects a substantive reengagement and rethinking of others that I have addressed previously, for example, in Hames-García, "What's at Stake in 'Gay' Identities?"

14. This chapter and the questions with which it grapples represent in many ways a continuation and deepening of some lines of inquiry in my previous single-author book. See Hames-García, *Fugitive Thought*.

15. Levinson and Fontana, *Oz*; Levinson, Fontana, and Finnerty, *Oz*.

1. Who Are Our Own People?

1. See Crenshaw, "Mapping the Margins," 358; Lugones, "Heterosexualism and the Colonial/Modern Gender System," 192–93.

2. See, for example, these women's contributions to the following: Anzaldúa, *Borderlands/La Frontera*; Anzaldúa, ed., *Making Face, Making Soul/Haciendo Caras*; Bambara, ed., *The Black Woman*; Boggs and Boggs, *Revolution and Evolution in the Twentieth Century*; Combahee River Collective, "A Black Feminist Statement"; Davis, *Women, Race, & Class*; hooks, *Ain't I a Woman*; Hull, Scott, and Smith, eds., *All the Women Are White, All the Blacks Are Men, but Some of Us*

Are Brave; Lorde, *Sister Outsider*; Mohanty, Russo, and Torres, eds., *Third World Women and the Politics of Feminism*; Moraga, *Loving in the War Years*; Moraga and Anzaldúa, eds., *This Bridge Called My Back*; Morales and Morales, *Getting Home Alive*; Parker, *Movement in Black*; Ramos, ed., *Compañeras*; Reagon, "Coalition Politics"; Smith, ed., *Home Girls*; Vance, ed., *Pleasure and Danger*; Wallace, *Black Macho and the Myth of the Black Superwoman*; Wong, Woo, and Yamada, *Three Asian American Writers Speak Out on Feminism.*

3. See Crenshaw, "Whose Story Is It, Anyway?"; Lugones, "Purity, Impurity, and Separation"; Moraga, *Loving in the War Years*, 50–59.

4. Nava, *The Hidden Law.*

5. Morrison, *Beloved*; Riggs, *Tongues Untied.*

6. I discuss distinctions between race and ethnicity further in chapter 2.

7. See, among others, Spelman, *Inessential Woman*, 133–37.

8. See Sedgwick, *Epistemology of the Closet*, 33; Crenshaw, "Demarginalizing the Intersection of Race and Sex," 141–52; Anzaldúa, *Borderlands*, 80–82.

9. See Spillers, "Interstices"; Lorde, *Sister Outsider*, 114–23.

10. Crenshaw, "Demarginalizing the Intersection of Race and Sex," 139, 140.

11. Lugones, "Heterosexualism and the Colonial/Modern Gender System," 192. Lugones's references to Crenshaw's thought draw primarily from Crenshaw, "Mapping the Margins."

12. Lugones, "Heterosexualism and the Colonial/Modern Gender System," 192–93.

13. Ibid., 193.

14. See, for example, the following: Carby, *Reconstructing Womanhood*; Martínez, "Dying to Know"; Muñoz, *Disidentifications*; Saldívar-Hull, *Feminism on the Border*; Smith, *The Truth That Never Hurts*; Smith, *Not Just Race, Not Just Gender*; Yarbro-Bejarano, *The Wounded Heart.*

15. Moraga, *The Hungry Woman*; Kenan, *A Visitation of Spirits.*

16. Barad, "Meeting the Universe Halfway"; Mohanty, "The Epistemic Status of Cultural Identity"; Mohanty, *Literary Theory and the Claims of History*; Moya, "Postmodernism, 'Realism,' and the Politics of Identity"; Moya, *Learning from Experience*; Roman, "White Is a Color!"; Siebers, "Disability in Theory"; Siebers, *Disability Theory.*

17. Alcoff, *Visible Identities*; Alcoff, Hames-García, Mohanty, and Moya, eds., *Identity Politics Reconsidered*; Dé, "Decolonizing Universality"; Grobman, "Postpositivist Realism in the Multicultural Writing Classroom"; Hames-García, *Fugitive Thought*; Martínez, "Dying to Know"; Martínez, "On Butler on Morrison on Language"; Moeller, "Marginalized Voices"; Moya and Hames-García, eds., *Reclaiming Identity*; Sánchez-Casal and Macdonald, eds., *Twenty-First-Century Feminist Classrooms*; Sánchez-Casal and Macdonald, eds., *Identity in Education*; Sandahl, "Black Man, Blind Man"; Stone-Mediatore, "Postmodernism, Realism,

and the Problem of Identity"; Tettenborn, "'Will the Big Boys Finally Love You'";
Teuton, "Placing the Ancestors"; Teuton, *Red Land, Red Power.*

18. See, for example, Castells, *The Power of Identity.*

19. On error, see Hau, "On Representing Others," esp. 136–37, 159–61; Nguyen,
"'It Matters to Get the Facts Straight,'" esp. 192–93.

20. See, for example, the following: Barad, "Meeting the Universe Halfway";
Barad, "Posthumanist Performativity," 817; Bohr, "Quantum Physics and Philoso-
phy"; Boyd, "How to Be a Moral Realist"; Gould, *The Mismeasure of Man*; Harding,
Whose Science? Whose Knowledge?; Kuhn, *The Structure of Scientific Revolutions.*

21. Some of the most influential statements informing this consensus include
the following: Baudrillard, *The Mirror of Production*; Butler, *Gender Trouble*; Butler and Scott, eds., *Feminists Theorize the Political*; Culler, *On Deconstruction*; De
Man, *Blindness and Insight*; Johnson, *The Critical Difference*; Johnson, *A World
of Difference*; Laclau and Mouffe, *Hegemony & Socialist Strategy*; Lyotard, *The
Postmodern Condition*; Lyotard, *The Différend*; Nicholson, ed., *Feminism/Post-
modernism*; Scott, "The Evidence of Experience"; Spivak, *In Other Worlds*; White,
Tropics of Discourse.

22. Boyd, "How to Be a Moral Realist," 195.

23. Mohanty, "The Epistemic Status of Cultural Identity," 39.

24. Ibid.

25. Ibid., 55–56.

26. Ibid., 36.

27. For several detailed accounts of what realists mean by "better and worse
knowledge" about the social world, see Hames-García, *Fugitive Thought*, xxvii–
xxxv, 21–33; Mohanty, *Literary Theory and the Claims of History*, 206–16; Moya,
Learning from Experience, 100–35.

28. Hau, "On Representing Others," 159–61; Mohanty, "The Epistemic Status of
Cultural Identity," 42.

29. Mohanty, "The Epistemic Status of Cultural Identity," 40; Harding, *Whose
Science? Whose Knowledge?*, 127.

30. See Martínez, "Dying to Know"; Mohanty, "Colonial Legacies, Multicultural Futures."

31. I am indebted to Anne Leighton for an e-mail exchange in which she first
brought these issues to my attention. That exchange proved useful to me in clarify-
ing how I understood my own use of multiplicity and its relation to DID. On DID,
see *Diagnostic and Statistical Manual of Mental Disorders*, 526–29.

32. Bombardieri, "Summers' Remarks on Women Draw Fire." For one of the
best journalistic discussions of the Summers incident, see O'Rourke, "Don't Let
Larry Summers Off the Hook Yet."

33. Wittgenstein, *Philosophical Investigations*, I, §66.

34. Boyd, "How to Be a Moral Realist," 196–99.

35. Lugones, "Purity, Impurity, and Separation," 477.

36. Moya, "Postmodernism, 'Realism,' and the Politics of Identity," 84.

37. Hames-García, *Fugitive Thought*, 25–27.

38. See, for example, Douglass, *The Oxford Frederick Douglass Reader*, 47–48; Jacobs, *Incidents in the Life of a Slave Girl*, 35–36, 51–52.

39. Kittay, "When Caring Is Just and Justice Is Caring"; Siebers, "Disability Studies and the Future of Identity Politics," 23–25.

40. Harding, "Rethinking Standpoint Epistemology"; Mohanty, "Colonial Legacies, Multicultural Futures," 110–17.

41. Hammett, *The Maltese Falcon*.

42. This most notably characterizes the third, fifth, and sixth novels in Nava's series: Nava, *How Town*; Nava, *The Death of Friends*; Nava, *The Burning Plain*.

43. Ortiz, "Pleasure and Power in the Novels of John Rechy, Arturo Islas, and Michael Nava," 123.

44. Rodríguez, *Brown Gumshoes*, 42.

45. For a further discussion of this claim, see Hames-García, "'Who Are Our Own People?'" 114–18.

46. Barad, "Meeting the Universe Halfway," 187; Roman, "White Is a Color!" 83.

47. Castells, *The Power of Identity*, 7.

48. Alcoff, "Cultural Feminism Versus Post-Structuralism," 432.

49. Ibid., 435.

50. Lugones, "Purity, Impurity, and Separation," 460.

51. Ibid., 474.

52. Ibid.

53. Ibid.

54. Ibid., 476; emphasis added.

55. Mohanty, "The Epistemic Status of Cultural Identity," 53–55.

56. Lugones, "Purity, Impurity, and Separation," 477.

57. Ibid.

58. Bowen, "Collect Yourself"; Saalfield, "On the Make."

59. House of Color, *I Object*.

60. Bowen, "Collect Yourself," 109.

61. García, "García Papers."

62. Banks et al., *America's Next Top Model*.

63. Ibid.

64. For another, related discussion of *America's Next Top Model*, see Hasinoff, "Fashioning Race for the Free Market on *America's Next Top Model*."

65. Banks et al., *America's Next Top Model*, cycle 3, episode no. 13. (This episode was directed by Luis Barreto, with writing credits given to Trice Barto, Heather Cocks, and Pam Suchman.)

66. Moraga, *Loving in the War Years*, 137.

67. García, "García Papers."

68. House of Color, *Probe*.

69. Lorde, *Sister Outsider*, 115–16.

70. Anzaldúa, *Borderlands/La Frontera*, 83–85; Henze, "Who Says Who Says?" 229–50; Pratt, *Rebellion*.

71. Smith, "Heteropatriarchy and the Three Pillars of White Supremacy," 69. I am indebted to Shireen Roshanravan's discussion of Smith in her dissertation; see Roshanravan, "South Asian American Identity Formation and the Politics of Women of Color."

72. See, for example, Imrie, "Oppression, Disability, and Access in the Built Environment," 129–46.

73. Garland-Thomson, *Extraordinary Bodies*, 4–10.

74. Baynton, "Disability and the Justification of Inequality in American History," 33–57.

75. Lorde, *Sister Outsider*, 111.

2. How Real Is Race?

1. The firestorm about "identity politics" and Sotomayor's confirmation hearings was ignited by a *New York Times* article quoting the following words from a speech she had given at the University of California, Berkeley: "I would hope that a wise Latina woman with the richness of her experiences would more often than not reach a better conclusion than a white male who hasn't lived that life." See Savage, "A Judge's View of Judging Is on the Record"; see also Sotomayor, "A Latina Judge's Voice."

2. In addition to the works I take up at length in this chapter, some examples of a general anti-identitarian position include the following: Butler, *Gender Trouble*; Gilroy, *Against Race*; Gitlin, *The Twilight of Common Dreams*; Hobsbawm, "Identity Politics and the Left"; Rorty, *Achieving Our Country*; Žižek, "A Leftist Plea for 'Eurocentrism.'"

3. "Proposition 54"; emphasis added.

4. El Nasser, "Voters Shoot Down Proposition on Collecting Racial Information."

5. Some important publications in this debate include the following: Alcoff, *Visible Identities*; Appiah, *In My Father's House*; Appiah, "Race, Culture, Identity"; Bell, Grosholz, and Stewart, *W.E.B. Du Bois on Race and Culture*; Glasgow, "Three Things Realist Constructionism About Race—or Anything Else—Can Do"; Outlaw, *On Race and Philosophy*; Sundstrom, "Race as a Human Kind"; Sundstrom, "'Racial' Nominalism"; Taylor, "Appiah's Uncompleted Argument"; Zack, *Thinking About Race*.

6. Brown, *States of Injury*, 54.

7. Ibid., 61.

8. Ibid., 65. See also Aronson, *After Marxism*; Hobsbawm, "Identity Politics and the Left." For some responses to this charge, see, among others, Hames-García, *Fugitive Thought*, 249–54; Kelly, *Yo' Mama's Disfunktional!* 103–24; Palumbo-Liu, "Multiculturalism Now"; Rosaldo, "Identity Politics."

9. Brown, *States of Injury*, 64. For Brown, oppression might be material, but identity is a psychological response to oppression, and an unproductive psychological response at that: "Revenge as a 'reaction,' a substitute for the capacity to act, produces identity as both bound to the history that produced it and as a reproach to the present which embodies that history. The will that 'took to hurting' in its own impotence against its past becomes (in the form of an identity whose very existence is due to heightened consciousness of the immovability of its 'it was,' its history of subordination) a will that makes not only a psychological but a political practice of revenge, a practice that reiterates the existence of an identity whose present past is one of insistently unredeemable injury. This past cannot be redeemed *unless* the identity ceases to be invested in it, and it cannot cease to be invested in it without giving up its identity as such, thus giving up its economy of avenging and at the same time perpetuating its hurt" (Brown, *States of Injury*, 73).

10. Ibid., 74.

11. Brown writes, "For if I am right about the problematic of pain installed at the heart of many contemporary contradictory demands for political recognition, all that such pain may long for—more than revenge—is the chance to be heard into a certain release, recognized into self-overcoming, incited into possibilities for triumphing over, and hence losing, itself" (Ibid., 74–75).

12. Ibid., 75.

13. "[T]he replacement—even the admixture—of the language of 'being' with 'wanting' would seek to exploit politically a recovery of the more expansive moments in the genealogy of identity formation . . . How might democratic discourse itself be invigorated by such a shift from ontological claims to these kinds of more expressly political ones?" (Ibid., 76).

14. Michaels, "Autobiography of an Ex-White Man," 125.

15. Ibid., 132–33.

16. Shiao, Tuan, and Rienzi, "Shifting the Spotlight," 1–16.

17. Michaels, "Autobiography of an Ex-White Man," 134–40.

18. Ibid., 142. Michaels's position thus goes much further than other considerations of the proposal simply to stop talking about race, such as philosopher Naomi Zack's discussion of racial "eliminativism" and the many practical barriers to it posed by the social reality of race. See Zack, *Thinking About Race*, 16–17.

19. Michaels, *The Shape of the Signifier*, 10.

20. See Wilkerson, "Is There Something You Need to Tell Me?" 272–75.

21. Morrison, "Unspeakable Things Unspoken," 26.

22. Gutiérrez-Jones, *Critical Race Narratives*, 48–65. For other scholarly criticisms of Michaels's work on race, see Elam, *Mixtries*; Glasgow, "Three Things Realist Constructionism About Race—or Anything Else—Can Do," 158–59.

23. See Bowen, Kurzweil, and Tobin, *Equity and Excellence in American Higher Education*, 161–93.

24. Castells, *The Power of Identity*, 1.

25. Ibid., 2.

26. Ibid., 8.

27. Ibid., 10.

28. Ibid., 11.

29. Ibid., 65.

30. Quijano, "Coloniality of Power, Eurocentrism, and Latin America," 533.

31. Ibid., 534.

32. Ibid., 545–56.

33. See also Aldrich, *Colonialism and Homosexuality*; Anzaldúa, *Borderlands/La Frontera*; Bhaskaran, *Made in India*; Marcos, *Taken from the Lips*; Massad, *Desiring Arabs*; McClintock, *Imperial Leather*; Najmabadi, *Women with Mustaches and Men without Beards*; Sigal, ed., *Infamous Desire*; Sigal and Chuchiak, eds., *Sexual Encounters/Sexual Collisions*; Smith, *Conquest*; Smith, "Heteropatriarchy and the Three Pillars of White Supremacy"; Somerville, *Queering the Color Line*; Stoler, *Carnal Knowledge and Imperial Power*; Teaiwa, "Bikinis and Other S/Pacific N/Oceans"; Trask, *From a Native Daughter*.

34. Lugones, "Heterosexualism and the Colonial/Modern Gender System."

35. Quijano, "Coloniality of Power, Eurocentrism, and Latin America," 538.

36. Ibid., 536.

37. Wolf, *Europe and the People without History*, 380–81.

38. Quijano, "Coloniality of Power, Eurocentrism, and Latin America," 541.

39. See, for example, Amin, *Eurocentrism*; Anzaldúa, *Borderlands/La Frontera*; Asad, ed., *Anthropology and the Colonial Encounter*; Bello, Cunningham, and Rau, *Dark Victory*; Bernal, *Black Athena*; Césaire, *Discourse on Colonialism*; Chakrabarty, *Provincializing Europe*; Clifford, *The Predicament of Culture*; Dussel, *The Underside of Modernity*; Escobar, *Encountering Development*; Fabian, *Time and the Other*; Fanon, *Black Skin, White Masks*; Fanon, *The Wretched of the Earth*; Ferreira da Silva, *Toward a Global Idea of Race*; Frank, *ReOrient*; Galeano, *Open Veins of Latin America*; McClintock, *Imperial Leather*; Massad, *Desiring Arabs*; Memmi, *The Colonizer and the Colonized*; Mignolo, *The Darker Side of the Renaissance*; Mudimbe, *The Invention of Africa*; Rodney, *How Europe Underdeveloped Africa*; Rosaldo, *Culture and Truth*; Said, *Orientalism*; Stoler, *Carnal Knowledge*; Wolf, *Europe and the People without History*.

40. Quijano, "Coloniality of Power, Eurocentrism, and Latin America," 551, 552.

41. Ibid., 555. See also, Mignolo, *Local Histories/Global Designs*, 114–16, 314–15.

42. Castells, *The Power of Identity*, 53.

43. Ibid., 53, 59, 65.

44. Ibid., 59.

45. On scientific racism, see Harding, ed., *The "Racial" Economy of Science*, 84–193.

46. Castells, *The Power of Identity*, 57. See also, West, *Race Matters*.

47. Castells, *The Power of Identity*, 53–55.

48. Mann, *Unequal Justice*, 219.

49. Baldus, Pulaski, and Woodworth, "Comparative Review of Death Sentences," 689–95, 707–10.

50. See, for example, Michaels, *The Shape of the Signifier*, 164; Zack, *Thinking About Race*, 44–45.

51. Steele and Aronson, "Stereotype Threat and the Intellectual Test Performance of African Americans," 800–808; Steele, Spencer, and Aronson, "Contending with Group Image," 382–84.

52. Stone, Sjomeling, Lynch, and Darley, "Stereotype Threat Effects on Black and White Athletic Performance"; Steele, Spencer, and Aronson, "Contending with Group Image," 386.

53. Gould, *The Mismeasure of Man*, esp. 26–36. See also Harding, ed., *The "Racial" Economy of Science*, 84–115 and 170–93; Hubbard and Wald, *Exploding the Gene Myth*, 13–38.

54. Graves, *The Race Myth*, 10.

55. Ibid., 226.

56. Ibid., 8. See also Barreiro et al., "Natural Selection Has Driven Population Differentiation in Modern Humans," 343; Graves, *The Race Myth*, 103–36; and Hubbard and Wald, *Exploding the Gene Myth*, 72–107.

57. Herrnstein and Murray, *The Bell Curve*. For two of the many critiques of *The Bell Curve* that also address genetics, heredity, and intelligence more generally, see Graves, *The Race Myth*, 172–84, and Gould, *The Mismeasure of Man*, 34–36, 367–90.

58. Barad, "Posthumanist Performativity," 809.

59. Ibid., 817.

60. Bohr, "Quantum Physics and Philosophy," 4; Barad, "Re(Con)Figuring Space, Time, and Matter," 82–83.

61. Barad, "Re(Con)Figuring Space, Time, and Matter," 88.

62. Omi and Winant, *Racial Formation in the United States from the 1960s to the 1990s*, 55–61.

63. Keith and Herring, "Skin Tone Stratification in the Black Community," 769–70.

64. Telles, *Race in Another America*, esp. 114–16; Arce, Murguía, and Frisbie, "Phenotype and Life Chances among Chicanos"; Darity, Hamilton, and Dietrich, "Bleach in the Rainbow"; Rodríguez, "The Effect of Race on Puerto Rican Wages."

65. Goldsmith, Hamilton, and Darity, "Shades of Discrimination," 244–45.

66. Blascovich et al., "African Americans and High Blood Pressure," 228; Steele, Spencer, and Aronson, "Contending with Group Image," 400–401.

67. On the fluctuating white and nonwhite status of Mexicans in the United States during the late nineteenth and early twentieth centuries, see Calderón-Zaks, "Constructing the 'Mexican Race.'"

68. Haney-López, *White by Law.*

69. For an overview of some of the debates around these issues, see Wylie, "Why Standpoint Matters." See also Alcoff and Potter, eds., *Feminist Epistemologies.*

70. Recently, the theoretical project of imaginatively and critically reconstructing identity has formed the undertaking of a multidisciplinary and multi-institution research project, The Future of Minority Studies. For more information, see Alcoff and Mohanty, "Reconsidering Identity Politics." Also see the website http://www.fmsproject.cornell.edu.

71. Sandahl, "Black Man, Blind Man," 584.

72. Siebers, "Disability as Masquerade," 13–16.

73. Sandahl, "Black Man, Blind Man," 588.

74. Ibid., 591.

75. For more on objectivity, see Moya and Hames-García, eds., *Reclaiming Identity*, 12–14, 39–41, 136–137, 200–202. See also, Wylie, "Why Standpoint Matters," 32–33.

76. Sandahl, "Black Man, Blind Man," 602.

77. Baynton, "Disability and the Justification of Inequality in American History"; Garland-Thomson, "Integrating Disability, Transforming Feminist Theory"; Siebers, "Disability Studies and the Future of Identity Politics"; Siebers, *Disability Theory.*

78. Moya and Hames-García, eds., *Reclaiming Identity*, 60–64, 186–87, 313–15.

79. Castells, *The Power of Identity*, 77, 78. Here, unlike elsewhere, Castells seems to consider ethnicity as a separate category from race.

80. Quijano, "Coloniality of Power, Eurocentrism, and Latin America," 533.

81. Mignolo, "The Zapatistas' Theoretical Revolution," 245.

82. Marcos and the Zapatista Army of National Liberation, *Shadows of Tender Fury*, 51. See also Marcos, *Conversations with Durito*; Marcos, *Desde las montañas del sureste mexicano*; Marcos, *¡Ya Basta!*.

83. Alcoff, *Visible Identities*, 227–84; Mignolo, *The Idea of Latin America*, 63–64, 135–41.

3. Are Sexual Identities Desirable?

1. See Price, "N.C. Guardsman Guilty in Iraqi Death"; Sain, "U.S. Soldier Claims Gay Panic Made Him Kill"; Sander and Ahmed, "Killing Drives Wedge between Troops."

2. Islamic Human Rights Commission, "IHRC Deplores Continued Abuses by Occupation Soldiers in Iraq."

3. Americans for Legal Immigration–PAC, "Possible Illegal Alien & U.S. Guardsman Killed Iraqi after Sex."

4. On the so-called gay panic defense, see Chen, "Provocation's Privileged Desire"; Comstock, "Dismantling the Homosexual Panic Defense"; Suffredini, "Pride and Prejudice."

5. For various accounts of the historical transformation of thinking about sexuality, see, among others, Aldrich, *Colonialism and Homosexuality*; Chauncey, *Gay New York*; D'Emilio, "Capitalism and Gay Identity"; Foucault, *The History of Sexuality*, 42–44; Greenberg, *The Construction of Homosexuality*; Halperin, *One Hundred Years of Homosexuality*; Hennessey, *Profit and Pleasure*, esp. 37–73; Mumford, *Interzones*; Sedgwick, *The Epistemology of the Closet*, esp. 44–48; Somerville, *Queering the Color Line*.

6. See, for example, Chauncey, *Gay New York*, 111–27.

7. For a thorough discussion of my own views on essentialism, see Hames-García, "What's at Stake in 'Gay' Identities?" 82–87. See also, among others, Bailey, *The Man Who Would Be Queen*; Battersby, *The Phenomenal Woman*; Frye, *The Politics of Reality*; Fuss, *Essentially Speaking*; Halwani, "Prolegomena to Any Future Metaphysics of Sexual Identity"; Kinsey, Pomeroy, and Martin, *Sexual Behavior in the Human Male*; Sigal, ed., *Infamous Desire*; Stein, ed., *Forms of Desire*; Wilkerson, "Is There Something You Need to Tell Me?"; Wilkerson, *Ambiguity and Sexuality*.

8. Kinsey, Pomeroy, and Martin, *Sexual Behavior in the Human Male*, 656.

9. Kushner, *Angels in America, Part One*, 45.

10. For the classic statement on political lesbianism, see Radicalesbians, "The Woman Identified Woman."

11. For a poignant discussion of this difficult process, see Martínez, "Dying to Know."

12. For further discussion of the politics of the MSM category, see Hames-García and Martínez, "Introduction," 7–8, 13–14; Roque Ramírez, "Gay Latino Cultural Citizenship," 178–85.

13. Wilkerson, "Is There Something You Need to Tell Me?" 266, 267.

14. Lugones, "Heterosexualism and the Colonial/Modern Gender System," 201–7.

15. Ibid., 202–3. Omise'eke Natasha Tinsley observes a similar point; see Tinsley, "Black Atlantic, Queer Atlantic," 209.

16. Lugones, "Heterosexualism and the Colonial/Modern Gender System," 201.

17. Ibid., 202. See also Anzaldúa, *Borderlands/La Frontera*; Estrada, "Chicanas/os, Homosexuality, and Two-Spirit Histories"; Hamilton, "The Flames of Namugongo"; Marcos, *Taken from the Lips*; Massad, *Desiring Arabs*; McClintock, *Imperial Leather*; Mohanty, Russo, and Torres, ed., *Third World Women and the Politics of Feminism*; Najmabadi, *Women with Mustaches and Men without Beards*; Sigal, ed., *Infamous Desire*; Sigal and Chuchiak, ed., *Sexual Encounters/Sexual Collisions*; Smith, *Conquest*; Smith, "Heteropatriarchy and the Three Pillars of White Supremacy"; Trask, *From a Native Daughter*.

18. Teaiwa, "Bikinis and Other S/Pacific N/Oceans," 97. See also Aiavao, "Who's Playing Naked Now?"; Trask, *From a Native Daughter*, 136–47.

19. Letellier, "Egyptians Decry 'Gay' U.S. Abusers in Iraq."

20. Michael, "Demonstrators Demand the Ejection of Egypt's U.S. Ambassador."

21. Jelinek, "Lawmakers View Disturbing Photos of Iraq Prison Abuse."

22. See "Top Al-Qaidah Leader in New Tape Criticizes U.S. 'Freedom'"; "Al-Jazeera TV Airs Parts of Al-Zawahiri Tape Criticizing USA."

23. "Al-Jazeera TV Airs Parts of Al-Zawahiri Tape Criticizing USA."

24. *Goodridge vs. Department of Public Health*; Izenberg, "Mazuz Backs Rights of Same-Sex Couples."

25. On the origins of English antisodomy laws, see Gorton, "The Origins of Anti-Sodomy Laws." On South Africa, see Goodman, "Beyond the Enforcement Principle."

26. Yawning Bread (Au Waipang), "The Map's Tale."

27. In 1990, Hong Kong repealed the antisodomy law it had inherited from the British; see Stormont, "Hong Kong Votes to Lift Penalties on Homosexual Acts." Yawning Bread omits Afghanistan from his map, although its government before Taliban rule also inherited a version of British colonial antisodomy law. The Taliban, however, replaced all civil law with sharia Islamic law after taking power.

28. In India, after numerous court battles spanning many years, the Delhi High Court overturned antisodomy laws in the National Capital Territory of Delhi in July 2009. The issue is now before the Indian Supreme Court, and same-sex sexual behavior remains criminalized at the federal level in the country. See Pinto, "Jai Ho!"

29. For an excellent discussion, see Bhaskaran, *Made in India*, 76–107. See also Mahapatra, "UN Body Slams India on Rights of Gays"; Ravindran, "New Sexual Revolution"; Thomas, "Delhi HC to Take Up PIL on Gay Rights."

30. Bhaskaran, *Made in India*, 86. See also Narrain and Dutta, "Male-to-Male Sex and Sexuality Minorities in South Asia," 7.

31. Overdorf, "Closet Drama."

32. Shing, "Saying No," 214–16.

33. See Amirthalingam, "Balancing Evidence and Rhetoric in Law Reform"; Ho, "It's Not a Big Deal for Most Singaporeans"; Ho, "There Are Gays, and There Are Gays . . ."; Shing, "Saying No."

34. Shing, "Saying No," 216–17.

35. Najmabadi, *Women with Mustaches and Men without Beards*, 33–41, 55–60.

36. Massad, *Desiring Arabs*, 51–98.

37. Najmabadi, *Women with Mustaches and Men without Beards*, 38.

38. Ibid., 59.

39. El-Rouayheb, *Before Homosexuality in the Arab-Islamic World, 1500–1800*, 21–33.

40. Najmabadi, *Women with Mustaches and Men without Beards*, 3.

41. Ibid., 56–57.

42. Foucault, *The History of Sexuality*, 57–58.

43. Said, *Orientalism*, 4–8.

44. See El-Rouayheb, *Before Homosexuality in the Arab-Islamic World, 1500–1800*; Massad, *Desiring Arabs*; Najmabadi, *Women with Mustaches and Men without Beards*; Ze'evi, *Producing Desire*.

45. See, among others, Dunne, "Power and Sexuality in the Middle East"; Murray and Roscoe, ed., *Islamic Homosexualities*; Schmitt and Sofer, ed., *Sexuality and Eroticism among Males in Moslem Societies*.

46. Almaguer, "Chicano Men"; Carrier, *De los Otros*; Lancaster, *Life Is Hard*; Murray, *Latin American Male Homosexualities*. For critiques of this view of Latin American, U.S. Latino, and Chicano men, see Bustos-Aguilar, "Mister Don't Touch the Banana"; Cantú, "Entre Hombres/Between Men"; Roque Ramírez, "Gay Latino Cultural Citizenship."

47. Abu-Lughod, "Writing Against Culture," 143.

48. Massad, "Re-Orienting Desire." This article was reprinted in Massad, *Desiring Arabs*.

49. Massad, "Re-Orienting Desire," 383–85.

50. Whitaker, *Unspeakable Love*, 204.

51. Ibid., 208.

52. Massad, "Re-Orienting Desire," 372, 72n40, 82, 84, 85.

53. Whitaker, *Unspeakable Love*, 212.

54. See Hames-García, "How to Tell a Mestizo from an Enchirito®."

55. Whitaker, *Unspeakable Love*, 216–23; Massad, "Re-Orienting Desire," 377, 382–83.

56. Whitaker, *Unspeakable Love*, 222, 223.

57. Narayan, *Dislocating Cultures*, 81–118.

58. Massad, "Re-Orienting Desire," 377.

59. Massad, *Desiring Arabs*, 37.

60. Massad, "Re-Orienting Desire," 383–85.

61. Massad, *Desiring Arabs*, 47.

62. Feinberg, *Lavender & Red*. See also, U.S. Department of State, Human Rights, and Labor, "Afghanistan."

63. Feinberg, *Lavender & Red*; Baer, "Kandahar."

64. Feinberg, *Lavender & Red*.

65. Stuever, "The Bomb with a Loaded Message," C01. I attempted to obtain a copy of this photo to reprint, but when I contacted the Associated Press with the relevant information for the photo as cited in the *Washington Post* article and in numerous online sources, where a reproduction of the original photo is available, I was directed to a different photo altogether, depicting a sailor writing on a different bomb with less inflammatory graffiti.

66. Ibid.

67. Loeb and Chandrasekaran, "Pentagon."

68. Feinberg, *Lavender & Red*; Stephen, "Startled Marines Find Afghan Men All Made up to See Them."

69. Stephen, "Startled Marines Find Afghan Men All Made up to See Them," 15.

70. See, for example, Massad, *Desiring Arabs*, ix–x.

71. See Castells, *The Power of Identity* and Alcoff et al., ed., *Identity Politics Reconsidered*.

72. al-Ghafari, "Is There a Lesbian Identity in the Arab Culture?" 88.

73. Ibid., 90.

74. Ibid., 86, 90.

75. Ibid., 90.

76. See Mecca, "It's All About Class"; Shepard, "Sylvia and Sylvia's Children."

77. Shahani, *Gay Bombay*, 283.

78. Ibid., 286.

79. Bhaskaran, *Made in India*, 97.

80. Altman, "Globalization and the International Gay/Lesbian Movement," 420.

81. Whitaker, *Unspeakable Love*, 216.

82. See, for example, Chowdhury, "Feminist Negotiations"; Karim, "Demystifying Micro-Credit."

83. D'Souza, *The Enemy at Home*, 2.

84. Ibid., 21, 173.

85. Ibid., 26.

86. Ibid., 27.

87. Ibid., 173.

88. El-Rouayheb, *Before Homosexuality in the Arab-Islamic World, 1500–1800*; Massad, *Desiring Arabs*; Najmabadi, *Women with Mustaches and Men without Beards*; Ze'evi, *Producing Desire*.

89. See Bhaskaran, *Made in India*; Shahani, *Gay Bombay*; and Srivastava, ed., *Sexual Sites, Seminal Attitudes*.

90. Massad, *Desiring Arabs*, 417–18.

91. See, for example, Chauncey, *Gay New York*; D'Emilio, "Capitalism and Gay Identity"; Davis, *Women, Race, & Class*; Faderman, *Surpassing the Love of Men*;

Feinberg, *Lavender & Red*; Foucault, *The History of Sexuality*; Greenberg, *The Construction of Homosexuality*; Halperin, *One Hundred Years of Homosexuality and Other Essays on Greek Love*; Mumford, *Interzones*; Sedgwick, *The Epistemology of the Closet*; Somerville, *Queering the Color Line*; Stoler, *Race and the Education of Desire*.

92. Warner, *The Trouble with Normal*, esp. 41–80.

93. My argument here bears much in common with Puar's critique of what she calls "homonationalism." See Puar, *Terrorist Assemblages*.

94. On the politics of gay tourism generally, see Alexander, "Imperial Desire/Sexual Utopias"; Boone, "Vacation Cruises"; Cantú, *"De Ambiente"*; Puar, "Circuits of Sexualities."

95. Ehrenreich, "What Abu Ghraib Taught Me."

96. Ibid.

97. Ibid.

98. See, for example, Apel, *Imagery of Lynching*.

99. See Attica Brothers Legal Defense, ed., *Fighting Back!*; Clark, *Attica*; New York State Special Commission on Attica, *Attica*; Oswald, *Attica*.

100. Massad, *Desiring Arabs*, 43.

101. Whitaker, *Unspeakable Love*, 42.

102. Personal interview with Rasha Moumneh, 18 September 2008.

103. Massad, *Desiring Arabs*, 43.

104. Personal interview with Rasha Moumneh, 18 September 2008.

105. Moumneh, "Helem at Montreal OutGames 2006."

106. *Baehr v. Lewin*.

107. *The Constitution of the State of Hawai'i*, Article I, Section 23.

108. American Friends Service Committee, "Making Respectful Travel Choices," 211–12.

109. Ibid., 210.

110. Na Mamo O Hawai'i, "Open Letter to the LGBT Community," 215.

111. American Friends Service Committee, "Making Respectful Travel Choices," 211.

112. Ibid., 213.

113. See Henríquez, *Juchitán de las locas*.

114. Zapatista Army of National Liberation (EZLN), "Sixth Declaration of the Selva Lacandona."

4. Do Prisons Make Better Men?

1. McGruder and Hudlin, "A Date with the Health Inspector."

2. Parenti, *Lockdown America*, 190–93.

3. Levinson and Fontana, *Oz*.

4. Kohan et al., *Will & Grace*; Cowen, Jonas, and Lipman, *Queer as Folk*.

5. On the threatened NAACP boycott, see Consoli, "Good Posture"; Doby, "Networks Bow to NAACP Heat"; McClellan, "NAACP Decries TV 'Whitewash'"; Wang, "NAACP Mulls Network Boycott"; Wynter, "Networks Need to Find a Better Balance with Minority Roles."

6. U.S. Department of Justice, *Prisoners in 2005*; U.S. Department of Justice, *Probation and Parole in the United States, 2005*; Pew Center on the States, *One in 100*, 6.

7. Some of the best recent work to address such analogies include Davis, *Are Prisons Obsolete?* 22–39; James, ed., *The New Abolitionists*; and Rodríguez, *Forced Passages*, 223–55.

8. See, for example, U.S. Department of Justice, *Prison and Jail Inmates at Midyear 2006*; U.S. Department of Justice, *Jails in Indian Country, 2004*.

9. Foundation for National Progress, "Debt to Society"; see also Prison Policy Initiative, "Racial Disparities in Incarceration by State, 2000." Data for Native Hawaiians and for Pacific Islanders are very difficult to obtain. The Foundation for National Progress, for example, appears to group Native Hawaiians with Asians when reporting incarceration rates in Hawai'i. According to a report by the Hawai'i Department of Public Safety, there was a daily average of 5127 inmates assigned to Hawaiian prisons and jails in 2000 (this number includes those contracted out to prisons on the mainland), while the population of the state that same year was 1,211,537. The Prison Policy Initiative, however, reports that in 2000, Native Hawaiians made up 9.4 percent of the population of the state (113, 884) and 22.3 percent of the population in the state's prisons and jails (1143). See Table 2-4, "Historical Population Assigned Counts," in Hawai'i (State of), *10-Year Corrections Master Plan Update*, 2-5; U.S. Census Bureau, "Hawai'i Quick Facts"; Wagner, "Native Hawaiians Are Overrepresented in Hawai'i's Prisons and Jails." See also Wagner, "Why Are So Many Native Hawaiians Incarcerated in Minnesota?"

10. Rumbaut et al., "Debunking the Myth of Immigrant Criminality."

11. Ibid., Table 3.

12. Wolf et al., *Law & Order*; Bruckheimer et al., *CSI: Crime Scene Investigation*; Kavanaugh et al., *America's Most Wanted*; Barbour, *Cops*.

13. A notable exception to the mainstream media blackout on prison issues was an article in the *New York Times* by Adam Liptak, published in 2008 as part of a series on aspects of the U.S. criminal justice system that are unique in comparison to other nations. See Liptak, "Inmate Count in U.S. Dwarfs Other Nations."

14. U.S. Department of Justice, *Prisoners in 2006*, 8. See also Mauer, *Race to Incarcerate*, 30–35 and 166–74.

15. See, for example, Ayers, *Vengeance and Justice*; Blomberg and Lucken, *American Penology*; Cohen, "Negro Involuntary Servitude in the South, 1865–1940"; Curtin, *Black Prisoners and Their World, Alabama, 1865–1900*; Davis, *Are*

Prisons Obsolete?; Foucault, *Discipline and Punish*; Freedman, *Their Sisters' Keepers*; Gilmore, *Golden Gulag*; Mauer, "The Causes and Consequences of Prison Growth in the United States"; Morris and Rothman, eds., *The Oxford History of the Prison*; Salvatore and Aguirre, ed., *The Birth of the Penitentiary in Latin America*; Shelden, "From Slave to Caste Society"; Staples, *The Culture of Surveillance*; Sullivan, *The Prison Reform Movement*; Wacquant, "The New 'Peculiar Institution.'"

16. See, among others, Baynton, "Disability and the Justification of Inequality in American History"; Davis, *Are Prisons Obsolete?* 67–68; and Garland-Thomson, "Integrating Disability, Transforming Feminist Theory."

17. See Davis, *Are Prisons Obsolete?* 45; Freedman, *Their Sisters' Keepers*, 10–11; and Zedner, "Wayward Sisters," 295–96.

18. See Bentham, *The Panopticon Writings*; Foucault, *Discipline and Punish*, 135–228; Rothman, "Perfecting the Prison"; and Rotman, "The Failure of Reform."

19. On the history and effects of this generalization of punishment, see Foucault, *Discipline and Punish*, 73–103, 293–308.

20. Caster, *Prisons, Race, and Masculinity*, 9. See also Patrick-Stamp, "Numbers That Are Not New."

21. Mauer, *Race to Incarcerate*, 5.

22. See Foucault, *Discipline and Punish*, 104–31; James, *Resisting State Violence*, 24–43.

23. On the informal racialization of Mexican Americans, see, among others, Michael Calderón-Zaks, "Constructing the 'Mexican Race.'"

24. For more extended accounts, see Rotman, "The Failure of Reform"; Rothman, "Perfecting the Prison."

25. See Wines, ed., *Transactions of the National Congress on Penitentiary and Reformatory Discipline*.

26. "Elmira: Nation's First Reformatory."

27. Salvatore and Aguirre, "The Birth of the Penitentiary in Latin America," 18. See also Aguirre, *The Criminals of Lima and Their Worlds*.

28. The dates for Reconstruction are generally uncontroversial, typically extending from the end of the Civil War in 1865 to the withdrawal of the last federal troops from the South by President Hayes in 1877. Dates for the Civil Rights Movement are the subject of much more debate. I have chosen to use the Supreme Court ruling against racially restrictive housing covenants, *Shelley v. Kraemer*, and the desegregation of the armed forces in 1948 as a starting point, ending in 1972 with the passage of the Equal Employment Opportunity Act, the acquittal of Black communist Angela Davis, and the release of Black Panther leader Huey P. Newton from prison in California.

29. Many scholars have written on the interrelation between the Black Codes, the convict lease system, and the racialization of prisons in the South during this period. See, for example, Cohen, "Negro Involuntary Servitude in the South,

1865–1940"; Curtin, *Black Prisoners and Their World, Alabama, 1865–1900*; Davis, *Are Prisons Obsolete?*, 22–39; Fierce, *Slavery Revisited*; Foner, *Reconstruction*; Lichtenstein, *Twice the Work of Free Labor*; Mancini, *One Dies, Get Another*; Oshinsky, *"Worse Than Slavery"*; Shelden, "From Slave to Caste Society"; Wilson, *The Black Codes of the South*.

30. Ayers, *Vengeance and Justice*, 61.

31. Fierce, *Slavery Revisited*, 148–49.

32. Curtin, *Black Prisoners and Their World, Alabama, 1865–1900*, 218n6.

33. Davis, *Are Prisons Obsolete?*, 33.

34. Fierce, *Slavery Revisited*, 111.

35. In addition to the works discussed at length in this section, see Davis, "Hell Factories in the Field"; Gilmore, *Golden Gulag*; Mauer, "The Causes and Consequences of Prison Growth in the United States"; Wacquant, "New 'Peculiar Institution.'"

36. See, among others, Blomberg, "Beyond Metaphors"; Blomberg and Lucken, *American Penology*, 224–29; Foucault, *Discipline and Punish*, 298–306; Hames-García, *Fugitive Thought*, 148–64; Rotman, "The Failure of Reform"; Staples, *The Culture of Surveillance*; Sullivan, *The Prison Reform Movement*.

37. Gilmore, "Globalisation and U.S. Prison Growth."

38. Andrews, "The Bretton Woods Agreement as an Invitation to Struggle," 91.

39. Cohen, "Bretton Woods System."

40. Triffin, *Gold and the Dollar Crisis*; Cohen, "Bretton Woods System"; and Gavin, "The Gold Battles within the Cold War."

41. *Mickey Spillane's Mike Hammer* (1958–59) constitutes an exception, due to its violence and vigilantism, but it met with strong criticism and only aired for two seasons. Indeed, at the time, the television journal *TV Guide* called it "easily the worst show on TV" (Nelson, "Darren McGavin, 83"). Patrick, *Perry Mason*; Meyer, Webb, and Meshekoff, *Dragnet*; Revue Studios, *Mickey Spillane's Mike Hammer*.

42. Examples include the following: Martin, *The F.B.I.* (1965–74); Webb, *Dragnet* (a reprisal, 1967–70); Chermak et al., *Ironside* (1967–75) (a major change of character for *Perry Mason* star Raymond Burr); Geller, *Mannix* (1967–75); Spelling and Thomas, *The Mod Squad* (1968–73); Webb, *Adam 12* (1968–75); Freeman and Leacock, *Hawaii Five-0* (1968–80).

43. See, for example, the following: Hargrove et al., *Columbo* (1971–78); Martin, *The Streets of San Francisco* (1972–77); Rapf and Mann, *Kojak* (1973–78); Gerber, *Police Story* (1973–78); Gerber, *Police Woman* (1974–78); Goldberg and Spelling, *S.W.A.T.* (1975–76); Cannell et al., *Baretta* (1975–78); Goldberg and Spelling, *Starsky & Hutch* (1975–79); Moessinger et al., *Quincy, M.E.* (1976–83); Rabwin and Rosner, *CHiPs* (1977–83).

44. Shows from this period include the following: Bochco and Kozoll, *Hill Street Blues* (1981–87); Spelling and Goldberg, *T. J. Hooker* (1982–86); Rosenzweig,

Cagney & Lacey (1982–88); Bernstein, *Mickey Spillane's Mike Hammer* (1984–87); Mann and Yerkovich, *Miami Vice* (1984–89); Huggins et al., *Hunter* (1984–91); Wilder, *Spenser for Hire* (1985–88); McAdams, *The Equalizer* (1985–89); Hasburgh and Cannell, *21 Jump Street* (1987–91); Silverman et al., *In the Heat of the Night* (1988–94).

45. Examples include the following: Goldberg and Spelling, *Charlie's Angels* (1976–81); Goldberg and Spelling, *Hart to Hart* (1979–84); Bellisario, Larson, and Selleck, *Magnum, P.I.* (1980–88); Gleason, *Remington Steele* (1982–87); Cannell and Lupo, *The A-Team* (1983–87); Fischer, Lansbury, and Moessinger, *Murder, She Wrote* (1984–96); Daniel and Caron, *Moonlighting* (1985–89); Silverman et al., *Matlock* (1986–95); Carter and Spotnitz, *The X-Files* (1993–2002); Breckman et al., *Monk* (2002–present).

46. See, for example, the following: Wolf et al., *Law & Order* (1990–present); Fontana, Levinson, and Bromell, *Homicide: Life on the Street* (1993–99); Bochco et al., *NYPD Blue* (1993–2005); Wolf, Kern, and Kurt, *New York Undercover* (1994–98).

47. In addition to numerous failed series, this period saw the successful debuts of the following: Kotcheff et al., *Law & Order: Special Victims Unit* (1999–present); Bruckheimer et al., *CSI: Crime Scene Investigation* (2000–present); Grazer et al., *24* (2001–present); Balcer et al., *Law & Order: Criminal Intent* (2001–present); Bruckheimer et al., *CSI: Miami* (2002–present); Kostroff-Noble, Simon, and Colesberry, *The Wire* (2002–2008); Littman et al., *Without a Trace* (2002–present); Littman et al., *Cold Case* (2003–present); Bellisario, Johnson, and Brennan, *NCIS: Naval Criminal Investigative Service* (2003–present); Bruckheimer et al., *CSI: NY* (2004–present); Josephson, Hanson, and Pontell, *Bones* (2005–present); Falacci et al., *Numb3rs* (2005–present); Spera et al., *Criminal Minds* (2005–present); Grammer et al., *Medium* (2005–present).

48. Littman et al., *Cold Case*; Heus and Kopp, *In Justice.*

49. Kavanaugh et al., *America's Most Wanted*; Barbour, *Cops.*

50. Parenti, *Lockdown America*, 12. The Haldeman quotation is from Haldeman, *The Haldeman Diaries*, 53.

51. Parenti, *Lockdown America*, 69–110. For more on the process and effects of housing discrimination during the mid-twentieth century, see Lipsitz, *The Possessive Investment in Whiteness*, 5–8, 25–33.

52. Sudbury, "Introduction," xvii.

53. Richie, "Queering Antiprison Work," 80. For other engagements specifically with homosexuality and prisons, see Burton-Rose, "The Anti-Exploits of Men against Sexism, 1977–78"; Kunzel, "Lessons in Being Gay"; Mead, "Men against Sexism."

54. Incite! ed., *Color of Violence*, 321.

55. From its website: *Incite!* http://www.incite-national.org (24 February 2008).

56. Critical Resistance and Incite! "Gender Violence and the Prison-Industrial Complex."

57. Díaz-Cotto, *Chicana Lives and Criminal Justice*, 21.

58. Ibid., 23.

59. See, for example, Sabo, Kupers, and London, "Gender and the Politics of Punishment"; Messerschmidt, "Masculinities, Crime, and Prison." For my own earlier attempt to address these and other related issues of masculinity and imprisonment, see my reading of the works of Piri Thomas and Miguel Piñero in Hames-García, *Fugitive Thought*, 141–89.

60. These claims are well established in empirical studies of sentencing and imprisonment. See, for example, Mann, *Unequal Justice*, 115–219; Mauer, *Race to Incarcerate*, 130–56; Shine and Mauer, *Does the Punishment Fit the Crime?*

61. Sabo, Kupers, and London, "Gender and the Politics of Punishment," 14.

62. Davis, *Are Prisons Obsolete?* 73.

63. See, for example, Freedman, *Their Sisters' Keepers*; Davis, *Are Prisons Obsolete?* 60–83.

64. See Patterson, *Slavery and Social Death*.

65. Levinson and Fontana, *Oz*.

66. Most criticism of *Oz* has focused on its violence and its "realism" or lack thereof. See, for example, Schuster, "Framing the (W)Hole," 99–153; Yousman, *Prime Time Prisons on U.S. TV*, 141–69.

67. Chase et al., *The Sopranos*.

68. Not coincidentally, *Oz* executive producers Tom Fontana and Barry Levinson also served as executive producers (with Henry Bromell) for *Homicide*. Fontana, furthermore, wrote or cowrote all fifty-six episodes of *Oz* and worked as a writer on just over half of the episodes of *Homicide*. The only other hour-long primetime dramatic series on a major network to have a cast with fifty percent or more nonwhite actors that I can find is *I Spy* (1965–68), which had only two regularly recurring characters: U.S. espionage agents played by Robert Culp and Bill Cosby. At least two other hour-long dramas before *Oz* had degrees of success with half people of color in leading roles, although they did not run on major networks in primetime. *Street Justice* (1991–93), another crime-related series, appeared in syndication, while a family drama series featuring all female leads, *Any Day Now* (1998–2002), ran on the Lifetime network. Of course, one of the most relevant television dramas since *Oz* in relation to race and sexuality is the HBO crime series, *The Wire* (2002–2008), which, like *Oz*, shared some production staff with *Homicide*. A fuller discussion of *The Wire* is, unfortunately, outside the scope of this chapter. See Mann and Yerkovich, *Miami Vice*; Hasburgh and Cannell, *21 Jump Street*; Fontana, Levinson, and Bromell, *Homicide*; Wolf, Kern, and Kurt, *New York Undercover*; Leonard, *I Spy*; Donahue, Glassner, and Levinson, *Street Justice*; Miller et al., *Any Day Now*; Kostroff-Noble, Simon, and Colesberry, *The Wire*.

69. Levinson and Fontana, *Oz*; Levinson, Fontana, and Finnerty, *Oz*.

70. See Yousman, *Prime Time Prisons on U.S. TV*, 143–56.

71. Levinson and Fontana, *Oz*, first season, episode no. 8, "A Game of Checkers."

72. Baum, *The Wizard of Oz*.

73. Levinson and Fontana, *Oz*, first season, episode no. 1, "The Routine," with commentary. See also Yousman, *Prime Time Prisons on U.S. TV*, 155.

74. Levinson and Fontana, *Oz*, first season, episode no. 1, "The Routine."

75. For a general overview of prison films and the conventions with which they work, see Rafter, *Shots in the Mirror*, 163–88.

76. Levinson and Fontana, *Oz*, first season, episode no. 1, "The Routine."

77. Levinson and Fontana, *Oz*, first season, episodes no. 3, "God's Chillin'" and no. 4, "Capital P."

78. Wlodarz, "Maximum Insecurity," 71.

79. Levinson and Fontana, *Oz*, first season, episodes no. 1, "The Routine," no. 3, "God's Chillin'," and no. 4, "Capital P."

80. Wlodarz, "Maximum Insecurity," 73. See Levinson and Fontana, *Oz*, first season, episode no. 7, "Plan B" and second season, episodes no. 1, "The Tip" and no. 2, "Ancient Tribes."

81. See, for example, Levinson and Fontana, *Oz*, second season, episode no. 6, "Strange Bedfellows."

82. Ferber, "Prisoners of Love," 46.

83. Ibid.

84. Wlodarz, "Maximum Insecurity," 84. See Levinson and Fontana, *Oz*, second season, episode no. 6, "Strange Bedfellows."

85. Yousman gives a slightly different interpretation of the role of sexuality and black masculinity in *Oz*. See Yousman, *Prime Time Prisons on U.S. TV*, 152–60.

86. Wlodarz, "Maximum Insecurity," 77.

87. Consider, for example, the cross-dressing HIV-positive murderer who for the most part lacks interiority, serving instead as a plot device to enable the death of a Mafia leader (Levinson and Fontana, *Oz*, third season, episodes no. 6, "Cruel and Unusual Punishments" and no. 7, "Secret Identities"). For Hanlon's character, see Levinson and Fontana, *Oz*, second season, episode no. 4, "Losing Your Appeal," and Levinson, Fontana, and Finnerty, third season, episode no. 4, "Unnatural Disasters."

88. Wlodarz, "Maximum Insecurity," 78.

89. Ibid., 86.

90. Ibid., 63.

91. See, for example, Carby, *Reconstructing Womanhood*; Hondagneu-Sotelo and Messner, "Gender Displays and Men's Power"; Lugones, "Heterosexualism and the Colonial/Modern Gender System"; Massad, *Desiring Arabs*; Najmabadi, *Women with Mustaches and Men without Beards*; Sigal, ed., *Infamous Desire*; Teaiwa, "Bikinis and Other S/Pacific N/Oceans."

92. Levinson and Fontana, *Oz*, first season, episode no. 2, "Visits, Conjugal and Otherwise."

93. See, for example, Siebers, *Disability Theory*, 135–75.

94. Siebers, "Disability as Masquerade," 13.

95. See Levinson and Fontana, *Oz*, first season, episode no. 3, "God's Chillin," and Levinson, Fontana, and Finnerty, *Oz*, fourth season, episode no. 3, "Bill of Wrongs."

96. Said's sentence is for arson, but his associated flashback merely shows an explosion, without any clear indication of his guilt. Levinson and Fontana, *Oz*, first season, episode no. 1, "The Routine."

97. Levinson, Fontana, and Finnerty, *Oz*, third season, episodes no. 4, "Unnatural Disasters" and no. 5, "U.S. Male," and Levinson, Fontana, and Finnerty, *Oz*, fourth season, episode no. 3, "The Bill of Wrongs."

98. Levinson, Fontana, and Finnerty, *Oz*, fourth season, episode no. 3, "The Bill of Wrongs."

99. Wlodarz, "Maximum Insecurity," 66, 80.

100. Díaz-Cotto, *Gender, Ethnicity, and the State*, 63. See also Hondagneu-Sotelo and Messner, "Gender Displays and Men's Power."

101. On the trope of black helper figures in white films, see Appiah, "'No Bad Nigger'"; Colombe, "White Hollywood's New Black Boogeyman"; Gabbard, *Black Magic*, 143–75; Hicks, "Hoodoo Economics"; Kempley, "Movies' 'Magic Negro' Saves the Day—but at the Cost of His Soul." I am grateful to Kathleen Karlyn for first suggesting to me the relevance of this figure for thinking about *Oz*.

102. Kempley, "Movies' 'Magic Negro' Saves the Day—but at the Cost of His Soul."

103. See, for example, the performances of Scatman Crothers in *The Shining* (1980); Whoopi Goldberg in *Ghost* (1990); Bill Cobbs in *The Hudsucker Proxy* (1994); Michael Clarke Duncan in *The Green Mile* (1999); Lawrence Fishburne in *The Matrix* (1999); Gloria Foster in *The Matrix* (1999) and *The Matrix Reloaded* (2003); Chris Rock in *Dogma* (1999); Gabriel Casseus in *Bedazzled* (2000); Don Cheadle in *The Family Man* (2000); Chris Thomas King and Lee Weaver in *O Brother Where Art Thou?* (2000); Will Smith in *The Legend of Bagger Vance* (2000); Mary Alice in *The Matrix Revolutions* (2003); and Morgan Freeman in *Bruce Almighty* (2003) and *Evan Almighty* (2007).

104. See, for example, Hattie McDaniel in *Gone with the Wind* (1939); Rex Ingram in *Sahara* (1943); James Baskett in *The Song of the South* (1946); Sidney Poitier in *The Defiant Ones* (1958), *Lilies of the Field* (1963), *To Sir, with Love* (1967), and *Guess Who's Coming to Dinner* (1967); Louis Gosset Jr. in *An Officer and a Gentleman* (1982); Whoopi Goldberg in *Clara's Heart* (1988) and *Sister Act* (1992); Morgan Freeman in *Driving Miss Daisy* (1989), *The Shawshank Redemption* (1994), *Se7en* (1995), and *Million Dollar Baby* (2004); Halle Berry in *Bulworth* (1998); Guy Torry in *American History X* (1998); and Cicely Tyson in *Because of Winn-Dixie* (2005).

105. These include the portrayals by McDaniel in *Gone with the Wind* (1939); Poitier in *Lilies of the Field* (1963); Gosset Jr. in *An Officer and a Gentlemen* (1982); Goldberg in *Ghost* (1990); and Freeman in *Million Dollar Baby* (2004). Berry's performance in *Monster's Ball* (2001) could make a debatable addition to this list.

106. Barber, Birnbaum, and Shyamalan, *Unbreakable*.

107. Kempley, "Movies' 'Magic Negro' Saves the Day—but at the Cost of His Soul"; emphasis added.

108. Williams, *Playing the Race Card*, 3–9, 301–08.

109. McRuer, *Crip Theory*, 6–28; Mark et al., *As Good as It Gets*.

110. McRuer, *Crip Theory*, 18.

111. Beecher and Keller, for example, are grouped with Hill in the "Others" category by Em City administrators in the second season (Levinson and Fontana, *Oz*, second season, episode no. 2, "Ancient Tribes"). On Beecher's close relationship to Said, see, for example, Levinson, Fontana, and Finnerty, *Oz*, third season, episode no. 6, "Cruel and Unusual Punishments."

112. Human Rights Watch, "Incarcerated America," 2.

113. Levinson and Fontana, *Oz*, second season, episode no. 2, "Ancient Tribes."

114. The theme of family is developed in relation to Alvarez's character from the outset of the series. See Levinson and Fontana, *Oz*, first season, episode no. 2, "Visits, Conjugal and Otherwise."

115. Mastro, Behm-Morawitz, and Kopacz, "Exposure to Television Portrayals of Latinos."

116. Fryberg et al., "Of Warrior Chiefs and Indian Princesses."

117. Stowe, *Uncle Tom's Cabin*. For such a reading of Stowe's novel, see Railton, "Black Slaves and White Readers." See also Williams, *Playing the Race Card*.

Conclusion

1. "Poll," 22.

2. Calem, Hershaff, and Wachter, "Neighborhood Patterns of Subprime Lending," 619.

3. DeNavas-Walt, Proctor, and Smith, "Income, Poverty, and Health Insurance Coverage in the United States," 8.

4. See, for example, Oliver and Shapiro, *Black Wealth/White Wealth*.

5. "Poll," 26.

6. Frank, "President Obama and Gay Rights."

7. Galinsky, "U.S. Gov't Set To Triple Immigration 'Audits'"; Egelko, "Group's Leader Urges New Strategy on Immigrant Rights."

8. The campaign address in question is the one that finally convinced me to vote for Obama; see Obama, "A More Perfect Union." See also Sappenfield, "Since Beer Summit, America Has Seen 'Two Good People.'"

9. Baker and Lewis, "Favorites of Left Don't Make Obama's Court List."

10. Sotomayor, "A Latina Judge's Voice," 92.

11. Lockhead, "Right Calls Sotomayor Racist Over Line in Talk."

12. Bravin and Koppel, "Nominee's Criminal Rulings Tilt to Right of Souter."

13. Zhu, "Renowned Af-Am Professor Gates Arrested for Disorderly Conduct."

14. Drash, "911 Caller in Gates Arrest Never Referred to 'Black Suspects.'"

15. Saltzman, "Sergeant at Eye of Storm Says He Won't Apologize."

16. Ford and Schapiro, "Sgt. James Crowley"; Goodnough, "Harvard Professor Jailed."

17. Colbert, "The Word—Neutral Man's Burden"; Dowd, "White Man's Last Stand"; Stewart, "White Men Can't Judge—Sotomayor."

18. Washington, "Latino Differences Muted in Sotomayor Celebration."

19. My thanks to Ernesto Martínez, Paula Moya, and Ramón Saldívar for conversations about Obama, Sotomayor, Gates, and the "post-race" moment in the United States during a writing retreat while I completed final edits to this book.

Bibliography

Abu-Lughod, Janet L. *Before European Hegemony: The World System A.D. 1250–1350.* New York: Oxford University Press, 1989.

Abu-Lughod, Lila. "Writing against Culture." In *Recapturing Anthropology: Working in the Present,* edited by Richard Gabriel Fox, 137–62. Santa Fe, N.Mex.: School of American Research Press/University of Washington Press, 1991.

Aguirre, Carlos. *The Criminals of Lima and Their Worlds: The Prison Experience, 1850–1935.* Durham, N.C.: Duke University Press, 2005.

Aiavao, Tunumafono Apelu. "Who's Playing Naked Now? Religion and Samoan Culture." *Pacific Perspective* 12, no. 2 (1983): 8–10.

al-Ghafari, Iman. "Is There a Lesbian Identity in the Arab Culture?" *Al-Raida* 20, no. 99 (2002–3): 86–90.

"Al-Jazeera TV Airs Parts of Al-Zawahiri Tape Criticizing USA." BBC Worldwide Monitoring, February 10, 2005.

Alcoff, Linda Martín. *Visible Identities: Race, Gender, and the Self.* New York: Oxford University Press, 2005.

———. "Cultural Feminism versus Post-Structuralism: The Identity Crisis in Feminist Theory." *Signs* 13, no. 3 (1988): 405–36.

Alcoff, Linda Martín, and Satya P. Mohanty. "Reconsidering Identity Politics: An Introduction." In *Identity Politics Reconsidered,* edited by Alcoff, Hames-García, Mohanty, and Moya, 1–9.

Alcoff, Linda Martín, and Elizabeth Potter, eds. *Feminist Epistemologies.* New York: Routledge, 1993.

Alcoff, Linda Martín, Michael Hames-García, Satya P. Mohanty, and Paula M. L. Moya, eds. *Identity Politics Reconsidered.* New York: Palgrave Macmillan, 2006.

Aldrich, Robert. *Colonialism and Homosexuality.* New York: Routledge, 2003.

Alexander, M. Jacqui. "Imperial Desire/Sexual Utopias: White Gay Capital and Transnational Tourism." In *Talking Visions: Multicultural Feminism in a Transnational Age,* edited by Ella Shohat, 281–305. Cambridge, Mass.: MIT Press, 1998.

Almaguer, Tomás. "Chicano Men: A Cartography of Homosexual Identity and Behavior." *differences: A Journal of Feminist Cultural Studies* 3, no. 2 (1991): 75–100.

Altman, Dennis. "Globalization and the International Gay/Lesbian Movement." In *Handbook of Lesbian & Gay Studies*, edited by Diane Richardson and Steven Seidman, 415–25. New York: Sage, 2002.

American Friends Service Committee. Hawaiʻi Area Program. Hawaiʻi Gay Liberation Program & National Community Relations [Division]. "Making Respectful Travel Choices: Honoring Kanaka Maoli (Indigenous Hawaiian) Sovereignty & Human Rights." *GLQ* 8, no. 1–2 (2002): 209–14.

Americans for Legal Immigration–PAC. "Possible Illegal Alien & U.S. Guardsman Killed Iraqi after Sex." December 20, 2004. http://www.alipac.us.

Amin, Samir. *Eurocentrism*. Translated by Russell Moore. New York: Monthly Review Press, 1989.

Amirthalingam, Kumaralingam. "Balancing Evidence and Rhetoric in Law Reform." *The Straights Times*, 5 December 2007.

Andrews, David M. "The Bretton Woods Agreement as an Invitation to Struggle." In *The Economy as a Polity: The Political Constitution of Contemporary Capitalism*, edited by Christian Joerges, Bo Stråth, and Peter Wagner, 77–98. London: UCL Press, 2005.

Anzaldúa, Gloria. *Borderlands/La Frontera: The New Mestiza*. San Francisco: Spinsters/Aunt Lute, 1987.

Anzaldúa, Gloria, ed. *Making Face, Making Soul/Haciendo Caras: Creative and Critical Perspectives by Feminists of Color*. San Francisco: Aunt Lute Books, 1995.

Apel, Dora. *Imagery of Lynching: Black Men, White Women, and the Mob*. New Brunswick, N.J.: Rutgers University Press, 2004.

Appiah, Kwame Anthony. *In My Father's House: Africa in the Philosophy of Culture*. Oxford: Oxford University Press, 1992.

——. "'No Bad Nigger': Blacks as the Ethical Principle in the Movies." In *Media Spectacles*, edited by Marjorie Garber, Jann Matlock, and Rebecca L. Walkowitz, 77–90. New York: Routledge, 1993.

——. "Race, Culture, Identity: Misunderstood Connections." In *Color Conscious: The Political Morality of Race*, by K. Anthony Appiah and Amy Gutmann, 30–105. Princeton, N.J.: Princeton University Press, 1996.

Arce, Carlos H., Edward Murguía, and W. Parker Frisbie. "Phenotype and Life Chances among Chicanos." *Hispanic Journal of Behavioral Sciences* 9, no. 1 (1987): 19–32.

Aronson, Ronald. *After Marxism*. New York: Guilford Press, 1995.

Asad, Talal, ed. *Anthropology and the Colonial Encounter*. Atlantic Highlands, N.J.: Humanities Press, 1973.

Attica Brothers Legal Defense, ed. and comp. *Fighting Back! Attica Memorial Book*. Buffalo, N.Y.: Attica Brothers Legal Defense, 1974.

Ayers, Edward L. *Vengeance and Justice: Crime and Punishment in the 19th-Century American South*. New York: Oxford University Press, 1984.

Baehr v. Lewin 852 P.2d 44 (Hawai'i 1993).

Baer, Brian James. "Kandahar: Closely Watched Pashtuns." *Gay & Lesbian Review Worldwide* 10, no. 2 (2003): 25–27.

Bailey, J. Michael. *The Man Who Would Be Queen: The Science of Gender-Bending and Transsexualism.* Washington, D.C.: Joseph Henry Press, 2003.

Baker, Peter, and Neil A. Lewis. "Favorites of Left Don't Make Obama's Court List." *New York Times,* May 26, 2009. http://www.nytimes.com.

Balcer, Rene, Peter Jankowski, Dick Wolf, Warren Leight, Fred Berner, Norberto Barba, John David Coles, Walon Green, Ed Zuckerman, and Robert Nathan, executive producers. *Law & Order: Criminal Intent* [Television Series]. USA: National Broadcasting Company (NBC), 2001–present.

Baldus, David C., Charles Pulaski, and George Woodworth. "Comparative Review of Death Sentences: An Empirical Study of the Georgia Experience." *Journal of Criminal Law and Criminology* 74, no. 3 (1983): 661–753.

Bambara, Toni Cade. *The Black Woman: An Anthology.* 1970. New York: Washington Square Press, 2005.

Banks, Tyra, Ken Mok, Anthony Dominici, and Daniel Soiseth, executive producers. *America's Next Top Model* [Television Series]. USA: United Paramount Network (UPN), 2003–6; CW Television Network, 2006–present.

Barad, Karen. "Meeting the Universe Halfway: Realism and Social Constructivism without Contradiction." In *Feminism, Science, and the Philosophy of Science,* edited by Lynn Hankinson Nelson and Jack Nelson, 161–94. Dordrecht, Netherlands: Kluwer, 1996.

———. "Posthumanist Performativity: Toward an Understanding of How Matter Comes to Matter." *Signs* 28, no. 3 (2003): 801–31.

———. "Re(Con)Figuring Space, Time, and Matter." In *Feminist Locations: Global and Local, Theory and Practice,* edited by Marianne DeKoven, 75–109. New Brunswick, N.J.: Rutgers University Press, 2001.

Barber, Gary, and Roger Birnbaum, executive producers, and M. Night Shyamalan, director. *Unbreakable* [Motion Picture]. USA: Buena Vista Pictures, 2000.

Barbour, Malcolm, executive producer. *Cops* [Television Series]. USA: Fox Network, 1989–present.

Barreiro, Luis B., Guillaume Laval, Hélène Quach, Etienne Patin, and Lluís Quintana-Murci. "Natural Selection Has Driven Population Differentiation in Modern Humans." *Nature Genetics* 40, no. 3 (2008): 340–45.

Battersby, Christine. *The Phenomenal Woman: Feminist Metaphysics and the Patterns of Identity.* New York: Routledge, 1998.

Baudrillard, Jean. *The Mirror of Production.* Translated by Mark Poster. St. Louis, Mo.: Telos Press, 1975.

Baum, L. Frank. *The Wizard of Oz.* 1900. New York: Bobbs-Merrill, 1944.

Baynton, Douglas C. "Disability and the Justification of Inequality in American

History." In *The New Disability History: American Perspectives*, edited by Paul K. Longmore and Lauri Umamsky, 33–57. New York: New York University Press, 2001.

Bell, Bernard, Emily Grosholz, and James Stewart, eds. *W. E. B. Du Bois on Race and Culture*. New York: Routledge, 1996.

Bellisario, Donald P., Chas. Floyd Johnson, Shane Brennan, executive producers. *NCIS: Naval Criminal Investigative Service* [Television Series]. USA: Columbia Broadcasting System (CBS), 2003–present.

Bellisario, Donald P., Glen A. Larson, and Tom Selleck, executive producers. *Magnum, P. I.* [Television Series]. USA: Columbia Broadcasting System (CBS), 1980–88.

Bello, Walden, Shea Cunningham, and Bill Rau. *Dark Victory: The United States and Global Poverty*. 2nd ed. London: Pluto Press, with Food First and Transnational Institute [TNI], 1999.

Bentham, Jeremy. *The Panopticon Writings*. Edited by Miran Božovič. London: Verso, 1995.

Bernal, Martin. *Black Athena: The Afroasiatic Roots of Classical Civilization, Volume 1: The Fabrication of Ancient Greece 1785–1985*. New Brunswick, N.J.: Rutgers University Press, 1987.

Bernstein, Jay, executive producer. *Mickey Spillane's Mike Hammer* [Television Series]. USA: Columbia Broadcasting System (CBS), 1984–87.

Bhaskaran, Suparna. *Made in India: Decolonizations, Queer Sexualities, Trans/National Projects*. New York: Palgrave Macmillan, 2004.

Blascovich, Jim, Steven J. Spencer, Diane Quinn, and Claude Steele. "African Americans and High Blood Pressure: The Role of Stereotype Threat." *Psychological Science* 12, no. 3 (2001): 225–29.

Blomberg, Thomas G. "Beyond Metaphors: Penal Reform as Net-Widening." In *Punishment and Social Control*, edited by Thomas G. Blomberg and Stanley Cohen, 45–62. Edison, N.J.: Transaction Publishers, 1995.

Blomberg, Thomas G., and Karol Lucken. *American Penology: A History of Control*. New York: Aldine de Gruyter, 2000.

Bochco, Steven, and Michael Kozoll, executive producers. *Hill Street Blues* [Television Series]. USA: National Broadcasting Company (NBC), 1981–87.

Bochco, Steven, Mark Tinker, David Milch, Matt Olmstead, Nicholas Wootton, Bill Clark, and William M. Finkelstein, executive producers. *NYPD Blue* [Television Series]. USA: American Broadcasting Company (ABC), 1993–2005.

Boggs, James, and Grace Lee Boggs. *Revolution and Evolution in the Twentieth Century*. New York: Monthly Review Press, 1974.

Bohr, Niels. "Quantum Physics and Philosophy: Causality and Complementarity." In *Essays 1958–1962 on Atomic Physics and Human Knowledge*, 1–7. New York: Interscience Publishers, 1963.

Bombardieri, Marcella. "Summers' Remarks on Women Draw Fire." *Boston Globe*, January 17, 2005. http://www.boston.com.

Boone, Joseph. "Vacation Cruises; or, the Homoerotics of Orientalism." In *Postcolonial, Queer: Theoretical Intersections*, edited by John C. Hawley, 43–78. Albany: State University of New York Press, 2001.

Bowen, Peter. "Collect Yourself." *Outweek*, June 27, 1990, 108–9. http://outweek.net.

Bowen, William G., Martin A. Kurzweil, and Eugene M. Tobin. *Equity and Excellence in American Higher Education*. Charlottesville: University of Virginia Press, 2005.

Boyd, Richard N. "How to Be a Moral Realist." In *Essays on Moral Realism*, edited by Geoffrey Sayre-McCord, 181–228. Ithaca, N.Y.: Cornell University Press, 1988.

Bravin, Jess, and Nathan Koppel. "Nominee's Criminal Rulings Tilt to Right of Souter." *The Wall Street Journal*, June 5, 2009. http://online.wsj.com.

Breckman, Andy, David Hoberman, Tony Shalhoub, Randall Zisk, and Rob Thompson, executive producers. *Monk* [Television Series]. USA: USA Cable Network, 2002–present.

Brown, Wendy. *States of Injury: Power and Freedom in Late Modernity*. Princeton, N.J.: Princeton University Press, 1995.

Bruckheimer, Jerry, Ann Donahue, Jonathan Littman, Carol Mendelsohn, Anthony E. Zuiker, Danny Cannon, Nancy Miller, Sam Strangis, David Black, and Stephen Zito, executive producers. *CSI: Miami* [Television Series]. USA: Columbia Broadcasting System (CBS), 2002–present.

Bruckheimer, Jerry, Carol Mendelsohn, Jonathan Littman, William Petersen, Cynthia Chvatal, Naren Shankar, Ann Donahue, Anthony E. Zuiker, and Danny Cannon, executive producers. *CSI: Crime Scene Investigation* [Television Series]. USA: Columbia Broadcasting System (CBS), 2000–present.

Bruckheimer, Jerry, Jonathan Littman, Anthony E. Zuiker, Pam Veasey, Peter M. Lenkov, Danny Cannon, Ann Donahue, Carol Mendelsohn, and Andrew Lipsitz, executive producers. *CSI: NY* [Television Series]. USA: Columbia Broadcasting System (CBS), 2004–present.

Burton-Rose, Daniel. "The Anti-Exploits of Men against Sexism, 1977–78." In *Prison Masculinities*, edited by Sabo, Kupers, and London, 224–29.

Bustos-Aguilar, Pedro. "Mister Don't Touch the Banana: Notes on the Popularity of the Ethnosexed Body South of the Border." *Critique of Anthropology* 15, no. 2 (June 1995): 149–70.

Butler, Judith. *Gender Trouble: Feminism and the Subversion of Identity*. New York: Routledge, 1990.

Butler, Judith, and Joan Wallach Scott, eds. *Feminists Theorize the Political*. New York: Routledge, 1992.

Calderón-Zaks, Michael. "Constructing the 'Mexican Race': Racial Formation and

Empire Building, 1886–1940." PhD diss., Binghamton University, State University of New York, 2008.

Calem, Paul S., Jonathan E. Hershaff, and Susan M. Wachter. "Neighborhood Patterns of Subprime Lending: Evidence from Disparate Cities." *Housing Policy Debate* 15, no. 3 (2004): 603–22.

Cannell, Stephen J., and Frank Lupo, executive producers. *The A-Team* [Television Series]. USA: National Broadcasting Company (NBC), 1983–87.

Cannell, Stephen J., Roy Huggins, Bernard L. Kowalski, Anthony Spinner, and Leigh Vance, executive producers. *Baretta* [Television Series]. USA: American Broadcasting Company (ABC), 1975–78.

Cantú, Lionel, Jr. "*De Ambiente:* Queer Tourism and the Shifting Boundaries of Mexican Male Sexualities." *GLQ* 8, no. 1–2 (2002): 139–66.

———. "Entre Hombres/Between Men: Latino Masculinities and Homosexualities." In Hames-García and Martínez, eds., *Gay Latino Studies*, 147–67.

Carby, Hazel V. *Reconstructing Womanhood: The Emergence of the Afro-American Woman Novelist.* New York: Oxford University Press, 1987.

Carrier, Joseph. *De los Otros: Intimacy and Homosexuality among Mexican Men.* New York: Columbia University Press, 1995.

Carter, Chris, and Frank Spotnitz, executive producers. *The X-Files* [Television Series]. USA: Fox Network, 1993–2002.

Castells, Manuel. *The Power of Identity.* Malden, Mass.: Blackwell, 1997.

Caster, Peter. *Prisons, Race, and Masculinity in Twentieth-Century U.S. Literature and Film.* Columbus: Ohio State University, 2008.

Césaire, Aimé. *Discourse on Colonialism.* c1972. Translated by Joan Pinkham. New York: Monthly Review Press, 2000.

Chakrabarty, Dipesh. *Provincializing Europe: Postcolonial Thought and Historical Difference.* Princeton, N.J.: Princeton University Press, 2000.

Chase, David, Brad Grey, Ilene S. Landress, Terence Winter, Mitchell Burgess, and Robin Green, executive producers. *The Sopranos* [Television Series]. USA: Home Box Office (HBO), 1999–2007.

Chauncey, George. *Gay New York: Gender, Urban Culture, and the Making of the Gay Male World, 1890–1940.* New York: HarperCollins, 1994.

Chen, Christina Pei-Lin. "Provocation's Privileged Desire: The Provocation Doctrine, 'Homosexual Panic,' and the Non-Violent Unwanted Sexual Advance Defense." *Cornell Journal of Law and Public Policy* 10, no. 1 (2000): 195–235.

Chermak, Cy, Frank Price, Joel Rogosin, and Collier Young, executive producers. *Ironside* [Television Series]. USA: National Broadcasting Company (NBC), 1967–75.

Chowdhury, Elora Halim. "Feminist Negotiations: Contesting Narratives of the Campaign against Acid Violence in Bangladesh." *Meridians: Feminism, Race, Transnationalism* 6, no. 1 (2005): 163–92.

Clark, Richard X. *The Brothers of Attica*. Edited by Leonard Levitt. New York: Links Books, 1973.

Clifford, James. *The Predicament of Culture: Twentieth-Century Ethnography, Literature, and Art*. Cambridge, Mass.: Harvard University Press, 1988.

Cohen, Benjamin J. "Bretton Woods System." In *The Routledge Encyclopedia of International Political Economy*, edited by R. J. Barry Jones, 95–102. New York: Routledge, 2002.

Cohen, William. "Negro Involuntary Servitude in the South, 1865–1940: A Preliminary Analysis." In *African American Life in the Post-Emancipation South*, edited by Nieman, 35–64.

Colbert, Stephen. "The Word—Neutral Man's Burden" [Online Video]. *The Colbert Report*, July 16, 2009. http://www.colbertnation.com.

Collins, Patricia Hill. *Black Feminist Thought: Knowledge, Consciousness, and the Politics of Empowerment*. Boston: Unwin Hyman, 1990.

Colombe, Audrey. "White Hollywood's New Black Boogeyman." *Jump Cut* 45 (Fall 2002). http://www.ejumpcut.org (accessed July 25, 2009).

Combahee River Collective. "A Black Feminist Statement." In *Capitalist Patriarchy and the Case for Socialist Feminism*, edited by Zillah R. Eisenstein, 362–72. New York: Monthly Review Press, 1979.

Comstock, Gary David. "Dismantling the Homosexual Panic Defense." *Law & Sexuality: A Review of Lesbian and Gay Legal Issues* 2 (1992): 81–102.

Consoli, John. "Good Posture." *Adweek Western Edition* 69, no. 46 (November 15, 1999): 52.

Constitution of the State of Hawai'i, Article I, Section 23.

Cowen, Ron, Tony Jonas, and Daniel Lipman, executive producers. *Queer as Folk* [Television Series]. USA: Showtime, 2000–2005.

Crenshaw, Kimberlé Williams. "Demarginalizing the Intersection of Race and Sex: A Black Feminist Critique of Antidiscrimination Doctrine, Feminist Theory, and Antiracist Politics." *University of Chicago Legal Forum* (1989): 139–67.

———. "Mapping the Margins: Intersectionality, Identity Politics, and Violence against Women of Color." *Stanford Law Review* 43, no. 6 (July 1991): 1241–99. Reprinted in *Critical Race Theory: The Key Writings That Formed the Movement*, edited by Kimberlé Crenshaw, Neil Gotanda, Gary Peller, and Kendall Thomas, 357–83. New York: The New Press, 1995.

———. "Whose Story Is It, Anyway? Feminist and Antiracist Appropriations of Anita Hill." In *Race-ing Justice, En-gendering Power: Essays on Anita Hill, Clarence Thomas, and the Construction of Social Reality*, edited by Toni Morrison, 402–40. New York: Pantheon, 1992.

Critical Resistance, and Incite! Women of Color Against Violence. "Gender Violence and the Prison-Industrial Complex." In *Color of Violence*, edited by Incite! 223–26.

Culler, Jonathan D. *On Deconstruction: Theory and Criticism after Structuralism.* Ithaca, N.Y.: Cornell University Press, 1982.

Curtin, Mary Ellen. *Black Prisoners and Their World, Alabama, 1865–1900.* Charlottesville: University Press of Virginia, 2000.

D'Emilio, John. "Capitalism and Gay Identity." In *The Lesbian and Gay Studies Reader,* edited by Henry Abelove, Michèle Aina Barale, and David M. Halperin, 467–76. New York: Routledge, 1993.

D'Souza, Dinesh. *The Enemy at Home: The Cultural Left and Its Responsibility for 9/11.* New York: Doubleday, 2007.

Daniel, Jay, and Glenn Gordon Caron, executive producers. *Moonlighting* [Television Series]. USA: American Broadcasting Company (ABC), 1985–89.

Darity, William, Jr., Darrick Hamilton, and Jason Dietrich. "Bleach in the Rainbow: Latino Preference for Whiteness." *Transforming Anthropology* 13, no. 2 (2005): 103–10.

Davis, Angela Y. *Are Prisons Obsolete?* New York: Seven Stories, 2003.

———. *Women, Race, & Class.* New York: Vintage Books, 1983.

Davis, Mike. "Hell Factories in the Field: A Prison-Industrial Complex." *The Nation* 260, no. 7 (1995): 229–34.

De Man, Paul. *Blindness and Insight: Essays in the Rhetoric of Contemporary Criticism.* Revised 2nd ed. Minneapolis: University of Minnesota Press, 1983.

Dé, Esha Niyogi. "Decolonizing Universality: Postcolonial Theory and the Quandary of Ethical Agency." *diacritics* 32, no. 2 (2002): 42–59.

DeNavas-Walt, Carmen, Bernadette D. Proctor, and Jessica C. Smith. (For the U.S. Department of Economics, Commerce, and Statistics Administration. U.S. Census Bureau.) "Income, Poverty, and Health Insurance Coverage in the United States: 2007." Washington, D.C.: GPO, 2008.

Diagnostic and Statistical Manual of Mental Disorders. 4th ed. text revision. Washington, D.C.: American Psychiatric Association, 2000.

Díaz-Cotto, Juanita. *Chicana Lives and Criminal Justice: Voices from El Barrio.* Austin: University of Texas Press, 2006.

———. *Gender, Ethnicity, and the State: Latina and Latino Prison Politics.* Albany: State University of New York Press, 1996.

Doby, Hersch. "Networks Bow to NAACP Heat." *Black Enterprise* 30, no. 9 (April 2000): 26.

Donahue, Ann, Jonathan Glassner, David Levinson, executive producers. *Street Justice* [Television Series]. USA: Stephen J. Cannell Productions, 1991–93.

Douglass, Frederick. *The Oxford Frederick Douglass Reader.* Edited by William L. Andrews. New York: Oxford University Press, 1996.

Dowd, Maureen. "White Man's Last Stand." *New York Times,* July 14, 2009: A25.

Drash, Wayne. "911 Caller in Gates Arrest Never Referred to 'Black Suspects.'" *CNN.com,* July 27, 2009. http://www.cnn.com.

Dunne, Bruce. "Power and Sexuality in the Middle East." *Middle East Report* no. 206 (Spring 1998): 8–11, 37.

Dussel, Enrique. *The Underside of Modernity: Apel, Ricoeur, Taylor and the Philosophy of Liberation*. Edited by Eduardo Mendieta. Atlantic Highlands, N.J.: Humanities Press, 1996.

Ehrenreich, Barbara. "What Abu Ghraib Taught Me." *Los Angeles Times*, May 19, 2004. http://www.latimes.com.

El Nasser, Haya. "Voters Shoot Down Proposition on Collecting Racial Information." *USA Today*, October 8, 2003. http://www.usatoday.com.

El-Rouayheb, Khaled. *Before Homosexuality in the Arab-Islamic World, 1500–1800*. Chicago: University of Chicago Press, 2005.

Elam, Michele. *Mixtries: Mixed Race in the New Millenium*. Palo Alto, Calif.: Stanford University Press, forthcoming.

Egelko, Bob. "Group's Leader Urges New Strategy on Immigrant Rights." *San Francisco Chronicle*, November 27, 2009. http://www.sfgate.com.

"Elmira: Nation's First Reformatory." *DOCS Today*, October 1998. http://www.correctionhistory.org.

Eng, David L., and Alice Y. Hom, eds. *Q & A: Queer in Asian America*. Philadelphia: Temple University Press, 1998.

Escobar, Arturo. *Encountering Development: The Making and Unmaking of the Third World*. Princeton, N.J.: Princeton University Press, 1995.

Estrada, Gabriel S. "Chicanas/os, Homosexuality, and Two-Spirit Histories." In *Gender and Native Societies in North America, 1400–1840*, edited by Fay Yarbrough and Sandra Slater. Oklahoma City: University of Oklahoma Press, forthcoming.

Fabian, Johannes. *Time and the Other: How Anthropology Makes Its Object*. New York: Columbia University Press, 1983.

Faderman, Lillian. *Surpassing the Love of Men: Romantic Friendship and Love between Women from the Renaissance to the Present*. New York: HarperCollins, 2001.

Falacci, Nicolas, Cheryl Heuton, Ridley Scott, Tony Scott, David W. Zucker, Don McGill, Ken Sanzel, Barry Schindel, Brooke Kennedy, and Alex Gansa, executive producers. *Numb3rs* [Television Series]. USA: Columbia Broadcasting System (CBS), 2005–present.

Fanon, Frantz. *Black Skin, White Masks*. New York: Grove Press, 1967.

———. *The Wretched of the Earth*. c1963. Translated by Richard Philcox. New York: Grove Press, 2004.

Feinberg, Leslie. *Lavender & Red*. Workers World, 2005. http://www.workers.org/lavender-red.

Ferber, Lawrence. "Prisoners of Love." *Advocate*, February 18, 2003, 46.

Ferguson, Roderick A. *Aberrations in Black: Toward a Queer of Color Critique*. Minneapolis: University of Minnesota Press, 2003.

Ferreira da Silva, Denise. *Toward a Global Idea of Race*. Minneapolis: University of Minnesota Press, 2007.

Fierce, Milfred C. *Slavery Revisited: Blacks and the Southern Convict Lease System, 1865–1933*. New York: Africana Studies Research Center-Brooklyn College, CUNY, 1994.

Fischer, Peter S., Angela Lansbury, and David Moessinger, executive producers. *Murder, She Wrote* [Television Series]. USA: Columbia Broadcasting System (CBS), 1984–96.

Foner, Eric. *Reconstruction: America's Unfinished Revolution, 1863–1877*. New York: Harper, 1988.

Fontana, Tom, Barry Levinson, and Henry Bromell, executive producers. *Homicide: Life on the Street* [Television Series]. USA: National Broadcasting Company (NBC), 1993–99.

Ford, Beverly, and Rich Schapiro. "Sgt. James Crowley, Cop Who Arrested Harvard Professor Henry Louis Gates Jr., Denies He's Racist." *New York Daily News*, July 24, 2009. http://www.nydailynews.com.

Foucault, Michel. *Discipline and Punish: The Birth of the Prison*. Translated by Alan Sheridan. New York: Vintage, 1979.

———. *The History of Sexuality: Volume 1, An Introduction*. Translated by Robert Hurley. New York: Vintage, 1990.

Foundation for National Progress. "Debt to Society: The Real Price of Prisons" (Racial Inequality Pop-up Window), July 10, 2001. http://www.motherjones.com (accessed July 27, 2007).

Frank, Andre Gunder. *ReOrient: Global Economy in the Asian Age*. Berkeley and Los Angeles: University of California Press, 1998.

Frank, Andre Gunder, and Barry K. Gills, eds. *The World System: Five Hundred Years or Five Thousand?* New York: Routledge, 1993.

Frank, Nathaniel. "President Obama and Gay Rights: Forgetting the Lessons of the Campaign." *Huffington Post*, November 5, 2009. http://www.huffingtonpost.com.

Freedman, Estelle B. *Their Sisters' Keepers: Women's Prison Reform in America, 1830–1930*. Ann Arbor: University of Michigan Press, 1984.

Freeman, Leonard, and Philip Leacock, executive producers. *Hawaii Five-0* [Television Series]. USA: Columbia Broadcasting System (CBS), 1968–80.

Fryberg, Stephanie, Hazel Rose Markus, Daphna Oyserman, and Joseph M. Stone. "Of Warrior Chiefs and Indian Princesses: The Psychological Consequences of American Indian Mascots." *Basic and Applied Social Psychology* 30 (2008): 208–18.

Frye, Marilyn. *The Politics of Reality*. Freedom, Calif.: Crossing Press, 1983.

Fuss, Diana. *Essentially Speaking*. New York: Routledge, 1990.

Gabbard, Krin. *Black Magic: White Hollywood and African American Culture*. New Brunswick, N.J.: Rutgers University Press, 2004.

Galeano, Eduardo H. *Open Veins of Latin America: Five Centuries of the Pillage of a Continent.* Translated by Cedric Belfrage. Chicago: Monthly Review Press, 1997.

Galinsky, Seth. "U.S. Gov't Set To Triple Immigration 'Audits.'" *The Militant* 73, no. 47 (December 7, 2009). http://themilitant.com.

García, Robert. "García Papers. Rare and Manuscript Collection #7574," Carl A. Kroch Library, Cornell University.

Garland-Thomson, Rosemarie. *Extraordinary Bodies: Figuring Physical Disability in American Culture and Literature.* New York: Columbia University Press, 1997.

———. "Integrating Disability, Transforming Feminist Theory." *NWSA Journal* 14, no. 3 (2002): 1–32.

Gaspar de Alba, Alicia, ed. *Velvet Barrios: Popular Culture & Chicana/o Sexualities.* New York: Palgrave Macmillan, 2003.

Gavin, Francis J. "The Gold Battles within the Cold War: American Monetary Policy and the Defense of Europe, 1960–1963." *Diplomatic History* 26, no. 1 (2002): 61–94.

Geller, Bruce, executive producer. *Mannix* [Television Series]. USA: Columbia Broadcasting System (CBS), 1967–75.

Gerber, David, executive producer. *Police Story* [Television Series]. USA: National Broadcasting Company (NBC), 1973–78.

———, executive producer. *Police Woman* [Television Series]. USA: National Broadcasting Company (NBC), 1974–78.

Gilmore, Ruth Wilson. "Globalisation and U.S. Prison Growth: From Military Keynesianism to Post-Keynesian Militarism." *Race & Class* 40, no. 2–3 (1998/1999): 171–88.

———. *Golden Gulag: Prisons, Surplus, Crisis, and Opposition in Globalizing California.* Berkeley: University of California Press, 2007.

Gilroy, Paul. *Against Race: Imagining Political Culture beyond the Color Line.* Cambridge, Mass.: Harvard University Press, 2001.

Gitlin, Todd. *The Twilight of Common Dreams: Why America Is Wracked by Culture Wars.* New York: Metropolitan Books, 1995.

Glasgow, Joshua. "Three Things Realist Constructionism About Race—or Anything Else—Can Do." *Journal of Social Philosophy* 38, no. 4 (2007): 554–68.

Gleason, Michael, executive producer. *Remington Steele* [Television Series]. USA: National Broadcasting Company (NBC), 1982–87.

Goldberg, Leonard, and Aaron Spelling, executive producers. *Charlie's Angels* [Television Series]. USA: American Broadcasting Company (ABC), 1976–81.

———, executive producers. *Hart to Hart* [Television Series]. USA: American Broadcasting Company (ABC), 1979–84.

———, executive producers. *S.W.A.T.* [Television Series]. USA: American Broadcasting Company (ABC), 1975–76.

———, executive producers. *Starsky & Hutch* [Television Series]. USA: American Broadcasting Company (ABC), 1975–79.

Goldsmith, Arthur H., Darrick Hamilton, and William Darity, Jr. "Shades of Discrimination: Skin Tone and Wages." *American Economic Review* 96, no. 2 (May 2006): 242–45.

Goodman, Ryan. "Beyond the Enforcement Principle: Sodomy Laws, Social Norms, and Social Panoptics." *California Law Review* 89, no. 3 (2001): 643–740.

Goodnough, Abby. "Harvard Professor Jailed; Office Is Accused of Bias." *New York Times*, July 20, 2009. http://www.nytimes.com.

Goodridge vs. Department of Public Health. 440 Mass. 309 (2003).

Gopinath, Gayatri. *Impossible Desires: Queer Diasporas and South Asian Public Cultures*. Durham, N.C.: Duke University Press, 2005.

Gorton, Don. "The Origins of Anti-Sodomy Laws." *Harvard Gay and Lesbian Review* 5, no. 1 (1998): 10–13.

Gould, Stephen Jay. *The Mismeasure of Man*. Revised and expanded ed. New York: Norton, 1996.

Grammer, Kelsey, Glenn Gordon Caron, Steve Stark, Ronald L. Schwary, René Echevarria, executive producers. *Medium* [Television Series]. USA: Columbia Broadcasting System (CBS), 2005–present.

Graves, Joseph L. *The Race Myth: Why We Pretend Race Exists in America*. New York: Dutton, 2004.

Grazer, Brian, Howard Gordon, Evan Katz, Kiefer Sutherland, Robert Cochran, Joel Surnow, Jon Cassar, Manny Coto, David Fury, and Tony Krantz, executive producers. *24* [Television Series]. USA: Fox Network, 2001–present.

Greenberg, David F. *The Construction of Homosexuality*. Chicago: University of Chicago Press, 1988.

Grobman, Laurie. "Postpositivist Realism in the Multicultural Writing Classroom: Beyond the Paralysis of Cultural Relativism." *Pedagogy* 3, no. 2 (2003): 205–25.

Grosfoguel, Ramón, and Ana Margarita Cervantes-Rodríguez, eds. *The Modern/Colonial/Capitalist World-System in the Twentieth Century: Global Processes, Antisystemic Movements, and the Geopolitics of Knowledge*. Westport, Conn.: Greenwood Press, 2002.

Gutiérrez-Jones, Carl. *Critical Race Narratives: A Study of Race, Rhetoric, and Injury*. New York: New York University Press, 2001.

Haldeman, H. R. *The Haldeman Diaries: Inside the Nixon White House*. New York: Putnam's Sons, 1994.

Halperin, David M. *One Hundred Years of Homosexuality and Other Essays on Greek Love*. New York: Routledge, 1990.

Halwani, Raja. "Prolegomena to Any Future Metaphysics of Sexual Identity: Recasting the Essentialism and Social Constructionism Debate." In *Identity Politics Reconsidered*, edited by Alcoff, Hames-García, Moya, and Mohanty, 209–27.

Hames-García, Michael. *Fugitive Thought: Prison Movements, Race, and the Meaning of Justice.* Minneapolis: University of Minnesota Press, 2004.

———. "How Real Is Race?" In *Material Feminisms,* edited by Stacy Alaimo and Susan Hekman, 308–39. Bloomington, Ind.: Indiana University Press, 2008.

———. "How to Tell a Mestizo from an Enchirito*: Colonialism and National Culture in Gloria Anzaldúa's *Borderlands/La Frontera.*" *diacritics* 30, no. 4 (2000): 102–22.

———. "Queer Theory Revisited." In *Gay Latino Studies,* edited by Hames-García and Martínez, 19–45.

———. "What's at Stake in 'Gay' Identities?" In *Identity Politics Reconsidered,* edited by Alcoff, Hames-García, Moya, and Mohanty, 78–95.

———. "'Who Are Our Own People?' Challenges for a Theory of Social Identity." In *Reclaiming Identity,* edited by Moya and Hames-García, 102–29.

Hames-García, Michael, and Ernesto Javier Martínez, eds. *Gay Latino Studies: A Critical Reader.* Durham, N.C.: Duke University Press, 2011.

———. "Introduction: Re-Membering Gay Latino Studies." In *Gay Latino Studies,* edited by Hames-García and Martínez, 1–18.

Hamilton, Kenneth Lewis. "The Flames of Namugongo: Postcolonial, Queer, and Thea/ological Reflections on the Narrative of the 1886 Ugandan Martyrdom." PhD diss., Union Institute and University, 2007.

Hammett, Dashiell. *The Maltese Falcon.* New York: Vintage Books, 1972.

Haney-López, Ian F. *White by Law: The Legal Construction of Race.* New York: New York University Press, 1998.

Harding, Sandra G. "Rethinking Standpoint Epistemology: 'What Is Strong Objectivity?'" In *Feminist Epistemologies,* edited by Linda Alcoff and Elizabeth Potter, 49–82. New York: Routledge, 1993.

———. *Whose Science? Whose Knowledge?: Thinking from Women's Lives.* Ithaca, N.Y.: Cornell University Press, 1991.

Harding, Sandra, ed. *The "Racial" Economy of Science: Toward a Democratic Future.* Bloomington: Indiana University Press, 1993.

Hargrove, Dean, Roland Kibbee, Richard Alan Simmons, and Richard Levinson, executive producers. *Columbo* [Television Series]. USA: National Broadcasting Company (NBC), 1971–78.

Hasburgh, Patrick, and Stephen J. Cannell, executive producers. *21 Jump Street* [Television Series]. USA: Fox Network, 1987–91.

Hasinoff, Amy Adele. "Fashioning Race for the Free Market on *America's Next Top Model,*" *Critical Studies in Media Communication* 25, no. 3 (2008): 324–43.

Hau, Caroline S. "On Representing Others: Intellectuals, Pedagogy, and the Uses of Error." In *Reclaiming Identity,* edited by Moya and Hames-García, 133–70.

Hawai'i (State of). Department of Accounting and General Services and Department of Public Safety. *10-Year Corrections Master Plan Update* (December 2003). http://hawaii.gov (accessed July 25, 2009).

Hennessey, Rosemary. *Profit and Pleasure: Sexual Identities in Late Capitalism.* New York: Routledge, 2000.

Henríquez, Patricio, director. *Juchitán: Queer Paradise* [DVD]. 2002. Chile and Canada: Filmmakers Library, 2003.

Henze, Brent R. "Who Says Who Says? The Epistemological Grounds for Agency in Liberatory Political Projects." In *Reclaiming Identity*, edited by Moya and Hames-García, 229–50.

Herrnstein, Richard J., and Charles Murray. *The Bell Curve: Intelligence and Class Structure in American Life.* New York: Free Press, 1994.

Heus, Richard, and Terri Kopp, co-executive producers. *In Justice* [Television Series]. USA: American Broadcasting Company (ABC), 2006.

Hicks, Heather J. "Hoodoo Economics: White Men's Work and Black Men's Magic in Contemporary American Film." *Camera Obscura* 18, no. 2 (2003): 26–55.

Ho, Andy. "It's Not a Big Deal for Most Singaporeans." *The Straits Times*, November 3, 2007. http://www.straitstimes.com.

———. "There Are Gays, and There Are Gays . . ." *The Straits Times*, November 10, 2007. http://www.straitstimes.com.

Hobsbawm, Eric. "Identity Politics and the Left." *New Left Review* (1996): 38–47.

Hondagneu-Sotelo, Pierrette, and Michael A. Messner. "Gender Displays and Men's Power: The 'New Man' and the Mexican Immigrant Man." In *Theorizing Masculinities*, edited by Harry Brod and Michael Kaufman, 200–218. Thousand Oaks, Calif.: Sage Publications, 1994.

hooks, bell. *Ain't I a Woman: Black Women and Feminism.* Boston: South End Press, 1981.

———. *Talking Back: Thinking Feminist, Thinking Black.* Boston: South End Press, 1989.

House of Color. *I Object* [Videocassette]. 1991. In García, "García Papers," V-129.

———. *Probe* [Videocassette]. 1992. In García, "García Papers," V-129.

Hubbard, Ruth, and Elijah Wald. *Exploding the Gene Myth: How Genetic Information Is Produced and Manipulated by Scientists, Physicians, Employers, Insurance Companies, Educators, and Law Enforcers.* Revised ed. Boston: Beacon Press, 1999.

Huggins, Roy, Fred Dryer, George Geiger, and Lawrence Kubik, executive producers. *Hunter* [Television Series]. USA: National Broadcasting Company (NBC), 1984–91.

Hull, Gloria T., Patricia Bell Scott, and Barbara Smith, eds. *All the Women Are White, All the Blacks Are Men, but Some of Us Are Brave: Black Women's Studies.* Old Westbury, N.Y.: Feminist Press, 1982.

Human Rights Watch. "Incarcerated America: Human Rights Watch Backgrounder," April, 2003. http://www.hrw.org (accessed July 25, 2009).

Imrie, Rob. "Oppression, Disability, and Access in the Built Environment." In *The*

Disability Reader: Social Science Perspectives, edited by Tom Shakespeare, 129–46. London: Cassell, 1998.

Incite! Women of Color Against Violence, ed. *Color of Violence: The Incite! Anthology*. Cambridge, Mass.: South End Press, 2006.

International Centre for Prison Studies, King's College London. "World Prison Brief." http://www.kcl.ac.uk (accessed December 1, 2009).

Islamic Human Rights Commission. "IHRC Deplores Continued Abuses by Occupation Soldiers in Iraq," December 23, 2004. http://www.ihrc.org.uk.

Izenberg, Dan. "Mazuz Backs Rights of Same-Sex Couples." *The Jerusalem Post*, December 9, 2004.

Jacobs, Harriet A. *Incidents in the Life of a Slave Girl*. Edited by Jean Fagan Yellin. Cambridge, Mass.: Harvard University Press, 1987.

James, Joy. *Resisting State Violence: Radicalism, Gender, and Race in U.S. Culture*. Minneapolis: University of Minneapolis Press, 1996.

James, Joy, ed. *The New Abolitionists: (Neo)Slave Narratives and Contemporary Prison Writings*. Albany: State University of New York Press, 2005.

Jelinek, Pauline. "Lawmakers View Disturbing Photos of Iraq Prison Abuse; Rumsfeld Defends Interrogation." *Associated Press Newswires*, May 12, 2004.

Johnson, Barbara. *The Critical Difference: Essays in the Contemporary Rhetoric of Reading*. Baltimore, Md.: The Johns Hopkins University Press, 1980.

———. *A World of Difference*. Baltimore, Md.: The Johns Hopkins University Press, 1987.

Johnson, E. Patrick. *Sweet Tea: Black Gay Men of the South*. Chapel Hill, N.C.: The University of North Carolina Press, 2008.

Johnson, E. Patrick, and Mae G. Henderson, eds. *Black Queer Studies: A Critical Anthology*. Durham, N.C.: Duke University Press, 2005.

Josephson, Barry, Hart Hanson, and Jonathan Pontell, executive producers. *Bones* [Television Series]. USA: Fox Network, 2005–present.

Karim, Lamia. "Demystifying Micro-Credit: The Grameen Bank, NGOs, and Neoliberalism in Bangladesh." *Cultural Dynamics* 20, no. 1 (2008): 5–29.

Kavanaugh, Dan, Michael Linder, Lance Heflin, and Greg Klein, series and executive producers. *America's Most Wanted* [Television Series]. USA: Fox Network, 1988–present.

Keith, Verna, and Cedric Herring. "Skin Tone Stratification in the Black Community." *American Journal of Sociology* 97 (1991): 760–78.

Kelly, Robin D. G. *Yo' Mama's Disfunktional! Fighting the Culture Wars in Urban America*. Boston: Beacon Press, 1997.

Kempley, Rita. "Movies' 'Magic Negro' Saves the Day—but at the Cost of His Soul." *The Black Commentator* 49 (July 3, 2003). http://www.blackcommentator.com.

Kenan, Randall. *A Visitation of Spirits*. New York: Vintage, 2000.

Kinsey, Alfred C., Wardell B. Pomeroy, and Clyde E. Martin. *Sexual Behavior in the Human Male*. Bloomington: Indiana University Press, 1998.

Kittay, Eva Feder. "When Caring Is Just and Justice Is Caring: Justice and Mental Retardation." *Public Culture* 13, no. 3 (2001): 557–79.

Kohan, David, Max Mutchnick, James Burrows, Jhoni Marchinko, Alex Herschlag, Jeff Greenstein, Greg Malins, and David Flebotte, executive producers. *Will & Grace* [Television Series]. USA: National Broadcasting Company (NBC), 1998–2006.

Kostroff-Noble, Nina, David Simon, and Robert F. Colesberry, executive producers. *The Wire* [Television Series]. USA: Home Box Office (HBO), 2002–8.

Kotcheff, Ted, Dick Wolf, Neal Baer, Peter Jankowski, Robert Palm, and David J. Burke, executive producers. *Law & Order: Special Victims Unit* [Television Series]. USA: National Broadcasting Company (NBC), 1999–present.

Kuhn, Thomas S. *The Structure of Scientific Revolutions.* 3rd ed. Chicago: University of Chicago Press, 1996.

Kunzel, Regina. "Lessons in Being Gay: Queer Encounters in Gay and Lesbian Prison Activism." *Radical History Review* 100 (2008): 10–37.

Kushner, Tony. *Angels in America, Part One: Millennium Approaches.* New York: Theatre Communications Group, 1993.

Laclau, Ernesto, and Chantal Mouffe. *Hegemony & Socialist Strategy: Towards a Radical Democratic Politics.* London: Verso, 1985.

Lancaster, Roger N. *Life Is Hard: Machismo, Danger, and the Intimacy of Power in Nicaragua.* Berkeley: University of California Press, 1992.

Leonard, Sheldon, executive producer. *I Spy* [Television Series]. USA: National Broadcasting Company (NBC), 1965–68.

Letellier, Patrick. "Egyptians Decry 'Gay' U.S. Abusers in Iraq." PlanetOut Network, May 17, 2004. http://www.planetout.com.

Levinson, Barry, and Tom Fontana, executive producers. *Oz: The Complete First Season* [Television Series on DVD]. 1997. USA: Home Box Office (HBO) Home Video, 2002.

Levinson, Barry, and Tom Fontana, executive producers. *Oz: The Complete Second Season* [Television Series on DVD]. USA: Home Box Office (HBO) Video, 2002.

Levinson, Barry, Tom Fontana, and Jim Finnerty, executive producers. *Oz: The Complete Third Season* [Television Series on DVD]. USA: Home Box Office (HBO) Video, 2004.

Levinson, Barry, Tom Fontana, and Jim Finnerty, executive producers. *Oz: The Complete Fourth Season* [Television Series on DVD]. USA: Home Box Office (HBO) Video, 2004.

Levinson, Barry, Tom Fontana, and Jim Finnerty, executive producers. *Oz: The Complete Fifth Season* [Television Series on DVD]. USA: Home Box Office (HBO) Video, 2004.

Levinson, Barry, Tom Fontana, and Jim Finnerty, executive producers. *Oz: The*

Complete Sixth Season [Television Series on DVD]. USA: Home Box Office (HBO) Video, 2006.

Lichtenstein, Alex. *Twice the Work of Free Labor: The Political Economy of Convict Labor in the New South.* London: Verso, 1996.

Lipsitz, George. *The Possessive Investment in Whiteness: How White People Profit from Identity Politics.* Philadelphia: Temple University Press, 1998.

Liptak, Adam. "Inmate Count in U.S. Dwarfs Other Nations." *New York Times,* April 23, 2008. http://www.nytimes.com.

Littman, Jonathan, Hank Steinberg, Jerry Bruckheimer, Jan Nash, Greg Walker, David Amann, and Ed Redlich, executive producers. *Without a Trace* [Television Series]. USA: Columbia Broadcasting System (CBS), 2002–present.

Littman, Jonathan, Jerry Bruckheimer, Meredith Stiehm, Jennifer Johnson, Greg Plageman, Veena Cabreros Sud, and Shaun Cassidy, executive producers. *Cold Case* [Television Series]. USA: Columbia Broadcasting System (CBS), 2003–present.

Lockhead, Carolyn. "Right Calls Sotomayor Racist Over Line in Talk." *San Francisco Chronicle,* May 29, 2009. http://www.sfgate.com.

Loeb, Vernon, and Rajiv Chandrasekaran. "Pentagon: U.S. Planes Mistakenly Bomb Red Cross Compound." *The Washington Post,* October 27, 2001. http://www.washingtonpost.com.

Lorde, Audre. *Sister Outsider: Essays and Speeches.* Freedom, Calif.: Crossing Press, 1984.

Lugones, María. "Heterosexualism and the Colonial/Modern Gender System." *Hypatia* 22, no. 1 (2007): 186–209

Lugones, María. *Pilgrimages/Peregrinajes: Theorizing Coalition against Multiple Oppressions.* New York: Rowman & Littlefield, 2003.

———. "Purity, Impurity, and Separation." *Signs* 19, no. 21 (1994): 458–79.

Lyotard, Jean-François. *The Différend: Phrases in Dispute.* Translated by Georges Van Den Abbeele. Minneapolis: University of Minnesota Press, 1988.

———. *The Postmodern Condition: A Report on Knowledge.* Translated by Geoff Bennington and Brian Massumi. Minneapolis: University of Minnesota Press, 1984.

Mahapatra, Dhananjay. "UN Body Slams India on Rights of Gays." *The Times of India,* April 25, 2008. http://timesofindia.indiatimes.com.

Manalansan, Martin F., IV. *Global Divas: Filipino Gay Men in the Diaspora.* Durham, N.C.: Duke University Press, 2003.

Mancini, Matthew J. *One Dies, Get Another: Convict Leasing in the American South, 1866–1928.* Columbia: University of South Carolina Press, 1996.

Mann, Coramae Richey. *Unequal Justice: A Question of Color.* Bloomington: Indiana University Press, 1993.

Mann, Michael, and Anthony Yerkovich, executive producers. *Miami Vice* [Television Series]. USA: National Broadcasting Company (NBC), 1984–89.

Marcos, Subcomandante. *Conversations with Durito: Stories of the Zapatistas and Neoliberalism.* Translated by Acción Zapatista Editorial Collective. Brooklyn, N.Y.: Autonomedia, 2005.

———. *Desde las montañas del sureste mexicano.* México, D.F.: Plaza & Janés Editores, 1999.

———. *¡Ya Basta! Ten Years of the Zapatista Uprising: Writings of Subcomandante Insurgente Marcos.* Translated by Irlandesa and others. Oakland, Calif.: AK Press, 2001.

Marcos, Subcomandante, and the Zapatista Army of National Liberation. *Shadows of Tender Fury: The Letters and Communiqués.* Translated by Frank Bardacke, Leslie López, and California Human Rights Committee Watsonville. New York: Monthly Review Press, 1995.

Marcos, Sylvia. *Taken from the Lips: Gender and Eros in Mesoamerican Religions.* Leiden, Netherlands: Brill, 2006.

Mark, Laurence, Richard Sakai, and Laura Ziskin, executive producers, and James L. Brooks, director. *As Good as It Gets* [Motion Picture]. USA: Sony Pictures Entertainment, 1997.

Martin, Quinn, executive producer. *The F.B.I.* [Television Series]. USA: American Broadcasting Company (ABC), 1965–74.

———, executive producer. *The Streets of San Francisco* [Television Series]. USA: American Broadcasting Company (ABC), 1972–77.

Martínez, Ernesto J. "Dying to Know: Identity and Self-Knowledge in Baldwin's *Another Country.*" *PMLA: Publications of the Modern Language Association* 124, no. 3 (May 2009): 782–97.

———. "On Butler on Morrison on Language." *Signs* 35, no. 4 (2010): 821–42.

Massad, Joseph A. *Desiring Arabs.* Chicago: The University of Chicago Press, 2007.

———. "Re-Orienting Desire: The Gay International and the Arab World." *Public Culture* 14, no. 2 (2002): 361–85.

Mastro, Dana E., Elizabeth Behm-Morawitz, and Maria A Kopacz. "Exposure to Television Portrayals of Latinos: The Implications of Aversive Racism and Social Identity Theory." *Human Communication Research* 34 (2008): 1–27.

Mauer, Marc. "The Causes and Consequences of Prison Growth in the United States." *Punishment and Society* 3, no. 1 (2001): 9–20.

———. *Race to Incarcerate.* Rev and updated ed. New York: The New Press, 2006.

McAdams, James Duff, executive producer. *The Equalizer* [Television Series]. USA: Columbia Broadcasting System (CBS), 1985–89.

McClellan, Steve. "NAACP Decries TV 'Whitewash.'" *Broadcasting & Cable* 129, no. 30 (July 19, 1999): 16.

McClintock, Anne. *Imperial Leather: Race, Gender, and Sexuality in the Colonial Contest.* New York: Routledge, 1995.

McGruder, Aaron, and Hudlin, Reginald, executive producers. "A Date with the Health Inspector." Directed by Joe Horne. Written by Aaron McGruder and Rodney Barnes. (First broadcast on December 4, 2005.) *The Boondocks: The Complete First Season* [Television Series on DVD]. USA: Sony Pictures Home Entertainment, 2006.

McRuer, Robert. *Crip Theory: Cultural Signs of Queerness and Disability.* New York: New York University Press, 2006.

Mead, Ed. "Men against Sexism." In *The New Abolitionists*, edited by James, 117–30.

Mecca, Tommi Avicolli. "It's All About Class." In *That's Revolting! Queer Strategies for Resisting Assimilation*, edited by Mattilda Bernstein Sycamore, 13–22. Brooklyn, N.Y.: Soft Skull Press, 2004.

Memmi, Albert. *The Colonizer and the Colonized.* Translated by Howard Greenfield. Boston: Beacon Press, 1965.

Messerschmidt, James W. "Masculinities, Crime, and Prison." In *Prison Masculinities*, edited by Sabo, Kupers, and London, 67–72.

Meyer, Stanley D., Jack Webb, and Michael Meshekoff, executive producers. *Dragnet* [Television Series]. USA: National Broadcasting Company (NBC), 1951–59.

Michael, Maggie. "Demonstrators Demand the Ejection of Egypt's U.S. Ambassador." *Associated Press Newswires*, May 12, 2004.

Michaels, Walter Benn. "Autobiography of an Ex-White Man: Why Race Is Not a Social Construction." *Transition* 73 (1997): 122–43.

———. *The Shape of the Signifier: 1967 to the End of History.* Princeton, N.J.: Princeton University Press, 2004.

Mignolo, Walter D. *The Darker Side of the Renaissance: Literacy, Territoriality, and Colonization.* Ann Arbor: University of Michigan Press, 1995.

———. *The Idea of Latin America.* Malden, Mass.: Blackwell Publishing, 2005.

———. *Local Histories/Global Designs: Coloniality, Subaltern Knowledges, and Border Thinking.* Princeton, N.J.: Princeton University Press, 2000.

———. "The Zapatistas' Theoretical Revolution: Its Historical, Ethical, and Political Consequences." *Review* 25, no. 3 (2002): 245–75.

Miller, Nancy, Bill Finnegan, Deborah Joy LeVine, Sheldon Pinchuk, and Gary A. Randall, executive producers. *Any Day Now* [Television Series]. USA: Lifetime Network, 1998–2002.

Moeller, Carol J. "Marginalized Voices: Challenging Dominant Privilege in Higher Education." In *Theorizing Backlash: Philosophical Reflections on the Resistance to Feminism*, edited by Anita M. Superson and Ann E. Cudd, 155–80. New York: Rowman & Littlefield, 2002.

Moessinger, David, Peter J. Thompson, Glen A. Larson, Richard Irving, Robert A. Cinader, Jud Kinberg, and Donald P. Bellisario, executive producers. *Quincy, M.E.* [Television Series]. USA: National Broadcasting Company (NBC), 1976–83.

Mohanty, Chandra Talpade, Ann Russo, and Lourdes Torres, eds. *Third World Women and the Politics of Feminism*. Bloomington: Indiana University Press, 1991.

Mohanty, Satya. "Colonial Legacies, Multicultural Futures: Relativism, Objectivity, and the Challenge of Otherness." *PMLA: Publications of the Modern Language Association* 110, no. 1 (1995): 108–18.

———. "The Epistemic Status of Cultural Identity: On *Beloved* and the Postcolonial Condition." In *Reclaiming Identity*, edited by Moya and Hames-García, 29–66.

———. *Literary Theory and the Claims of History: Postmodernism, Objectivity, Multicultural Politics*. Ithaca, N.Y.: Cornell University Press, 1997.

Moraga, Cherríe. *The Hungry Woman*. Albuquerque, N.Mex.: West End Press, 2001.

———. *Loving in the War Years: Lo que nunca pasó por sus labios*. Boston: South End Press, 1983.

Moraga, Cherríe, and Gloria Anzaldúa, eds. *This Bridge Called My Back: Writings by Radical Women of Color*. 2nd ed. New York: Kitchen Table/Women of Color Press, 1983.

Morales, Aurora Levins, and Rosario Morales. *Getting Home Alive*. Ithaca, N.Y.: Firebrand Books, 1986.

Morris, Norval, and David J. Rothman, eds. *The Oxford History of the Prison*. New York: Oxford University Press, 1998.

Morrison, Toni. *Beloved*. New York: Knopf, 1987.

———. "Unspeakable Things Unspoken: The Afro-American Presence in American Literature." In *The Black Feminist Reader*, edited by Joy James and T. Denean Sharpley-Whiting, 24–56. Malden, Mass.: Blackwell, 2000.

Moumneh, Rasha. "Helem at Montreal OutGames 2006," http://www.youtube.com.

Moya, Paula M. L. *Learning from Experience: Minority Identities, Multicultural Struggles*. Berkeley: University of California Press, 2002.

———. "Postmodernism, 'Realism,' and the Politics of Identity: Cherríe Moraga and Chicana Feminism." In *Reclaiming Identity*, edited by Moya and Hames-García, 67–101.

Moya, Paula M. L., and Michael Hames-García, eds. *Reclaiming Identity: Realist Theory and the Predicament of Postmodernism*. Berkeley: University of California Press, 2000.

Mudimbe, V. Y. *The Invention of Africa: Gnosis, Philosophy, and the Order of Knowledge*. Indianapolis: Indiana University Press, 1988.

Mumford, Kevin J. *Interzones: Black/White Sex Districts in Chicago and New York in the Early Twentieth Century*. New York: Columbia University Press, 1997.

Muñoz, José Esteban. *Disidentifications: Queers of Color and the Performance of Politics*. Minneapolis: University of Minnesota Press, 1999.

Murray, Stephen O. *Latin American Male Homosexualities*. Albuquerque: University of New Mexico Press, 1995.

Murray, Stephen O., and Will Roscoe, eds. *Islamic Homosexualities: Culture, History, and Literature.* New York: New York University Press, 1997.

Na Mamo O Hawai'i. "Open Letter to the LGBT Community." *GLQ* 8, no. 1–2 (2002): 215–16.

Najmabadi, Afsaneh. *Women with Mustaches and Men without Beards: Gender and Sexual Anxieties of Iranian Modernity.* Berkeley: University of California Press, 2005.

Narayan, Uma. *Dislocating Cultures: Identities, Traditions, and Third World Feminism.* New York: Routledge, 1997.

Narrain, Arvind, and Brototi Dutta. "Male-to-Male Sex and Sexuality Minorities in South Asia: An Analysis of the Politico-Legal Framework." Naz Foundation International, 2006.

Nava, Michael. *The Burning Plain.* New York: G. P. Putnam's Sons, 1997.

———. *The Death of Friends.* New York: G. P. Putnam's Sons, 1996.

———. *The Hidden Law.* New York: Ballantine Books, 1994.

———. *How Town.* New York: Ballantine Books, 1990.

Nelson, Valier J. "Darren McGavin, 83." *Los Angeles Times,* February 27, 2006, online edition.

New York State Special Commission on Attica. *Attica: The Official Report of the New York State Special Commission on Attica.* New York: Bantam Books, 1972.

Nguyen, Minh T. "'It Matters to Get the Facts Straight': Joy Kogawa, Realism, and Objectivity of Values." In *Reclaiming Identity,* edited by Moya and Hames-García, 171–204.

Nicholson, Linda, ed. *Feminism/Postmodernism.* New York: Routledge, 1990.

Nieman, Donald G., ed. *African American Life in the Post-Emancipation South, 1861–1900.* New York: Garland, 1994.

Obama, Barack. "A More Perfect Union." *NPR,* March 18, 2008. http://www.npr.org.

Oliver, Melvin L., and Thomas M. Shapiro. *Black Wealth/White Wealth: A New Perspective on Racial Inequality.* 2nd ed. New York: Routledge, 2006.

Omi, Michael, and Howard Winant. *Racial Formation in the United States from the 1960s to the 1990s.* New York: Routledge, 1994.

O'Rourke, Meghan. "Don't Let Larry Summers Off the Hook Yet: Why the Harvard President's Tactless Social Science Was a Bad Idea." *Slate,* January 28, 2005. http://www.slate.com (accessed 26 July 2009).

Ortiz, Ricardo L. "Pleasure and Power in the Novels of John Rechy, Arturo Islas, and Michael Nava." *Journal of Homosexuality* 26, no. 2/3 (1993): 111–26.

Oshinsky, David M. *"Worse Than Slavery": Parchman Farm and the Ordeal of Jim Crow Justice.* New York: Free Press, 1996.

Oswald, Russell G. *Attica—My Story.* Garden City, N.Y.: Doubleday, 1972.

Outlaw, Lucius T., Jr. *On Race and Philosophy.* New York: Routledge, 1996.

Overdorf, Jason. "Closet Drama." *Far Eastern Economic Review,* October 3, 2002. http://feer.wsj.com.

Palumbo-Liu, David. "Multiculturalism Now: Civilization, National Identity, and Difference Before and After September 11." In *Identity Politics Reconsidered,* edited by Alcoff, Hames-García, Mohanty, and Moya, 126–41.

Parenti, Christian. *Lockdown America: Police and Prisons in the Age of Crisis.* London: Verso, 2000.

Parker, Pat. *Movement in Black: The Collected Poetry of Pat Parker, 1961–1978.* Ithaca, N.Y.: 1978.

Patrick, Gail, executive producer. *Perry Mason* [Television Series]. USA: Columbia Broadcasting System (CBS), 1957–66.

Patrick-Stamp, Leslie. "Numbers That Are Not New: African Americans in the Country's First Prison, 1790–1835." *Pennsylvania Magazine of History and Biography* 119, no. 1–2 (1995): 95–128.

Patterson, Orlando. *Slavery and Social Death: A Comparative Study.* Cambridge, Mass.: Harvard University Press, 1982.

Pew Center on the States. *One in 100: Behind Bars in America, 2008.* Washington, D.C.: Pew Center on the States, 2008.

Pinto, Jerry. "Jai Ho!" *The Advocate* no. 1030 (September 2009): 15.

"Poll." *New York Times*/CBS News, October 25–29, 2008. http://www.nytimes.com.

Pratt, Minnie Bruce. *Rebellion: Essays, 1980–1991.* Ithaca, N.Y.: Firebrand Books, 1991.

Price, Jay. "N.C. Guardsman Guilty in Iraqi Death." *Raleigh News & Observer,* October 7, 2004. http://www.newsobserver.com.

Prison Policy Initiative. "Racial Disparities in Incarceration by State, 2000," http://www.prisonpolicy.org.

"Proposition 54: Classification by Race, Ethnicity, Color, or National Origin: Initiative Constitutional Amendment." In *State of California Official Voter Information Guide.* 2003. http://vote2003.sos.ca.gov/propositions/2-3-prop-54.html.

Puar, Jasbir Kaur. "Circuits of Sexualities." *GLQ* 8, no. 1–2 (2002): 101–37.

———. *Terrorist Assemblages: Homonationalism in Queer Times.* Durham, N.C.: Duke University Press, 2007.

Quijano, Aníbal. "Coloniality of Power, Eurocentrism, and Latin America." Translated by Michael Ennis. *Nepantla: Views from the South* 1, no. 3 (2000): 533–80.

Quiroga, José. *Tropics of Desire: Interventions from Queer Latino America.* New York: New York University Press, 2000.

Rabwin, Paul, and Rick Rosner, producers. *CHiPs* [Television Series]. USA: National Broadcasting Company (NBC), 1977–83.

Radicalesbians. "The Woman Identified Woman." In *The Second Wave: A Reader in Feminist Theory,* edited by Linda Nicholson, 153–57. New York: Routledge, 1997.

Rafter, Nicole. *Shots in the Mirror: Crime Films and Society.* New York: Oxford University Press, 2006.

Railton, Stephen. "Black Slaves and White Readers." In *Approaches to Teaching Stowe's Uncle Tom's Cabin*, edited by Elizabeth Ammons and Susan Belasco, 104–10. New York: Modern Language Association, 2000.

Ramos, Juanita, ed. *Compañeras: Latina Lesbians: An Anthology.* New York: Routledge, 1994.

Rapf, Matthew, and Abby Mann, executive producers. *Kojak* [Television Series]. USA: Columbia Broadcasting System (CBS), 1973–78.

Ravindran, Nirmala. "New Sexual Revolution." *India Today,* March 10, 2008. http://indiatoday.intoday.in.

Reagon, Bernice Johnson. "Coalition Politics: Turning the Century." In *Home Girls*, edited by Smith, 356–68.

Revue Studios, producer. *Mickey Spillane's Mike Hammer* [Television Series]. USA: Studios USA Television, 1958–59.

Richie, Beth. "Queering Antiprison Work: African American Lesbians in the Juvenile Justice System." In *Global Lockdown*, edited by Sudbury, 73–85.

Riggs, Marlon, director. *Tongues Untied* [DVD]. 1990. USA: Frameline/Strand Releasing, 2008.

Rodney, Walter. *How Europe Underdeveloped Africa.* Washington, D.C.: Howard University Press, 1981.

Rodríguez, Clara E. "The Effect of Race on Puerto Rican Wages." In *Hispanics in the Labor Force: Issues and Policies*, edited by Edwin Meléndez, Clara E. Rodríguez, and Janis B. Figueroa, 77–96. New York: Plenum Press, 1991.

Rodríguez, Dylan. *Forced Passages: Imprisoned Radical Intellectuals and the U.S. Prison Regime.* Minneapolis: University of Minnesota Press, 2006.

Rodríguez, Juana. *Queer Latinidad: Identity Practices, Discursive Spaces.* New York: New York University Press, 2003.

Rodríguez, Ralph. *Brown Gumshoes: Detective Fiction and the Search for Chicana/o Identity.* Austin: University of Texas Press, 2005.

Roman, Leslie G. "White Is a Color! White Defensiveness, Postmodernism, and Anti-Racist Pedagogy." In *Race, Identity, and Representation in Education*, edited by Cameron McCarthy and Warren Crichlow, 71–88. New York: Routledge, 1993.

Roque Ramírez, Horacio N. "Gay Latino Cultural Citizenship: Predicaments of Identity and Visibility in San Francisco in the 1990s." In *Gay Latino Studies*, edited by Hames-García and Martínez, 175–97.

Rorty, Richard. *Achieving Our Country: Leftist Thought in Twentieth-Century America.* Cambridge, Mass.: Harvard University Press, 1998.

Rosaldo, Renato. *Culture and Truth.* 2nd ed. Boston: Beacon, 1993.

———. "Identity Politics: An Ethnography by a Participant." In *Identity Politics Reconsidered*, edited by Alcoff, Hames-García, Mohanty, and Moya, 118–25.

Rosenzweig, Barney, executive producer. *Cagney & Lacey* [Television Series]. USA: Columbia Broadcasting System (CBS), 1982–88.

Roshanravan, Shireen. "South Asian American Identity Formation and the Politics of Women of Color." PhD diss., Binghamton University, State University of New York, 2007.

Rothman, David J. "Perfecting the Prison: United States, 1789–1865." In *The Oxford History of the Prison*, edited by Morris and Rothman, 100–116.

Rotman, Edgardo. "The Failure of Reform: United States, 1865–1965." In *The Oxford History of the Prison*, edited by Morris and Rothman, 151–77.

Rumbaut, Rubén G., Roberto G. Gonzales, Golnaz Komaie, and Charlie V. Morgan. "Debunking the Myth of Immigrant Criminality: Imprisonment among First- and Second-Generation Young Men." *Migration Information Source* (June 2006). http://www.migrationinformation.org.

Saalfield, Catherine. "On the Make: Activist Video Collectives." In *Queer Looks: Perspectives on Lesbian and Gay Film and Video*, edited by Martha Gever, John Greyson, and Pratibha Parmar, 21–37. New York: Routledge, 1993.

Sabo, Don, Terry A. Kupers, and Willie London. "Gender and the Politics of Punishment." In *Prison Masculinities*, edited by Sabo, Kupers, and London, 3–18.

Sabo, Don, Terry A. Kupers, and Willie London, eds. *Prison Masculinities*. Philadelphia, Penn.: Temple University Press, 2001.

Said, Edward. *Orientalism*. New York: Vintage, 1979.

Sain, Ken. "U.S. Soldier Claims Gay Panic Made Him Kill." *New York Blade Online,* January 7, 2005.

Saldívar-Hull, Sonia. *Feminism on the Border: Chicana Gender Politics and Literature*. Berkeley: University of California Press, 2000.

Saltzman, Jonathan. "Sergeant at Eye of Storm Says He Won't Apologize." *The Boston Globe*, July 23, 2009. http://www.boston.com.

Salvatore, Ricardo D., and Carlos Aguirre. "The Birth of the Penitentiary in Latin America: Toward an Interpretive Social History of Prisons." In *The Birth of the Penitentiary in Latin America*, edited by Salvatore and Aguirre, 1–43.

Salvatore, Ricardo D., and Carlos Aguirre, eds. *The Birth of the Penitentiary in Latin America: Essays on Criminology, Prison Reform, and Social Control, 1830–1940*. Austin: University of Texas Press, 1996.

Sánchez-Casal, Susan, and Amie A. Macdonald, eds. *Identity in Education*. New York: Palgrave Macmillan, 2009.

Sánchez-Casal, Susan, and Amie A. Macdonald, eds. *Twenty-First-Century Feminist Classrooms: Pedagogies of Identity and Difference*. New York: Palgrave Macmillan, 2002.

Sandahl, Carrie. "Black Man, Blind Man: Disability Identity Politics and Performance." *Theatre Journal* 56, no. 4 (2004): 579–602.

Sander, Edmund, and Suhail Ahmed. "Killing Drives Wedge between Troops." *Los Angeles Times,* October 18, 2004. http://www.latimes.com.

Sappenfield, Mark. "Since Beer Summit, America Has Seen 'Two Good People.'" *Christian Science Monitor,* August 2, 2009. http://www.csmonitor.com.

Savage, Charlie. "A Judge's View of Judging Is on the Record." *New York Times,* May 15, 2009, A21.

Schmitt, Arno, and Jehoeda Sofer, eds. *Sexuality and Eroticism among Males in Moslem Societies.* New York: Harrington Park, 1992.

Schuster, Heather. "Framing the (W)Hole: Representing the Prison in the Era of United States Mass Imprisonment, 1972–Present." PhD diss., New York University, 2001.

Scott, Joan Wallach. "The Evidence of Experience." *Critical Inquiry* 17 (1991): 773–97.

Sedgwick, Eve. *The Epistemology of the Closet.* Berkeley: University of California Press, 1990.

Shahani, Parmesh. *Gay Bombay: Globalization, Love, and (Be)Longing in Contemporary India.* New Delhi: Sage Publications, 2008.

Shelden, Randall G. "From Slave to Caste Society: Penal Changes in Tennessee, 1830–1915." In *African American Life in the Post-Emancipation South,* edited by Nieman, 300–316.

Shepard, Benjamin. "Sylvia and Sylvia's Children: A Battle for a Queer Public Space." In *That's Revolting! Queer Strategies for Resisting Assimilation,* edited by Mattilda Bernstein Sycamore, 97–112. Brooklyn, N.Y.: Soft Skull Press, 2004.

Shiao, Jiannbin Lee, Mia Tuan, and Elizabeth Rienzi. "Shifting the Spotlight: Exploring Race and Culture in Korean-White Adoptive Families." *Race and Society* 7 (2004): 1–16.

Shine, Cathy, and Marc Mauer. *Does the Punishment Fit the Crime?: Drug Users and Drunk Drivers, Questions of Race and Class.* Washington, D.C.: The Sentencing Project, 1993.

Shing, Lynette J. Chua Kher. "Saying No: Sections 377 and 377a of the Penal Code." *Singapore Journal of Legal Studies* (2003): 209–61.

Siebers, Tobin. "Disability as Masquerade." *Literature and Medicine* 23, no. 1 (2004): 1–22.

———. "Disability in Theory: From Social Constructionism to the New Realism of the Body." *American Literary History* 13, no. 4 (2001): 737–54.

———. "Disability Studies and the Future of Identity Politics." In *Identity Politics Reconsidered,* edited by Alcoff, Hames-García, Moya, and Mohanty, 10–30.

———. *Disability Theory.* Ann Arbor: University of Michigan Press, 2008.

Sigal, Pete, ed. *Infamous Desire: Male Homosexuality in Colonial Latin America.* Chicago: University of Chicago Press, 2003.

Sigal, Pete, and John F. Chuchiak, IV, eds. *Sexual Encounters/Sexual Collisions: Alternative Sexualities in Colonial Mesoamerica.* Special issue of *The Journal of the American Society for Ethnohistory* 54, no. 1 (2007).

Silverman, Fred, Carroll O'Connor, David Moessinger, and Juanita Bartlett, executive producers. *In the Heat of the Night* [Television Series]. USA: National Broadcasting Company (NBC), 1988–94

Silverman, Fred, Joel Steiger, Dean Hargrove, and Andy Griffith, executive producers. *Matlock* [Television Series]. USA: National Broadcasting Company (NBC), 1986–93.

Smith, Andrea. *Conquest: Sexual Violence and American Indian Genocide.* Cambridge, Mass.: South End Press, 2005.

———. "Heteropatriarchy and the Three Pillars of White Supremacy: Rethinking Women of Color Organizing." In *The Color of Violence,* edited by Incite! 66–73.

Smith, Barbara. *The Truth That Never Hurts: Writings on Race, Gender, and Freedom.* New Brunswick, N.J.: Rutgers University Press, 1998.

Smith, Barbara, ed. *Home Girls: A Black Feminist Anthology.* New York: Kitchen Table/Women of Color Press, 1983.

Smith, Valerie. *Not Just Race, Not Just Gender: Black Feminist Readings.* New York: Routledge, 1998.

Somerville, Siobhan. *Queering the Color Line: Race and the Invention of Homosexuality in American Culture.* Durham, N.C.: Duke University Press, 2000.

Sotomayor, Sonia. "A Latina Judge's Voice." *Berkeley La Raza Law Journal* 13, no. 1 (2002): 87–93.

Spelling, Aaron, and Danny Thomas, executive producers. *The Mod Squad* [Television Series]. USA: American Broadcasting Company (ABC), 1968–73.

Spelling, Aaron, and Leonard Goldberg, executive producers. *T. J. Hooker* [Television Series]. USA: American Broadcasting Company (ABC), 1982–85.

Spelman, Elizabeth V. *Inessential Woman: Problems of Exclusion in Feminist Thought.* Boston: Beacon, 1988.

Spera, Deborah, Edward Allen Bernero, Mark Gordon, and Jeff Davis, executive producers. *Criminal Minds* [Television Series]. USA: Columbia Broadcasting System (CBS), 2005–present.

Spillers, Hortense J. "Interstices: A Small Drama of Words." In *Pleasure and Danger,* edited by Vance, 73–100.

Spivak, Gayatri Chakravorty. *In Other Worlds: Essays in Cultural Politics.* New York: Routledge, 1987.

Srivastava, Sanjay, ed. *Sexual Sites, Seminal Attitudes: Sexualities, Masculinities, and Culture in South Asia.* New Delhi: Sage Publications, 2004.

Staples, William G. *The Culture of Surveillance: Discipline and Social Control in the United States.* New York: St. Martin's Press, 1997.

Steele, Claude M., and Joshua Aronson. "Stereotype Threat and the Intellectual

Test Performance of African Americans." *Journal of Personality and Social Psychology* 69, no. 5 (1995): 797–811.

Steele, Claude M., Steven J. Spencer, and Joshua Aronson. "Contending with Group Image: The Psychology of Stereotype and Social Identity Threat." In *Advances in Experimental Social Psychology*, 34, edited by Mark Hanna, 379–440. San Diego, Calif.: Academic Press, 2002.

Stein, Edward, ed. *Forms of Desire: Sexual Orientation and the Social Constructionist Controversy.* New York: Routledge, 1992.

Stephen, Chris. "Startled Marines Find Afghan Men All Made Up to See Them." *The Scotsman*, May 24, 2002. http://www.scotsman.com.

Stewart, Jon. "White Men Can't Judge—Sotomayor: Judgment Days" [Online Video]. *The Daily Show with Jon Stewart*, July 16, 2009. http://www.thedaily show.com.

Stoler, Laura Ann. *Carnal Knowledge and Imperial Power: Race and the Intimate in Colonial Rule.* Berkeley: University of California Press, 2002.

———. *Race and the Education of Desire: Foucault's History of Sexuality and the Colonial Order of Things.* Durham, N.C.: Duke University Press, 1995.

Stone-Mediatore, Shari. "Postmodernism, Realism, and the Problem of Identity." *Diaspora: A Journal of Transnational Studies* 11, no. 1 (2002): 125–38.

Stone, Jeff, Mike Sjomeling, Christian I. Lynch, and John M. Darley. "Stereotype Threat Effects on Black and White Athletic Performance." *Journal of Personality and Social Psychology* 77, no. 6 (1999): 1213–27.

Stormont, Diane. "Hong Kong Votes to Lift Penalties on Homosexual Acts." *Reuters News*, July 11, 1990.

Stowe, Harriet Beecher. *Uncle Tom's Cabin.* Edited by Henry Louis Gates, Jr. and Hollis Robbins. New York: Norton, 2007.

Stuever, Hank. "The Bomb with a Loaded Message; for Gays in America, Even Heroism Isn't a Ticket to Inclusion." *Washington Post*, October 27, 2001. http://www.washingtonpost.com.

Sudbury, Julia. "Introduction: Feminist Critiques, Transnational Landscapes, Abolitionist Visions." In *Global Lockdown*, edited by Sudbury, xi–xxviii.

Sudbury, Julia, ed. *Global Lockdown: Race, Gender, and the Prison-Industrial Complex.* New York: Routledge, 2005.

Suffredini, Kara S. "Pride and Prejudice: The Homosexual Panic Defense." *Boston College Third World Law Journal* 21 (2001): 279–314.

Sullivan, Larry E. *The Prison Reform Movement: Forlorn Hope.* Boston: Twayne, 1990.

Sundstrom, Ronald R. "Race as a Human Kind." *Philosophy & Social Criticism* 28, no. 1 (2002): 91–115.

———. "'Racial' Nominalism." *Journal of Social Philosophy* 33, no. 2 (2002): 193–210.

Taylor, Paul C. "Appiah's Uncompleted Argument: W. E. B. Du Bois and the Reality of Race." *Social Theory and Practice* 26, no. 1 (2000): 103–28.

Teaiwa, Teresia K. "Bikinis and Other S/Pacific N/Oceans." *The Contemporary Pacific* 6, no. 1 (1994): 87–109.

Telles, Edward E. *Race in Another America: The Significance of Skin Color in Brazil.* Princeton, N.J.: Princeton University Press, 2004.

Tettenborn, Éva. "'Will the Big Boys Finally Love You': The Impossibility of Black Male Homoerotic Desire and the Taboo of Black Homosexual Solidarity in Thomas Glave's 'Whose Song?'" *Callaloo* 26, no. 3 (2003): 855–66.

Teuton, Sean Kicummah. "Placing the Ancestors: Postmodernism, 'Realism,' and American Indian Identity in James Welch's *Winter in the Blood." The American Indian Quarterly* 25, no. 4 (2001): 626–50.

———. *Red Land, Red Power: Grounding Knowledge in the American Indian Novel.* Durham, N.C.: Duke University Press, 2008.

Thomas, Shibu. "Delhi HC to Take Up PIL on Gay Rights." *The Times of India,* May 20, 2008. http://timesofindia.indiatimes.com.

Tinsley, Omise'eke Natasha. "Black Atlantic, Queer Atlantic: Queer Imaginings of the Middle Passage." *GLQ: A Journal of Lesbian and Gay Studies* 14, no. 2–3 (2008): 191–215.

"Top Al-Qa'idah Leader in New Tape Criticizes U.S. 'Freedom.'" BBC Worldwide Monitoring, February 10, 2005.

Trask, Haunani-Kay. *From a Native Daughter: Colonialism and Sovereignty in Hawai'i.* Revised ed. Honolulu: University of Hawai'i Press, 1999.

Triffin, Robert. *Gold and the Dollar Crisis: The Future of Convertibility.* New Haven, Conn.: Yale University Press, 1960.

U.S. Census Bureau. "Hawai'i Quick Facts," http://quickfacts.census.gov.

U.S. Department of Justice. Bureau of Justice Statistics. *Jails in Indian Country, 2004.* Washington, D.C.: GPO, 2006.

———. *Prison and Jail Inmates at Midyear 2006.* Washington, D.C.: GPO, 2007.

———. *Prisoners in 2005.* Washington, D.C.: GPO, 2006.

———. *Prisoners in 2006.* Washington, D.C.: GPO, 2007.

———. *Prisoners in 2007.* Washington, D.C.: GPO, 2008.

———. *Probation and Parole in the United States, 2005.* Washington, D.C.: GPO, 2006.

U.S. Department of State, Human Rights, and Labor. Bureau of Democracy. "Afghanistan: Country Reports on Human Rights Practices—2000." Washington, D.C.: GPO, 2001.

Vance, Carole S. *Pleasure and Danger: Exploring Female Sexuality.* Boston: Routledge, 1984.

Wacquant, Loïc. "The New 'Peculiar Institution': On the Prison as Surrogate Ghetto." *Theoretical Criminology* 4, no. 3 (2000): 337–89.

Wagner, Peter. "Native Hawaiians Are Overrepresented in Hawai'i's Prisons and Jails." Prison Policy Initiative. http://www.prisonpolicy.org.

———. "Why Are So Many Native Hawaiians Incarcerated in Minnesota?" Prisoners of the Census. http://www.prisonersofthecensus.org.

Wallace, Michele. *Black Macho and the Myth of the Black Superwoman*. New York: Dial Press, 1979.

Wallerstein, Immanuel. *The Modern World-System I: Capitalist Agriculture and the Origins of the European World Economy in the Sixteenth Century*. New York: Academic Press, 1975.

———. *The Modern World-System II: Mercantilism and the Consolidation of the European World-Economy, 1600–1750*. New York: Academic Press, 1980.

———. *The Modern World-System III: The Second Era of Great Expansion of the Capitalist World-Economy, 1730–1840s*. San Diego, Calif.: Academic Press, 1989.

———. *World-Systems Analysis: An Introduction*. Durham, N.C.: Duke University Press, 2004.

Wang, Karissa S. "NAACP Mulls Network Boycott." *Electronic Media* 20, no. 5 (January 1, 2001): 36.

Warner, Michael. *The Trouble with Normal: Sex, Politics, and the Ethics of Queer Life*. Cambridge, Mass.: Harvard University Press, 2000.

Washington, Jesse. "Latino Differences Muted in Sotomayor Celebration." *Seattle Times*, May 27, 2009. http://seattletimes.nwsource.com.

Webb, Jack, executive producer. *Adam 12* [Television Series]. USA: National Broadcasting Company (NBC), 1968–75.

———, executive producer. *Dragnet* [Television Series]. USA: National Broadcasting Company (NBC), 1967–70.

West, Cornel. *Race Matters*. c1993. Boston: Beacon Press, 2001.

Whitaker, Brian. *Unspeakable Love: Gay and Lesbian Life in the Middle East*. Berkeley: University of California Press, 2006.

White, Hayden. *Tropics of Discourse: Essays in Cultural Criticism*. Baltimore, Md.: The Johns Hopkins University Press, 1978.

Wilder, John, executive producer. *Spenser for Hire* [Television Series]. USA: American Broadcasting Company (ABC), 1985–88.

Wilkerson, William S. *Ambiguity and Sexuality: A Theory of Sexual Identity*. New York: Palgrave Macmillan, 2007.

———. "Is There Something You Need to Tell Me? Coming Out and the Ambiguity of Experience." In *Reclaiming Identity*, edited by Moya and Hames-García, 251–78.

Williams, Linda. *Playing the Race Card: Melodramas of Black and White from Uncle Tom to O. J. Simpson*. Princeton, N.J.: Princeton University Press, 2002.

Williams, Patricia J. *The Alchemy of Race and Rights: Diary of a Law Professor*. Cambridge, Mass.: Harvard University Press, 1991.

Wilson, Theodore Brantner. *The Black Codes of the South*. Birmingham: University of Alabama Press, 1965.

Wines, E. C., ed. *Transactions of the National Congress on Penitentiary and Reformatory Discipline*. Albany, N.Y.: Weed, Parsons, 1871.

Wittgenstein, Ludwig. *Philosophical Investigations*. Translated by G. E. M. Anscombe. New York: Macmillan, 1967.

Wlodarz, Joe. "Maximum Insecurity: Genre Trouble and Closet Erotics in and out of HBO's *Oz*." *Camera Obscura* 20, no. 58 (2005): 58–105.

Wolf, Dick, Brad Kern, and Don Kurt, executive producers. *New York Undercover* [Television Series]. USA: Fox Network, 1994–98.

Wolf, Dick, Jeffrey L. Hayes, Jim Ellis, Rene Balcer, Edwin Sherin, Peter Jankowski, Michael S. Chernuchin, Matthew Penn, Eric Overmyer, Roz Weinman, Walon Green, Joseph Stern, Barry Schindel, Nicholas Wootton, Fred Berner, William M. Finkelstein, and Arthur Penn, executive producers. *Law & Order* [Television Series]. USA: National Broadcasting Company (NBC), 1990–present.

Wolf, Eric R. *Europe and the People without History*. 2nd ed. Berkeley: University of California Press, 1997.

Wong, Nellie, Merle Woo, and Mitsuye Yamada. *Three Asian American Writers Speak Out on Feminism*. San Francisco: SF Radical Women, 1979.

Wylie, Alison. "Why Standpoint Matters." In *Science and Other Cultures: Issues in Philosophies of Science and Technology*, edited by Robert Figueroa and Sandra G. Harding, 26–48. New York: Routledge, 2003.

Wynter, Leon E. "Networks Need to Find a Better Balance with Minority Roles." *Wall Street Journal*, September 8, 1999. http://online.wsj.com.

Yarbro-Bejarano, Yvonne. *The Wounded Heart: Writing on Cherríe Moraga*. Austin: University of Texas Press, 2001.

Yawning Bread (Au Waipang). "The Map's Tale." Yawning Bread, 2004. http://www.yawningbread.org.

Yousman, Bill. *Prime Time Prisons on U.S. TV: Representation of Incarceration*. New York: Peter Lang, 2009.

Zack, Naomi. *Thinking About Race*. Belmont, Calif.: Wadsworth, 1998.

Zapatista Army of National Liberation (EZLN). "Sixth Declaration of the Selva Lacandona." *XCP: Cross-Cultural Poetics* no. 15/16 (2006): 104–14.

Zedner, Lucia. "Wayward Sisters: The Prison for Women." In *The Oxford History of the Prison*, edited by Morris and Rothman, 295–324.

Zeevi, Dror. *Producing Desire: Changing Sexual Discourse in the Ottoman Middle East, 1500–1900*. Berkeley: University of California Press, 2006.

Zhu, Peter F. "Renowned Af-Am Professor Gates Arrested for Disorderly Conduct." *Harvard Crimson*, July 20, 2009. http://www.thecrimson.com.

Žižek, Slavoj. "A Leftist Plea for 'Eurocentrism.'" *Critical Inquiry* 24 (1998): 988–1007.

Index

prisons: Alaskan Natives and, 117–18; Asian Americans and, 117–18, 132; blacks and, 114–18, 121, 123–25, 129, 149; capitalism and, 125–27, 129; Civil Rights Movement and, 125, 127, 128; class and, 120–21; colonial/ modern gender system and, xvii, 113–14, 129, 132; cultural representation of, 113–14, 119; gender and, 129; history of, 120–29; homophobia and, 129, 137; homosexuality and, 1–4, 136–37; incarceration rates and, 114–20; Latin America and, 123; Latinas and Latinos and, 114, 116–18, 130, 132, 149–50; masculinity and, 1–4, 129, 131–32; media and, 176n13; multiplicity and, xvii; mutual constitution and, xvii; Native Americans and, 117–18, 132; Native Hawaiians and, 117–18, 132, 176n9; Pacific Islanders and, 117–18, 176n9; race and, 115–19, 120–21, 123–25, 128–32; rape and, 113, 129, 136–37; Reconstruction and, 123–24; reform and, 120–23, 125; sexism and, 129; sexuality and, 129; slavery and, 114–15; transformation of, 122–23, 125; violence and, 134; whiteness and, 120–21; women and, 113, 120–21, 129–31, 132. See also Oz
privilege, 34–35
Puar, Jasbir, 175n93
Puerto Ricans. See Latinas and Latinos

Quijano, Aníbal, 51–54, 55, 65, 77

race: beliefs and, 56; biology and, 44–46, 57–62, 76; Chicanas and Chicanos and, 76–77, 170n67; class and, 151–52; criminal sentencing and, 55; criticism of, 39–41, 44–49,

54–55; cultural representation and, 140–50; death penalty and, 55–56; disease and, 57–58; economic reality of, 55–56; ethnicity and, 45, 47, 54, 163n6; freedom and, 120; genetic distance and, 57–58; history of, 51–54; indeterminacy of, 46–47; indigenous identity and, 65–66; meaning of, 61–62; Mexico and, 76–77; mutual constitution of, 40; Oz and, 133, 134; police profiling and, 154; prisons and, 115–19, 120–21, 123–25, 128–32; reality of, xvi, 55–62, 65–67; reason and, 120; social construction of, 44–46; as a social location, 62–63; as a standpoint, 62–63; television and, 133; wages and, 60. See also colonial/ modern gender system
Racial Privacy Initiative, 39–40
racism, 55–56, 153–55; gay identity and, 8–9; race and, 62; scientific, 51, 56, 57–58, 62; sexuality and, 138–39, 141; television and, 114
rape: prison and, 113, 129, 136–37
Reagan, Ronald, 128
Reagon, Bernice Johnson, 6
realism, postpositivist: knowledge and, 16–17; social identity and, 14–15, 18–21
reference. See knowledge
relativism, 16, 19, 20, 25
Renna, Cathy, 94
restriction: domination and oppression and, 7–8, 20–21; multiplicity and, 7–9, 14; resistance to, 33–37; self and, 7–9; social identities and, 20
revision. See social identity: verification and revision of
Reyes-Santos, Irmary, xv
Rice, Condoleezza, 47–48

MICHAEL HAMES-GARCÍA is professor of ethnic studies at the University of Oregon. He is the author of *Fugitive Thought: Prison Movements, Race, and the Meaning of Justice* and the coeditor of *Reclaiming Identity: Realist Theory and the Predicament of Postmodernism, Identity Politics Reconsidered,* and *Gay Latino Studies: A Critical Reader.*